Global
Dreams

Global
Dreams

Class, Gender, and Public Space in Cosmopolitan Cairo

Anouk de Koning

The American University in Cairo Press
Cairo   New York

First published in Egypt in 2009 by
The American University in Cairo Press
113 Sharia Kasr el Aini, Cairo, Egypt
420 Fifth Avenue, New York 10018
www.aucpress.com

Dar el Kutub No. 16760/08
ISBN 978 977 416 249 7

Dar el Kutub Cataloging-in-Publication

de Koning, Anouk
        Global Dreams: Class, Gender, and Public Space in Cosmopolitan Cairo /
    Anouk de Koning.—Cairo: The American University in Cairo Press, 2008
        p.   cm.
        ISBN 977 416 249 8
        1. Middle Class—Egypt   I. Title
        305.55

1 2 3 4 5 6 7 8   14 13 12 11 10 09

Designed by Fatiha Bouzidi
Printed in Egypt

This book is dedicated to my grandmother Agnes (Sioe Tjoe) Groothuizen-Lauw and my grandfather Bert Groothuizen.

Contents

Acknowledgments

When I first came to Cairo, I knew few people and little about the city. Now, after years of research and personal visits, Cairo has become a second home, thanks to all those who helped educate me, sharing their stories and their friendship. Numerous people have, in one way or another, contributed to my understanding of contemporary Cairo as it is laid out in this study. Some I met only once, others have become close friends. I can only mention a few of these people, but remain indebted to all who have shown me such good-natured support and kindness. It is their insights on which this study rests. I can only hope that they recognize some of their own contributions, and that I, in some small way, have offered some new insights as well.

I thank Gamal and Yehia for helping me get started, Adel Abdel Moneim for teaching me Egyptian Arabic so effectively, and Ghada Tantawi for helping me explore some of the Egyptian literature on the middle class. I am grateful to Noha and Maisa for their support and friendship, and their families for their generosity and warmth. I feel lucky to have Dina, Samir, and Tamer as colleagues and friends. The members of al-Khayaal al-Sha'bi provided me with a home away from home. Shaker, Marwa, Dina, and Naama were always willing to help out, talk things over and share some of their experiences and contacts. I am also grateful to Nivin for our long talks about the trials and tribulations of life in Cairo, and to Mona for making me a part of her life. I want to thank Mostafa, Ahmed, Ferial, Iman, Heidi, Yasser, and Alaa for their invaluable contributions and their frankness. From the start of the research I have been able to sound out my ideas to Mohamed Waked, who always had new stories to tell about the crazy times in which we live. I would like to thank him for suffering my endless queries patiently and straightening out my transliterations. Mostafa Wafy kept me afloat through difficult times with his kindness and steadfast optimism. He has helped me in more ways than I can tell. I am happy that my friendships with these individuals have carried on beyond the period of research and, in some cases, into places other than Cairo.

The Amsterdam School of Social Science Research not only generously financed the PhD research on which this book is based, but also provided a welcoming and intellectually stimulating environment. Its staff's commitment to the students made it more than merely an academic institute. The Dutch Organization for Scientific Research generously supported a follow-up research trip and financed a fellowship at the International Center for Advanced Studies (ICAS), New York University, in winter/spring 2006, which gave me the luxury of being an academic flaneur. I am grateful to Timothy Mitchell and the ICAS residents for their collegiality at this time.

This study would not have been possible without the enthusiasm, support, and intellectual input of my friends, colleagues, and professors in Amsterdam. I would like to express my gratitude to Annelies Moors for the intellectual freedom she granted me, and Peter Geschiere, Birgit Meyer, and Frances Gouda for their support and enthusiasm. I also want to thank all the members of the Anthropology Club, which provided a constructive forum for frank discussions and, at times, heated debates. Ines Trigo de Sousa shared many of the trials and tribulations of this journey, while Miriyam Aouragh shared my engagement with the Middle East. Pia di Matteo was the closest witness of the madness of writing a dissertation. I am grateful for her support and friendship throughout. Yatun Sastramidjaja's camaraderie and her thoughtful and incisive presence were much appreciated, as was Vazira Zamindar's committed and intelligent company. Wieke Vink lent me her critical eye and helped me develop more effective arguments. Despite the distance, Julia Hornberger remained a close friend and much appreciated academic sparring partner. Eileen Moyer has stood by me from the start, as a colleague and a friend. She helped me see the relevance of urban studies to the issues I confronted in Cairo. She also taught me much about the intricacies of language by editing an early version of this manuscript, which Irfan Ahmad, Rivke Jaffe, and Andrew Gebhardt subsequently helped me revise. I am grateful to my editors at AUC Press for the enthusiasm they brought to the publication of this book. A version of Chapter Five appears as "Gender, Public Space and Social Segregation in Cairo: Of Taxi Drivers, Prostitutes and Professional Women," in *Antipode: A Journal of Radical Geography* 41(3) (June 2009). I thank the editorial board of *Antipode*, and Wiley-Blackwell Publishers for allowing me to publish them side by side.

Finally, I could not have done without the unconditional love and support that my parents, Tom and Marijke de Koning-Groothuizen, gave me. My grandparents have inspired me in more indirect ways. From early on, their transnational story provided me with a sense of wonder and love for social history. Agnes (Sioe Tjoe) Groothuizen-Lauw had the ability to move between worlds in an amazing down-to-earth manner, while Bert Groothuizen found ways to be kind despite the severe trials in his life. Both taught me about a world in which everyone, in the end, is only human. I dedicate this book to them.

A Note on Transliteration

Since almost all Arabic words in the text are Cairene colloquial expressions, I have chosen a transliteration system that reflects local pronunciations. I follow the system adopted in *A Dictionary of Egyptian Arabic* by El-Said Badawi and Martin Hinds (Beirut: Librarie du Liban, 1986). I have however simplified the transcription of the Arabic alphabet, in order to make it more easily accessible to readers who are not familiar with Arabic. I thus use:

[s] for both س and ص
[h] for both ح and هـ
[t] for ط and ت
[d] for د and ض
[z] for ز and ظ
[sh] for ش
[kh] for خ
[gh] for غ
['] for ع
['] for ء and for ق, when the ق is replaced by a glottal stop, as in *'ahwa*.

Long vowels are represented by double vowels; doubled consonants are similarly represented by double consonants in English (e.g., *muhaggabaat*). Proper names and place names have been written according to their usual spelling in English.

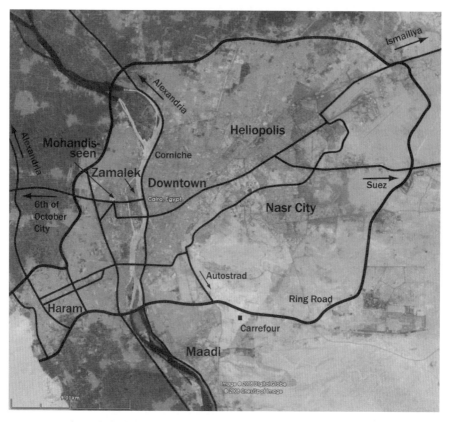

Map of Cairo highlighting a number of middle and upper class areas and major thoroughfares. Based on Google map imagery, adapted by Martijn de Koning.

Introduction

Young Professionals and the City

If we stop dreaming, we'll die,
If we insist, we'll be able to pass
If we cross once, it's done
If we shy back, all will be lost

A bit of endurance, a bit of enthusiasm
And the dream will have color and sound

Muhammad Mounir, "If We Stop Dreaming, We'll Die"
(From the album *Open Your Heart*; my translation)

If I were to tell the story of this study, one evening in November 2001 would certainly provide a good starting point. I had been in Cairo for a few months, and had made the leftist, progressive Downtown scene of artists, journalists, activists, and hopefuls my home base. That evening, however, I made my way to a five-star hotel in Zamalek, Cairo's old elite neighborhood, where I encountered a crowd of elegantly and formally dressed young Cairenes. They were members of SaharaSafaris, an internet-based community founded a few months previously, which brought people together for trips to the desert and more mundane social outings in the city. The gathering was held in preparation for our upcoming trip to Siwa, an oasis in Egypt's

1

Western Desert. While there were several Cairo-based internet groups that organized forums and a range of social activities for upper-middle class professionals, SaharaSafaris was one of the best known and most active groups. Meeting likeminded people, particularly of the opposite sex, was one of its more potent attractions.

The group's fast-growing membership largely consisted of young upper-middle class professionals employed in multinational companies, consultancy firms, NGOs, marketing agencies, and so on, that comprise the up-market segment of the urban economy. Most had attended 'language schools,' private schools that teach much of the curriculum in a European language, and were relatively fluent in English. Most conversations were held in a mixture of Arabic and English, which was the vernacular of Cairo's young, professional upper-middle class. While thoroughly familiar with cosmopolitan requirements and tastes, most members seemed to heed class-specific norms of respectability and religious propriety. They constituted part of a class that fit the upper segments of the labor market, Cairo's transnational workspaces, and the media representations of Egypt's future generation.

The initial contacts I made on SaharaSafaris outings introduced me to a number of loosely knit networks of upper-middle class professionals. Being roughly the same age, and, like them able to easily combine Arabic and English repertoires, I was an easygoing companion on outings. These outings took me to a Cairo that I was quite unfamiliar with. I soon found myself visiting upscale coffee shops like Cilantro, Beano's, and the Retro Café located in affluent areas like Mohandisseen, Zamalek, Maadi, and Heliopolis on an almost daily basis. These coffee shops stood out because of their Western menus, fancy designs, immaculate cleanliness, and air-conditioned climate, as well as their mixed-gender publics. I learned that these venues had become central urban spaces for the social life of many relatively affluent urban professionals.

My encounter with a group of professionals so unlike the middle class people I had met before raised a host of questions concerning social divisions in Cairo's middle class landscape. This study is my attempt to map and explain these social divisions. It thereby speaks to the everyday of class in what has been called Egypt's new liberal era (Denis 1997), and examines Cairo's experience of economic liberalization in an era of globalization. I trace the ways new inequalities insert themselves into, and thereby reconfigure, earlier forms of stratification. I track this reshaping of inequality and distinction across the interconnected domains of education, the labor market, leisure spaces, and the wider urban landscape. Contrasts between explicitly localized and conspicuously cosmopolitan reverberate across these domains.

ANOUK DE KONING (2004)

Cairo on the banks of the Nile

From National Development to New Liberalism

At the start of the twenty-first century, Cairo's cityscape had acquired a spectacular global touch. The luxurious five-star hotels, high-rise office buildings, immaculately clean new malls, and the many fancy, up-market coffee shops serving caffè lattes and Caesar salads seemed to herald Cairo's status as a global city. The budding upscale gated communities, hotels, golf courses, and foreign educational institutions in the desert around Cairo offered affluent Cairenes transnational products and experiences, as well as a perfect, socially homogeneous world that the city with its high poverty rates, crowdedness, and pollution could not offer (cf. Denis 2006). This spectacular Cairo is one of the clearest expressions of three decades of economic liberalization. Although the most extravagant accruements of Egypt's new liberal era are to be found in Cairo's new desert expanses, more established urban areas have also undergone drastic changes. While the glamour and shiny surfaces of the latest version of urban modernity clamor for attention, it is crucial to examine in what ways Cairene society has been reconfigured beyond this spectacular façade.

The stories of everyday life in middle class Cairo speak to Egypt's larger shift from a developmental to a neoliberal state. They chart some of the everyday effects of the move from a national economy dominated by public enterprises and state directives to a reliance on the private sector and integration into global networks. The Nasser-era project of state-led development has increasingly been replaced by policies that seek to reduce the deep-seated patronage role of the state and rewrite the earlier social contract between state and people. At the same time, the state takes on a new developmental role meant to bring privileged segments of the nation up to speed with the global.

In the years following the 1952 Revolution the Egyptian state assumed an increasingly central and dominant role in the national economy. As was the case in a number of leading nonaligned countries, this formative period in Egyptian history was characterized by its own brand of socialism and a national development project with the state as its prime agent. State policies fostered a large urban middle class, most notably through the democratization of education and the provision of government jobs to all graduates (Abdel-Fadil 1980). Cairo's professional middle class became a central protagonist in narratives of national progress and modernity. From the mid-1970s onward, Egypt witnessed the withdrawal of the state from its previous role as the primary agent of national development. Egypt was, at least in theory, to become a liberal market economy integrated into the global market and conforming to neoliberal precepts. This reorientation sped up significantly in the 1990s with the adoption of structural adjustment policies. Eric Denis argues that Egypt has entered a new liberal age, reminiscent of its earlier pre-Second World War liberal era (1997, 2006). Given its historically strong connection with the Nasserist project and state, the professional middle class in particular has felt the impact of the new social divisions and cultural distinctions of Egypt's new liberal age.

As the older Nasserite narrative and project are abandoned in favor of attempts to bring the nation up to speed with globally dominant standards and fashions, dreams that are connected to the Nasser era are increasingly countered by hostile realities. Meanwhile, new dreams of a First World Egypt are within reach of those young urban professionals who are able to negotiate the conspicuously cosmopolitan realms of up-market Cairo. They are presented as the successful mediators between the 'local' and the 'global,' not unlike India's 'new middle class,' which, as Leela Fernandes argues, is constructed as "the social group that is able to negotiate India's new relationship with the global economy in both cultural and economic terms" (2000b:91).

The Divided City

Saskia Sassen (2001) has made the by now paradigmatic argument that economic globalization gives rise to an increasingly dense network of global cities that harbor the material nodes of control for spatially dispersed production processes and are production sites for the specialized business services that make such control possible. The urban sectors that are involved in such global coordination functions become increasingly disconnected from the surrounding economic landscape. This disjunction in the urban economy is accompanied by changing class configurations, and increasingly disparate urban geographies and modes of inhabiting and consuming the city.

Sassen's analysis of 'global city formation' addresses changes in the socio-economic landscapes of New York, London, and Tokyo. In their recent discussion of economic and spatial developments in Cairo, Leïla Vignal and Eric Denis argue that global city models, though useful in understanding "archipelago economies of globalizing cities and urban nodes," offer limited insights into the complexities of globalization in Third World cities. They particularly point to the singular focus on financial and service sector activities at the expense of "continuing, but transformed, industrial and manufacturing sectors of cities" (Vignal and Denis 2006:101). The global networks in which Southern cities like Cairo are entangled are not only more diverse, but also place such cities "at quite the opposite end of the command and control continuum of global city functions" (Robinson 2002:547; cf. Dawson and Edwards 2004). It is telling that Cairo's 'global movers' not only include multinational companies, but also, significantly, the development industry—international organizations and the semilocal NGOs they finance—as well as tourism. Such dependent positioning has a long history. As Ashley Dawson and Brent Hayes Edwards argue, "old imperial maps still influence the circuits of culture and capital, underneath and in tension with the 'new imperialism' of economic globalization" (2004:3; cf. King 1990).

Despite these crucial differences in historical trajectories, socioeconomic structures, and contemporary positioning in global networks, Sassen's work invites us to explore connections between economic globalization and the social and cultural transformation of cityscapes, whether North or South. Sassen argues that one of the central features of the sociocultural transformations that accompany "global city formation" is social and economic polarization, which particularly impacts the middle classes. These changing class configurations resonate with Cairene realities. Social inequalities have markedly widened in the course of the 1980s and 1990s. The city has witnessed the rise of a new bourgeoisie, as well as the growth of a relatively affluent professional upper-middle class whose members are employed in the more internationally oriented segments of the urban economy. In the social landscape beyond these few more fortunate groups, real wages have been in steady decline while the withdrawal of a whole range of government subsidies and services has made life increasingly expensive. In the mid-1990s half of the Egyptian population was estimated to be poor or on the margins of poverty.[1] The broad urban professional middle class that was fostered under Nasser has become increasingly divided between professionals whose more localized qualifications have lost much of their previous value and others whose formal and informal cosmopolitan qualifications allow them to compete for relatively lucrative jobs in Egypt's upscale workspaces.

This social polarization is related to Egypt's economic restructuring and the endorsement of a private sector integrated in global economic networks (Mitchell 2002). An up-market segment of internationally oriented companies and institutions has emerged in Cairo's urban economy. The upper-middle class professionals employed in managerial and professional positions in this internationally oriented segment constitute the Cairene equivalent of the stratum of high-income earners discussed by Sassen. They receive relatively good wages compared to the meager pay of the highly insecure private sector jobs or low-level government jobs of young professionals from less privileged middle class strata (cf. Abdel Moati 2002:324–30). While in 2002 salaries in the latter employments ranged from 150 to 1,000 Egyptian pounds (LE) per month, wages in the up-market segment started at LE1,000, but could exceed LE10,000.[2] Many older professionals were cushioned from such segmentation by the continued existence of older economic structures, but younger professionals were confronted with a strongly segmented labor market and urban economy.

The emergence of this Cairene equivalent of Sassen's high-income professional class is the focus of the greater part of this study. I call them upper-middle class to highlight the significant differences from professionals of other middle class strata in terms of income, lifestyle, and social worlds. What most clearly sets these upper-middle class professionals apart from other middle class professionals is what I call 'cosmopolitan capital': familiarity with globally dominant, First World repertoires and standards—for example, fluency in English—as well as the ability to participate in conspicuously cosmopolitan lifestyles that have become the prerogative of Cairo's upper-middle class and elites. Whereas the urban professional middle class, symbolized by the engineer and the doctor, was the main protagonist of Nasserite Egypt, young upper-middle class professionals employed in the technologically advanced offices of internationally oriented companies have become iconic of the national narratives and projects of Egypt's new liberal era. Equipped with the latest fashions and technology, they are the ones who can match global standards and can staff transnational workspaces.

These new social inequalities materialize in the urban landscape in the form of spatial and sociocultural segregation (cf. Singerman and Amar 2006). Cairo's cityscape has become marked by a high degree of segmentation in the spheres of production and consumption (cf. Amin 1999). Most Cairenes must consume the products and services provided by informal markets of consumption and leisure that accommodate their limited buying power. They have to seek out the sparse remaining benefits of the Nasserite subsidized system and buy cheap Chinese imports. Still, many find it difficult to make ends meet. Meanwhile, the urban landscape also speaks of the existence of another Cairo. Gated communities are built in the desert around Cairo, the streets are filled with luxury cars, and upscale Mohandisseen is steadily replacing Wist il-Balad (literally: Downtown) as city center for those who can afford its comparatively steep prices (Armbrust 1999; Denis 2006). Moreover, as a result of the declining quality of government services and the simultaneous existence of relative affluence among Cairo's upper and upper-middle classes, Cairo has witnessed a duplication of social services and institutions (cf. Amin 1999). Cairo now has an ever-growing number of private schools, institutes, and universities, as well as private hospitals. Moreover, in upscale districts like Mohandisseen, Heliopolis, and Maadi, spotlessly clean supermarkets like Metro and Alfa Market offer the commodities necessary for first-class lifestyles, while upscale coffee shops and restaurants provide new public spaces that intimate First World pleasures and belonging.

Sassen argues that the global city's high-income workers pioneer new consumption practices, which significantly affect the urban landscape of these cities (2001:341). The consumption patterns and lifestyles of young upper-middle class Cairenes have similarly contributed to the emergence of new public spaces for consumption and leisure, as well as shifting axes of centrality in the city at large. They inhabit and consume the spaces of upscale Cairo and have carved out a specific young, upper-middle class professional presence in the urban landscape, first and foremost in the upscale coffee shops I discuss in Chapters Four and Five.

Cosmopolitan Capital

In Cairo claims of knowledge and connections to the 'outside' (*barra*: the West, the First World, the global) have a long history as markers of elite belonging, just as rootedness, locality, and authenticity have served to identify what are called 'the popular classes' (*ish-sha'b*). In many colonial and postcolonial settings like Cairo, cosmopolitan or 'westernized' elite practices have been taken to indicate modernity and sophistication. Emanuela Guano, for example, observes that in late nineteenth-century Argentina, "the localization of transnational dynamics—and especially the conspicuous consumption of European culture—played a pivotal role in legitimizing the elite of Buenos Aires as 'modern'" (Guano 2002:182). With respect to Brazilian middle classes, Maureen O'Daugherty similarly notes that middle class Brazilians take the availability of foreign goods as an indication of the country's development and its inclusion on the world stage (2002:130–31). In Cairo such cosmopolitan referencing not only intimates elite standing and sophistication, but it can also be taken as a sign of alienation and rootless westernization, which is associated with moral looseness. The charge of westernization has been around for over a century, and has been used to criticize the perceived cultural and moral corruption of the upper class (Armbrust 1996, 1999; cf. Baraka 1998).

The term 'cosmopolitan' has been deployed in different ways, in and outside of academia (see, e.g., Calhoun 2003; Robbins 1998; Cheah 1998). Some authors have focused on the vernacular cosmopolitanisms of ordinary folk, who in dealing with a globalizing world have created their own ways of living multiplicity (see, for Cairo, Ghannam 2002; Singerman and Amar 2006). Even though I recognize the existence of vernacular cosmopolitanisms, my use of the term cosmopolitan is meant to highlight the longstanding relation between claims of connectedness and elite membership in Egypt. In his study of mine workers in the Zambian Copperbelt, James Ferguson (1999) argues that the 'local' and the 'cosmopolitan' present two locally available styles. A choice for one or the other reflects a specific stance within the local context. Adoption of a local style indicates allegiance to kin and local networks, while conversely the choice for a cosmopolitan style indicates a withdrawal from such networks into a more anonymous urban life. Following Ferguson, I understand the 'local' and the 'cosmopolitan' as local repertoires that are taken up in personal strategies and performances. These distinct repertoires signify specific choices, allegiances, and modes of belonging in the local context. In Cairo such choices are heavily inflected by the conflation of explicitly localized (*sha'bi* or *baladi*) repertoires with the working class and conspicuously cosmopolitan repertoires with the elite.

Notwithstanding their transnational references, cosmopolitan repertoires are locally generated and derive their significance from desires for First World sophistication and inclusion, as well as from their longstanding function as class markers (Armbrust 1999; Abaza 2001). During the first half of the twentieth century, France provided central reference points for such local, distinctive cosmopolitan practices and lifestyles (Abaza 2001). The Nasser period initiated a partial shift away from ready identifications of cosmopolitan lifestyles with elite membership. In Egypt's new liberal age, with its attempted integration into global networks and markets, and its striving for First World standards and appearances, such conspicuous cosmopolitanism has again become a potent marker of elite belonging and distinctiveness. Only now, the United States has overtaken France as reference for such distinctive cosmopolitan practices.

Repeating longstanding themes in Egypt's class-divided society, claims of connectedness to the 'outside' and being conversant with global standards and fashions serve to distinguish elites from what is imagined as the locally rooted culture of the popular classes, as well as from the irredeemable outdatedness of the Nasserite middle class with its local degrees and limited command of English (cf. Armbrust 1996). I use the term 'cosmopolitan capital' for those forms of cultural capital that are marked by familiarity with and mastery of globally dominant cultural codes. In Cairo's new liberal age, this kind of cultural capital is an important component of Cairo's upper-middle class and elite subcultures. Such cosmopolitan capital most clearly entails fluency in English and an ability to use the mix of Arabic and English common in upper and upper-middle class circles, as well as Western diplomas or degrees from educational institutes that are associated with Western knowledge, for example, private language schools or the American University in Cairo. It also entails knowledge of the West, Western consumer culture, and prevailing elite dress codes that reference global fashions. Such cosmopolitan capital has come to designate social and cultural worth across the different domains discussed in this study. It is a crucial marker of private language schools and up-market offices, as well as upscale consumption and leisure venues like malls, cinemas, and coffee shops.

Anthropology and Egypt's New Liberal Era

Despite the central role of the urban middle class in Egypt's national imagery, few ethnographic studies have focused on Cairo's middle class. The rich popular (sha'bi) and largely informal worlds of Cairo's working class have been studied more extensively (e.g., Singerman 1995; Hoodfar 1999; Wikan 1980, 1996). Most pertinent to my study of middle class Cairo were ethnographic studies of Egyptian popular culture, film, and television that extensively discuss cultural elaborations of class. Walter Armbrust (1996, 1998, 1999) and Lila Abu-Lughod (1993, 1995, 2004) analyze Egyptian television and film as important carriers of national narratives and imaginations, and as part of what Lila Abu-Lughod calls a 'national pedagogy.' The urban middle class has been a main protagonist in these narratives. Particularly Armbrust's work on mass culture and modernism provides excellent discussions of being middle class in Egypt, as well as insightful analyses of connections between culture and class in Cairo.

The rise of Islamic movements as well as more grassroots forms of piety has been hotly debated in Egypt and has drawn much attention in Western academia and media. The increased importance of religiosity in Cairo and the ways it has impacted both Egyptian subjectivities and public institutions has been taken up by, among others, Saba Mahmood (2005), Charles Hirschkind (2006), and Gregory Starrett (1998). Yet even if political Islam and the increased dominance of religious discourses are important issues in contemporary Cairo, they are not the only sources of social identifications and contestations. The slow but sure dismantling of the Nasserist legacy and the concurrent rise of vast new social inequalities present equally fundamental themes. Moreover, it is crucial to take Egypt's political and economic reorientation and the resulting class configurations into account if one wants to understand the dynamics of sociocultural life in Cairo. This is apparent, for example, in the way new forms of religiosity are taken up in highly divergent ways by, say, working class and elite women (see MacLeod 1991 on the class dynamics of the new veiling).

Egypt's new liberal era has only recently become the subject of ethnographic study. Elyachar discusses the role of 'development' (2005), Abaza that of consumption (2001, 2006), while Winegar (2006) discusses global–local frictions in Cairo's art world. The larger contours of the emerging realities of new liberal Egypt are most thoroughly addressed in the field of urban studies and political economy (see the contributions to Singerman and Amar 2006; Denis 1997; Mitchell 1999, 2005). I explore how the developments that are noted in this literature materialize on the ground in everyday contestations of inequality, the redrawing of sociocultural distinctions, and new forms of social segregation and urban exclusivity.

Class is a pervasive everyday reality in Cairo, both on account of the vast social inequalities among Cairenes and because of the strong associations between class and culture, which create contrasting yet intricately connected cultural worlds. Such everyday manifestations and contestations of class in Cairo's divided cityscape have, however, rarely been addressed. Even though many ethnographic studies of Egyptian society are actually situated in Cairo, few take up its complexly stratified social life as their primary theme (yet see, e.g., Ghannam 2002, Armbrust 1998). This study focuses on such negotiations and contestations of class in the spaces of liberalizing Cairo. It first explores the institutional spaces of education and the labor market, and then moves into the public life that unfolds in Cairo's coffee shops and streets. The everyday of class entails situational performances of superiority and deference, and senses of belonging and nonbelonging. Particular class performances determine in which parts of the city one can feel at home, and how one is seen and treated in different spaces on Cairo's class-segmented map (cf. Ghannam 2002:83). Not only do physical and social locations in metropolitan Cairo differ significantly, but mappings, codes and allowed and expected behaviors are also highly differentiated (see, e.g., Battesti 2006). These different ways of inhabiting the city meet in Cairo's urban spaces and give rise to the urban social life marked by cross-class encounters that I consider typical of Cairo. While much of this study focuses on the more affluent middle class Cairo, I have tried to retain a feel of the constitutive and often conflictive presence of other social worlds in these same urban spaces. As I explore the emergence of a young, upper-middle class Cairo, I try not to loose sight of the underlying denials and conflicts that are the silent constituents of these areas of apparent affluence and ease.

My understanding of contemporary middle class Cairo owes much to the expertise and knowledge of my middle class contacts, who routinely negotiate Cairo's everyday realities. Many of the social changes that they noticed are extremely hard to document quantitatively, since data is unavailable, inaccessible, notoriously inaccurate, or not detailed enough to indicate changes within the city's professional middle class.[3] The recent date of most of these changes and the speed with which they reconfigure the existing urban landscape add another level of complication. The new divisions, lifestyles, and urban spaces I explore in this study are part of an emergent urban landscape.

Combining urban ethnography of a Southern global city, analysis of changing patterns of social stratification, and exploration of new middle class lifestyles, this study is above all an in-depth examination of a particular moment in Cairo's, and Egypt's, social history. It asks what happened to a postcolonial middle class that was once the carrier of national dreams and aspirations. While the radical changes in Cairo's economy, social fabric, and cityscape are sufficient reason for such an exploration, the story of middle class Cairo in new liberal times also speaks to transformations underway in other major postcolonial cities. After independence, many postcolonial countries similarly pioneered large projects of state-building, and have, in the last three decades, turned to neoliberal precepts in a globalizing world. Manifestations of spectacular urbanism and social segmentation in Cairo's urban landscape echo trends found in numerous global cities of the South. My analysis of the everyday manifestations of economic liberalization in Cairo thus speaks to the fate of postcolonial societies in an era of neoliberal globalization. The story of Cairo's younger generation of professionals likewise resonates with stories of their peers in other major postcolonial cities, who may similarly remember some of the earlier promises of a respectable middle class life, may be equally tantalized by prospects of being up-to-date with global standards and fashions and First World membership, but also find that entrance tickets to this new generation are ever more unequally disbursed.

Young, Professional, and Middle Class

This study is based on twenty months of ethnographic research among young professional Cairenes. The fieldwork was carried out from September 2001 to February 2003, and from May 2004 to July 2004. It included participant observation and interviews with differently positioned middle class professionals, mostly in their mid-twenties to early thirties. As Walter Armbrust argues, in Cairo being middle class was figured primarily in terms of education. To be middle class meant having an education, being acquainted with modern institutions, and enjoying a 'clean' life, removed from Cairo's lower class existence (Armbrust 1999). In line with these local conceptions of being middle class, my delineation of the professional middle class relies on education. I focus on those Cairenes who, as university-educated professionals, depend on their educational capital for their livelihood. This professional middle class makes up about 30 percent of Cairo's population.[4]

As both Armbrust and John Waterbury argue, being part of the Egyptian middle class did not necessarily imply a certain minimum life-standard (Armbrust 1999:111, Waterbury 1983:262). Incomes in the middle class ranged from a few hundred to tens of thousands of pounds per month. This 'middle class' included educated professionals who barely made enough to keep out of poverty. Their financial circumstances did not contradict their middle class identification or the social salience of their education and office jobs. It rather reflected the precarious situation of large sections of the educated middle class, most notably poorly paid civil servants and unemployed university graduates. Cairo's professional middle class has long encompassed significant differences in income, life standard, and lifestyle, yet such differences have widened and hardened in Egypt's new liberal era. Though I use the labels 'lower-middle class,' 'middle class,' and 'upper-middle class' to intimate such differences in financial situation and social worlds, these terms do not connote clearly distinct social segments or mutually exclusive realities. At the start of the twenty-first century, the composition of and divisions in Cairo's middle class were changing as a result of the processes described in this study. Older social and economic hierarchies fed into new divisions, yet were significantly transformed in the process, while processes of class formation were still tentative.

Almost all my middle class contacts had graduated from university and were active participants in the labor force, even though some were unemployed or underemployed. While labor force participation was nearly universal among men, labor force participation among women varied strongly according to educational status and region. According to figures for 1998, some 88 percent of single women with a university education participated in the urban labor force, compared to 40 percent of those with intermediate education. Of their married counterparts, 66 percent were active participants in the urban labor force (Assaad 2002:24). This means that almost all urban, single, university-educated women, and a significant share of married women, were employed or actively looking for a job. Employment and professional identities and aspirations were clearly as much a part of these women's lives as they were of men's. Some of the couples who were contemplating marriage did have tense discussions about women's employment after marriage. These contestations concerned ideas about proper masculinity and femininity and gender roles in the family, especially the wife's ability to combine outside work with her family duties and the husband's ability to provide for her without her taking on a job.

Most of these professionals were not married at the time of research and lived with their parents. Many also remained financially dependent on their parents. While this was obviously the case for those who were unemployed or worked in ill-paid jobs, even many upper-middle class professionals had to rely on their family to be able to afford their upper-middle class lifestyles. This held particularly true for those who were actively looking for possible marriage partners with whom they could 'open a home.' Marriage requires large financial contributions of particularly the groom's family.

Fieldwork in Middle Class Cairo

In Cairo, extensive personal networks constitute the social capital that is crucial in getting a job, marrying or, in my case, doing research. Forging ties of friendship rather than informant–researcher relationships proved to be a major condition for more intimate knowledge of middle class life in Cairo. My frequent references to 'friends' and 'acquaintances' rather than 'informants' reflects the personalized nature of the relationships that were instrumental to my research. Participant observation opened up a world of stories, gossip, social performances, and implicit knowledge and codes. I learned much from informal discussions, fleeting comments, trips to different parts of the city, or personal talks in a coffee shop. My growing ease in spoken Egyptian Arabic, *'ammiyya*, was crucial in this respect.[5] I conducted all research in *'ammiyya*, or in upper-middle class gatherings, in a mix of *'ammiyya* and English.

Being a European foreigner, *agnabiyya*, who was knowledgeable with respect to local class-specific languages, styles, and norms for social interaction facilitated my participation in these networks. As a female professional in her late twenties who could easily combine Egyptian and 'foreign' repertoires, I could easily blend in, especially in upper-middle class circles, where such mixing of local and Western repertoires was the norm. Since much of young middle-class social life took place in mixed-gender spaces and networks, I had the opportunity to meet and become friends with both men and women, though my closest contacts were with women. This explains my focus on women's urban trajectories in the last part of this study. Being not quite white helped in this respect, since it allowed me to blend into Cairo's cityscape and share some of the urban experiences of my female friends and acquaintances in Cairo's coffee shops, transport systems, streets, and markets.

Even if my upper-middle class networks and upscale coffee shops came to constitute primary research sites, I was most at home in the middle-class intellectual and activist scene located in Downtown Cairo. This leftist scene brought together journalists, activists, artists, and many other men and women who were attracted by its comparatively lenient spaces. Contacts in this Downtown group presented other important routes for networking, and provided ample partners for discussions on contemporary Cairo. This study is largely written as a dialogue with these knowledgeable local counterparts.

With the exception of a number of close friends, I would generally participate in people's public social lives, which in the case of upper-middle class Cairenes, primarily played themselves out in upscale coffee shops. My focus on public spaces reflects the public nature of much of their social lives. My friends and acquaintances were part of extensive, rapidly shifting social networks. The fleeting nature of networks and the public character of my encounters lends this research a decidedly urban touch. It discusses a social life that is marked by "the continual brushing against strangers and the experience of observing bits of the 'stories' men and women carry with them, without ever knowing their conclusions," a quality Elizabeth Wilson considers characteristic of metropolitan life (2001:86). All these middle class Cairenes had stories and lives other than those in which I participated. This held particularly true with respect to family life.

Most of these single middle class professionals tried to maintain a distance between their familial lives and their social lives outside of the family realm. Generational differences in attitudes and beliefs, especially regarding mixed-gender contacts and social and sexual codes, called for a separation between these different spheres. Introducing personal friends to family was likely to breach this separation and open an otherwise bracketed social life away from home to critique or questioning. Moreover, notwithstanding the importance of the family in the lives of my informants, their family backgrounds and family lives were rarely a topic of conversation or discussion. In my upper-middle class circles I seldom heard people publicly inquire into the social background of their conversation partners. However, much like public secrets, whispers about people's family, reputation, or material worth abounded. This simultaneous absence and presence of the family reflects the ambivalent position of many unmarried professionals who lived with their families until marriage. Since many did not marry until in their late twenties or early thirties, they spent a considerable part of their adult working lives in their family homes, where their professional and independent status was partially negated by their filial position in the family.

Besides participant observation I rely on more formal interviews on schooling and the labor market, as well as the leisure culture that has developed in upscale coffee shops and, more generally, negotiations of public space. In addition to the young middle class professionals who constituted the majority of my informants, I also interviewed a number of 'specialists': coffee shop owners/managers and waiters, teachers, older professionals and business consultants, as well as the editors of two English-language magazines that target upper-middle class professionals.

Itineraries

So what has happened to middle class Cairo in Egypt's new liberal era? In this study I ask what lines of inclusion and exclusion confronted young, middle class professionals in the early twenty-first century and track how these new divisions materialized in the urban landscape.

The first chapter explores Egypt's new liberal age as a particular moment in its social history and introduces new imaginations of a Cairo with global aspirations. It continues by outlining some of their materializations in the built environment. The educational system and the labor market are primary fields for the production of new sociocultural divisions and distinctions. New lines of nobility based on combinations of educational, cultural, and social capital increasingly differentiate those who are able to participate in exclusive, conspicuously cosmopolitan up-market circuits of consumption and production from those who cannot. Chapter Two therefore discusses the imbrications of education and class in the making of Cairene social hierarchies. A national project aimed at the creation of a broad, highly educated middle class has given way to a more competitive and exclusionary system of private schools that coexists with increasingly decrepit public schooling. Not only has private schooling expanded markedly, it has also become one of the prime mechanisms of division and distinction in Cairo's professional middle class. Chapter Three, which discusses the labor market, highlights the ways in which these educational qualifications become effective in Cairo's strongly segmented economy.

These new divisions and distinctions are imprinted on *and* elaborated in the urban landscape. Chapters Four and Five discuss the ways in which young upper-middle class professionals negotiated the city. In Chapter Four I discuss Cairo's changing landscapes of leisure, focusing on the phenomenon of the up-market coffee shop and the sociabilities that unfold in these upscale spaces. These upscale coffee shops carve out specifically upper-middle class spaces in Cairo's urban landscape, which are marked by a great degree of class closure. I argue that such coffee shops allow for new matrices of belonging *and* distance in Cairo's cityscape. They thereby strengthen tendencies toward a slicing of physical and social space and a fragmentation of city life. In the last chapter I explore some of the footprints of social segregation in Cairo by looking at the urban trajectories of upper-middle class women. I follow the high-powered routines that take them from home to work to coffee shop and explore what these trajectories can tell us about present-day Cairo. I argue that significations and fears surrounding upper-middle class femininity have come to legitimize social segregation. I surmise that the bodies of upper-middle class women have become a battleground for new class configurations and contestations, literally embodying both power and fragility of Cairo's upper-middle class.

By way of conclusion I return to the global dreams that take center stage in Egypt's new liberal era. I argue that Egypt's new liberalism contains a recipe for a divided nation, eliciting simultaneous materializations of a First and a Third World in the spaces of an increasingly divided city. "If we stop dreaming, we'll die," sang Egyptian singer Muhammad Mounir, addressing a public struggling to hold on to their dreams of something better in the face of adverse circumstances. Those dreams differ significantly from global dreams of a life of affluence and ease in conspicuously cosmopolitan Cairo. The question is whose dreams count.

Chapter 1

Dreams of a Global Cairo

History, Present and Future

In December 2002 the opening of a French hypermarket on the outskirts of Cairo was a hot topic in my upper-middle class circles. Everyone seemed to be talking about the new Carrefour, located close to the exclusive *compound* (gated community) of Qattamiya Heights outside of up-market Maadi (see map). Maha, an upper-middle class friend in her late twenties, excitedly invited me to come along to see the new hypermarket-cum-shopping mall. In the first weeks after the opening we paid a visit to one of Maha's friends who worked as a store designer at City Center Mall, the official name of the greater complex that housed the Carrefour hypermarket (see Elsheshtawy 2006).

After we managed the congested traffic of inner-city Cairo, traveled along the eight-lane Munib Bridge, and continued for a few minutes on the highway, we arrived at what for the moment had become one of Cairo's hotspots. A huge square hangar-like building rose before us out of the desert. Since the complex was located at a distance from the city along a crossroads of highways, and was only accessible by car, its location promised an exclusive public. We entered a spacious, clean, and brightly lit hall that seemed to be insulated from reminders of Egypt's poverty and dust. One side of the main corridor was occupied by a long row of Carrefour checkout counters. Along the other side of the corridor, a number of upscale shops seduced passersby with premium goods in enticing window displays. These stores included Timberland, a sports shop that sold Nike and Adidas, as well as a Mobaco shop selling elegant, locally produced clothing. Visitors who tired of shopping could take a break in the Cilantro coffee shop with its modern, minimalist steel and leather décor. Though the food court and the children's play park Magic Land were not yet open, Carrefour was already a complete shopping experience, set apart from the more ambiguous social landscape of the city.

The excitement generated by Carrefour could not have been about the products on offer. Up-market supermarkets like Metro and Alfa Market had been catering to elite tastes for some ten years. Nor was it because of the promise of a clean, even antiseptic environment, which was a major feature of most up-market establishments. A large part of the thrill seemed related to the mere idea that a French formula for shopping/living had come to Cairo, providing for an unusual shopping experience. The City Center Mall was a joint project of Dubai-based Majid Al-Futtaim Group and the French Carrefour concern. Yasser Elsheshtawy mentions that "the Egyptian local press largely downplays the Dubai connection and the fact that the entire center is based on a Dubai model. In fact, more emphasis is placed on the French connection, in a sense suggesting that Egypt will become Western by constructing centers such as these" (2006:245). Rather than a Gulf-based investment, Carrefour was welcomed as the latest manifestation of what Emanuela Guano has described as "the free market with its tantalizing promise of participation in the privileged Western modernity to be found in the northern hemisphere—still so distant from the south of the world" (2002a:197). The location added to the allure of this shopping experience. Since the complex was set apart from the city, a trip to Carrefour could provide the feel of a visit to a foreign country. A huge sign over the Nile on the newly extended Munib Bridge said: "Carrefour, only 5 minutes away," inviting those still lingering in the city to taste this newest edition of First World inclusion. Maha's friend enthusiastically told us that it was a wonderful place, not only because it was still so new and clean, but also since its public was so select. "Only *clean* people come here," she told us emphatically. Complete, exclusive, perfect.

Carrefour is part of the conspicuously cosmopolitan Cairo of affluence and ease described in the Introduction. This up-market Cairo is located in wealthier districts like Zamalek, Mohandisseen, Heliopolis, Nasr City, and Maadi. While most Cairenes suffered the withdrawal of state support for basic foodstuffs and were forced to rely on informal markets of consumption, leisure, and housing that accommodated their limited buying power, the urban landscape also harbored striking affluence. This upscale city consisted of well-designed and maintained, spotlessly clean venues that offered a comprehensive range of products and services that shared an emphasis on First World standards and quality and comparatively high prices. To illustrate, in 2003 coffee in a *'ahwa baladi* (male-dominated sidewalk café) cost anywhere between LE0.5 and LE1, whereas a caffè latte in an upscale coffee shop was at least LE5 (excluding 5 percent taxes and 12 percent service charge). This upscale city represents Cairo's "reterritorializations of the metropole" (Guano 2002:183). It speaks both to Egypt's new liberal striving and to deep-seated desires for a First World existence. As Vignal and Denis note, "the popular majority focuses on survival, while . . . a thin layer of city dwellers consumes on a world scale, affording a lifestyle that is increasingly similar to those in other international cities" (2006:111).

Carrefour, then, was merely the latest addition to the expanding landscape of up-market Cairo. The introduction of Carrefour raised much momentary excitement. Older malls no longer conveyed such feelings of renewed inclusion into much-desired First World consumption and lifestyles. The fast incorporation of malls, coffee shops, and up-market restaurants into the daily lives of affluent Cairenes signals the consolidation and normalization of such reterritorializations of the First World. At the start of the twenty-first century, this conspicuously cosmopolitan Cairo had become the self-evident backdrop of the lives of affluent Cairenes.

In this chapter I explore Cairo's changing landscape in the context of Egypt's new liberal age. The political and economic reorientation away from Nasser's state-led development originates in the mid-1970s with Sadat's *infitaah* (open-door) policies that initiated a gradual liberalization of the economy. In the 1990s it significantly sped up as a result of the adoption of a structural adjustment policy package. I first examine this shift away from the Nasser-era state-led development. I then turn to Egypt's new liberal era, characterized by structural adjustment policies and an emphasis on the private sector and integration into global economic networks. I ask what new national narratives and imaginations accompany this shift to neoliberal policies. Finally, I explore the material expressions of these new national policies and dreams in Cairo's urban landscape.

Egypt's Social Contract

In the years following the 1952 Revolution the state assumed an increasingly central and dominant role in the Egyptian economy, particularly after the nationalizations that followed the 1956 Suez Crisis. The new Nasser-led regime initiated agrarian land reforms that significantly reduced the landed properties of the largest landowners and redistributed part of the sequestered land (Jankowski 2000:148–49). Under Nasser's strongly centralized and authoritarian regime, Egypt embarked on an ambitious program of industrialization geared toward import substitution. Cairo's citizens benefited from greatly improved access to educational and health facilities, as well as an exponential growth of jobs in the new public sector industries and the expanding state bureaucracy. Many of these policies were geared toward the creation of a large urban middle class, most notably through the democratization of education and the provision of government jobs to all graduates (Abdel-Fadil 1980). In the early 1960s Egypt was officially declared a socialist state. The state became the dominant actor in the national economy, as well as the main employer. In the early 1980s over half of the nonagricultural workforce was employed by the state (Richards and Waterbury 1996:184).

In 1969, Janet Abu-Lughod wrote that Cairo's urban landscape seemed to be in a process of ongoing homogenization. The older elite presence in the city had been decimated, while "consumption patterns, ways of dress, and leisure time activities which were once the prerogative of a somewhat westernized middle class have been diffusing down the social structure. One rarely sees the *jallabiyah*. . . . Almost no women are veiled" (J. Abu-Lughod 1971:238–39). Differences between urban neighborhoods were rapidly erased, she argued, and Downtown shops that sold prestigious foreign goods began selling the same locally produced goods sold in other places. Looking back at the Nasser era, James Jankowski argues, "economic disparities did decrease from 1952 to 1970; the social opportunities available to many Egyptians expanded over the same period. The Nasser era left a legacy of commitment to 'the people' and to socioeconomic egalitarianism which many Egyptians recall with fondness" (2000:152).

The Nasser era also created its own class hierarchies (Abdel-Fadil 1980, Moore 1994). It gave rise to a new bourgeoisie, which "could be defined as those officials who by virtue of their managerial positions and special skills 'owned' the means of converting public into private resources, together with their allies in the private sector" (Moore 1994:122). Clement Henry Moore (1994) and Mahmoud Abdel-Fadil (1980) moreover note that there was a large measure of social continuity with the prerevolutionary period, since relatively privileged families were well placed to capitalize on new avenues of social mobility in and through state institutions.

Toward the end of the 1960s it became apparent that many of the ambitious aims and programs of Nasserite developmentalism would prove untenable. John Waterbury writes that, in the context of economic stagnation in the late 1960s and 1970s, "the goals of extending basic services to all

Egyptians had to be quietly abandoned," along with some of the central tenets of the Nasser regime (1983:223). The Nasserite social contract between the state and the populace that promised welfare provisions in exchange for political passivity could, however, not easily be overturned (Jankowski 2000:187ff.). Despite a shift toward economic liberalization from the mid-1970s onward, and the concomitant erosion of Nasser-era arrangements, it remains a central framework for state policies and popular reactions to such policies. It is still a crucial yardstick for public and private discussions of the state and its policies, and continues to inform imaginations of the relation between the state, the nation, and its citizens.

After Nasser's death Sadat embarked on a course of economic liberalization and rapprochement with the West. Under the label *infitaah*, 'opening,' a number of new laws was set down, which "on the one hand attempted to make Egypt a more hospitable environment for international capital; on the other, gave the local private sector more freedom domestically and more encouragement to work in collaboration with foreign enterprises" (Jankowski 2000:171). The late 1970s and the early 1980s were a period of relative prosperity, not so much because of the expanded private sector or foreign presence in the economy, but because of a surge in revenues from external resources: oil, the Suez Canal, and tourism, as well as increased sums of Western, especially American, foreign aid and the sizable remittances of the estimated 1.5 million Egyptians working in the Gulf states (Jankowski 2001:173). Working in one of the richer Arab states became the major way to increase family incomes for the educated and uneducated alike (Ibrahim 1982).

The *infitaah* gave rise to a stratum of nouveaux riches that was able to capitalize on the opening of the economy to foreign investors and foreign goods and the expanded leverage granted to the private sector. These were often top-level bureaucrats who could use their control of state enterprises to ensure favorable starting positions in the newly invigorated private sector. Old and new elites—the aristocracy of the prerevolution years, the military technocratic elite of the Nasser period, and the commercial nouveaux riches of the *infitaah*—started to converge in a new upper class (Ayubi 1982:403). At the same time, labor migration created new divisions within the existing professional middle class between those who were able to work for extended periods abroad and significantly improve their family's economic situation, and those who were unable or chose not to leave their comparatively ill-paid jobs in Egypt.

In everyday life the *infitaah* materialized first and foremost as an opening to imported luxury consumption goods.[6] Wealth and conspicuous consumption were once again on display in the streets of Cairo. Max Rodenbeck writes that in 1980s Cairo a new cosmopolitanism began to flourish. "International chain stores, high-tech discos, theme restaurants and shopping centers appeared," catering to tourists and burgeoning strata of affluent Egyptians (Rodenbeck 1999:244). At the same time, inflation steadily eroded real wages of salaried workers in Egypt. Food subsidies provided the major buffer against rapid impoverishment; expenditure on food subsidies grew from less than 8 percent in 1970 to a staggering 60 percent of government expenditure in 1980 (Jankowski 2000:174).

Outside middle class areas, discontent grew as more and more youths found that the withering of Nasser-style institutions and the 'open door' to the private sector and the West left them to face a grim future. Meanwhile, the political climate under Sadat gave room to "the expression of an alternative Islamic vision of society," which largely took the form of Islamic social activism and an increased prominence of religious discourses in different areas of life (Jankowski 2000:176). This religious revival also led to bouts of Islamist violence from the mid-1970s onward. By the mid-1990s, the state was on the winning end, and Islamist militant activity decreased significantly (Jankowski 2000: 87–89).

The 1980s reliance on income from workers' remittances, tourism, oil, the Suez Canal, and foreign aid left the Egyptian economy highly vulnerable to fluctuations in the world economy and increasingly dependent on the wishes of foreign donors, most notably the United States (Abdelrahman 2004, Mitchell 2002). In the 1980s, the drop in oil prices diminished possibilities for labor migration to oil-rich Arab countries. In 1990 the Gulf war moreover led to the immediate return of many labor migrants. Though labor migration resumed in the early 1990s, the opportunities for labor migration to other Arab states never returned to its previous level (Abdel Moati 2002:336–38)[7]. The shortfall in revenue in the 1980s led to rising foreign debts to the extent that debt servicing became threatened. At the end of the 1980s, after a number of partial and hesitant attempts at macrostabilization and structural adjustment, the government could no longer avoid accepting an extensive IMF/World Bank structural adjustment package. In 1991, the Egyptian state began implementing structural adjustment policies that included financial austerity measures, a depreciation of the exchange rate, elimination of price controls and subsidies, and public sector reform and privatization (Kienle 2002:144ff.). This policy package was aimed at transforming Egypt into a liberal market economy integrated into global economic networks.

Neoliberalist Faiths

Neoliberal tenets proclaim the superiority of the global market as an allocating and regulating force in economies and societies around the world. The free reign of the global market was said to bring about higher affluence for all who dare to brave global competition, while failure to do so spells inevitable economic slowdown. Such tenets become self-fulfilling prophecies as they influence policies of state and nonstate actors on a local, national, and global scale. States around the world rewrite their laws and redesign their budgets and national economic policies to conform to global standards of neoliberal economics. These neoliberal policies and new regulatory regimes are presented in terms of apolitical scientific rationality and efficiency (Peck and Tickell 2002:400). As Timothy Mitchell rightly argues, "The continuous political struggles under way in places such as Egypt are not the consequences of a more global logic, but an active political process whose significance is repeatedly marginalized and overlooked in reproducing the simple narratives of globalization . . ." (2002:298).

For 'developing countries' like Egypt with state debts that skyrocketed in the 1980s, such policies were commonly implemented under pressure from the IMF and the World Bank and were framed as structural adjustment packages. Such by and large standard packages were generally comprised of "privatization of public assets, severely reduced social expenditures, wage reduction, currency devaluation, liberalization of trade and investment laws and export enhancement" (McMichael 1998:107, cf. Veltmeyer et al. 1997). Egypt's structural adjustment program not only entailed the state's withdrawal from social welfare provisions, but also the establishment of the internationally funded semi-governmental Social Fund for Development, which was meant to ease Egypt through the pains of structural adjustment. It moreover included significant state subsidies to the private sector in the form of massive loans to businessmen from public banks, tax holidays for business ventures, and investments in infrastructure that benefited new production sites (Mitchell 1999, 2002).

The actual implementation of these reforms has been partial. Despite fifteen years of structural adjustment, the Nasser-era social contract between state and society continues to loom large. As Lila Abu-Lughod argues, "supporting privatization and multinational corporations does not sit easily with a governing elite's self-justification in terms of continuing rhetoric of national development whose keystone was social development and the wider social good" (2005:18–19). Notwithstanding its neoliberal policies and commitments, official statements regularly rehearsed the government's commitment to the poor and goals of social equality. Since earlier attempts to drastically cut subsidies resulted in a popular uprising that left parts of the city in ruins, the government chose to slowly dismantle Nasser-era institutions, rather than outright abolish such welfare arrangements. Privatization did not gain momentum until the end of the 1990s. Civil service employment has grown steadily (Assaad 1997) and the government regularly claimed the success of governmental job provision schemes.[8] The extension of food subsidy programs in 2003 and 2004 represented a similar digression from set policies.[9] The widespread disaffection of many Egyptians after years of economic crisis and inflation has repeatedly forced the government to resort to state interventions that were supposed to be a thing of the past.

Even if a comprehensive critical account of the past two decades of economic restructuring and neoliberal policies in Egypt has yet to be written, the record seems rather grim. Egypt's performance was initially hailed as a textbook example of IMF reforms, and macroeconomic indicators were cited to demonstrate the success of the reforms: a low inflation rate, significantly reduced state deficit and foreign debt, as well as reasonable growth figures. Yet, as Timothy Mitchell convincingly demonstrates, these figures in fact tell a more sobering story of the short-lived influx of speculative financial flows and financial injections, which led to a building boom geared toward a small section of affluent Egyptians instead of reinvigorated production or the expansion of exports (Mitchell 2002:273ff.). These subsidies to the private sector did not reap the expected benefits. The most painful reminders of this failure are abandoned construction sites (cf. Vignal and Denis 2006:134) and high-profile cases against businessmen who have been prosecuted for their failure to service outstanding public bank loans.

Mitchell (2002) and Kienle (2002) claim that social inequality and poverty rose in Egypt throughout the 1980s and suggest that these likely became more pronounced in the 1990s as a consequence of structural adjustment policies. They moreover argue that neoliberal reforms have resulted in the further concentration of wealth in the hands of a few with powerful resources and state connections. Available statistics indicate that social inequality has become especially pronounced in metropolitan Cairo.[10] Ragui Assaad and Malak Rouchdy tentatively conclude that in the mid-nineties a quarter of the Egyptian population was poor by any standard, while another quarter was on the margins of poverty (1999:11). Unemployment had been on the rise, while real wages decreased throughout the 1980s and 1990s (see Assaad 2002, Awad 1999). It is likely that in the following years, the situation had grown even worse, since the Egyptian economy experienced a severe economic crisis with high levels of inflation.

So far I have emphasized the 'negative' policies that are characteristic of structural adjustment: withdrawal of the state from economic and social interventions, budget cuts, and the abolishment of barriers to 'open markets.' Such a portrayal downplays the continuing dominance of the Egyptian state. While the Egyptian state might have been curtailed by the 'transnational governmentality' of international organizations and internationally funded 'local' NGOs (Ferguson and Gupta 2002), it has retained an important role in managing these nonstate actors and their policy prescriptions (Abdelrahman 2004). The state moreover remains a central arbiter of resource allocation (cf. Mitchell 2002), the major employer in the formal sector, and the provider of crucial public goods, even if they are of low quality. The Nasser-era social contract between state and population still provides an important frame for popular expectations and demands vis-à-vis the state, even if the latter does not live up to these expectations. Lila Abu-Lughod rightly notes that the nation-state continues to provide the primary context for the everyday lives and social imaginations of most Egyptians (2005:26).

The 1990s have seen a reorganization and redeployment of the state, rather than its withering. Diane Singerman and Paul Amar highlight the violent, repressive nature of 'liberalization' in Egypt. They characterize the 'liberal' state as one "run in the interests of an elite, state-subsidized ring of Cairo-based capitalists who call themselves liberals or globalizers or democratizers because they facilitate foreign investment in the economic sphere, even as they insist on repression, the extension of the Emergency Law, and police-state practices in the political sphere" (2006:9). The Egyptian state has played a crucial role in the creation and securing of 'market conditions' and the implementation of neoliberal policies (Mitchell 2002, cf. Sassen 1998, Chapter Ten). As I argue in the following section, the state actively took up the facilitation, promotion, and even creation of new urban economy sites, and made major infrastructural investments meant to create a world-class environment in the country's capital.

Global City Imperatives

Egypt has long been a highly centralized country. In 1996, metropolitan Cairo housed an estimated 15 million, some 17 percent of Egypt's population (Vignal and Denis 2006:121, 123). Its centrality, however, far exceeds that suggested by its share of the country's population. Cairo's centrality to the Egyptian nation-state is perhaps best illustrated by the fact that in colloquial Egyptian, the name for the capital city and the country are one and the same: *Masr.* Almost all major state institutions and most major economic activities are concentrated in the capital (see Vignal and Denis 2006). This is exceedingly true for up-market, internationally oriented economic activities, which are almost exclusively located in the Greater Cairo area.

The changes brought about by Egypt's neoliberal reforms and quest for integration into the global market are primarily effected through, and felt in, Cairo's urban landscape. The urban landscape of the capital bears the imprint of Egypt's new national project. Private sector and state initiatives have been directed at the creation of a globally appropriate city that can cater to transnational business and the lifestyles of affluent Cairenes (see, e.g., Vignal and Denis 2006, Ghannam 2002, Mitchel 1999, Yousry et al. 1998). These efforts materialized in investments in infrastructure and the building of new-economy production sites, such as Media City and the ICT complex, as well as housing and leisure facilities for those employed in these sectors (see Denis 2006; Elsheshtawy 2006). At the start of the twenty-first century, the ring road circling the city had been completed; gated communities had sprouted up along the highways that formed new axes of centrality in the expanding metropolitan area. A new private university seemed to open its doors every year. Cairo's landscape increasingly catered to those groups who fit the neoliberal project and whose relative affluence allowed them to leave their mark on the landscape in the form of conspicuously cosmopolitan consumption practices and uses of urban space. The inhabitants of this upscale Cairo are not only the wealthy elites, but also the upper-middle class professionals who staff its upscale, internationally oriented workspaces.

"Office towers housing multinational corporations, transnational banks, world trade centers, and five-star hotels, once the exclusive hallmark of a small number of 'world cities,' now signify the integration of almost every major metropolis into global capitalism," Ayse Öncü and Petra Weyland note (1997:1). The signs of the turn to neoliberalism and the global market are similarly inscribed in the landscape of Cairo. The Nile City Towers located along the Nile Corniche north of Downtown are striking emblems of neoliberal Cairo. These thirty-three-story Orascom headquarters function as a signpost of Cairo's entrance into a global era.

Such obvious convergences in urban landscapes around the world speak of the emergence of a circuit of interconnected global spaces set within oftentimes impoverished, and increasingly marginalized, surroundings. Saskia Sassen (2000, 2001) argues that cities have gained importance as the nodes of coordination and control of dispersed global production. They harbor materializations of the global that are increasingly disconnected from the rest of the urban landscape. This (perceived) centrality of cities has created its own dynamic. Robinson argues that the 'global city' has been translated into a 'regulating fiction' that promises new urban wealth, and threatens with a global disconnect (2002, cf. M.P. Smith 2001). Neil Smith argues that the concentration of production on the metropolitan scale has given rise to "a new urbanism" (2002:434).

Nile City Towers

This new urbanism entails competition among city governments to capture a share of global business and ameliorate their city's ranking in the ubiquitous indices of global city hierarchy. According to Smith this 'quest for the global' generally involves a major shift in resource allocation toward infrastructure and showcase projects, as well as subsidies to global corporations to entice them to locate or remain located in a particular city, subsidies he pointedly calls 'geobribes' (2002:427–28).

Such showcase investments in cities are, however, not only related to competition for global business. Dawson and Edwards rightly warn against neglecting the dialectical relationship between "economic global city functions" and "political global city functions" in the "cultures of globalization" (Dawson and Edwards 2004:2). As Abidin Kusno (2004) argues, life in capital cities is often made to stand for the life of the nation. The resultant 'nationalist urbanism' entails large investments in the urban landscape of these capital cities in order to represent national ambitions. This has long been the case in Egypt. Cairo's belle-époque Downtown, for example, still stands as a reminder of late nineteenth-century ambitions of Khedive Ismail. Such showcase projects can also be seen as attempts to intimate the country's move from Third to First World status, as Anthony D. King has argued with respect to China's frequent use of the high-rise tower (2004, Chapter One).

Talaat Harb Square, Downtown Cairo

An article by Egyptian city planner Khaled El-Khishin exemplifies such 'global city' logic. El-Khishin argues that Cairo had better speed up its quest for global city status in order to secure vital resources for its financial health. He sums up the features of Cairo's infrastructure he considers conducive to such a bid for global city status: "a multi-million dollar National Museum, a Stock Exchange Complex, a new French university, a smart/hi-tech research park . . . the inauguration of the second and third subway lines, and a ring road." He moreover mentions as assets the "exclusive residential estates [that] have sprung up around the city," as well as the fact that "entertainment, leisure and international events have been served by the construction of an Opera House, a $200 million Media City, a 'City Stars' shopping mall and residential complex, a 'Dreamland' theme park, four world-class golf courses [and] four new five-star hotels . . ." (El-Khishin 2003:129–30). This list reads like an upper or upper-middle class itinerary. The celebration of these specific amenities highlights the intimate connection between this quest for the global and Cairo's upper and upper-middle classes. It also illustrates the irrelevance of the majority of the city's spaces and inhabitants to a globally appropriate Cairo and displays a worrying absence of concern for questions of social equity, even survival.

Farha Ghannam argues that Cairo's urban landscape became the object of a search for the global in the late 1970s (2002, see also Ibrahim 1987). "The plan to build a modern Cairo placed great emphasis on the visual image of urban space," she argues. "Aiming to imitate Western modernity, Sadat's policies privileged the gaze of tourists and upper-class Egyptians" (Ghannam 2002:31). President Anwar Sadat wrote in his 1974 'October Paper' that he intended to create "a city that fits its international position through providing it with the necessary infrastructure, modern communication systems, and the facilities needed for work as well as economic and touristic activities" (cited in Ghannam 2002:29). As Saad Eddin Ibrahim notes, Sadat's favorite models were Los Angeles and Houston, rather than Paris (1987:214). The construction of a modern capital suited to the more external orientation of the *infitaah* period not only entailed new construction and the upgrading of the city's infrastructure, but also the removal of 'popular' areas in central locations in the name of national interest, development, and modernity (Ghannam 2002:33–38).

Subsequent interventions geared at the creation of a globally appropriate Cairo in the 1980s and 1990s coincided with neoliberal economic restructuring and attempts at integration into the global market. The government played an active role in the restructuring of the urban landscape. As Mahmoud Yousry et al. argue,

> To adapt the investment environment to globalization trends and
> to provide economic space for investors in the new global market,
> the Egyptian government . . . [acquired] extensive foreign technical
> and financial assistance . . . to upgrade the infrastructure and
> transportation and communication networks of Cairo to enhance its
> target role as a world city. (1998:277–78)

In 1975, a central agency took on the task of upgrading Cairo's infrastructure, aided by World Bank expertise and financing. Massive investments were made in roads, flyovers, and a ring road. At the end of the 1980s, the first of three metro lines was completed; the second was completed at the end of the 1990s. The agency also worked toward upgrading public utilities and communication networks (Yousry et al. 1998). It is telling that while investment in transportation projects in 1992/1993 amounted to over LE150 million, only LE10 million had been assigned to the upgrading of 'degraded' areas, which housed over half of all Cairenes (Yousry et al. 1998:282, 300).

The massive investments in Cairo's infrastructure have done much to improve living conditions in Cairo. Electricity and water supply have become far more reliable. Whereas the waiting times and baksheesh needed to get a phone line used to be legendary (Rodenbeck 1999:230–31), telephone connections can now be installed in a matter of weeks. The two metro lines provide

HOSSAM FADL (2008)

crucial means of public transport for many Cairenes. The major infrastructure plan to improve traffic inside and around Cairo has been completed. A ring road and inner-city highways connect Sixth of October City, the major site for new economic showcase projects like Media Production City and the ICT complex, with diverse outlying parts of Cairo. This new infrastructure 'incidentally' connects different up-market areas of Cairo, significantly speeding up movement between these outlying areas, including the new cities and compounds in the desert (see map of Cairo). Though it has done much to improve the previously notorious traffic situation, these flyover bridges and highways have also created the conditions for a further disjunction between the spaces of up-market Cairo and less affluent parts of the city. An intricate network of inner-city highways and the ring road allow affluent car-owners to move from one part of up-market Cairo to the next, without descending into the disorder, crowdedness, and poverty of Cairo's poorer spaces. The lives of affluent Cairenes are increasingly located along Cairo's three major transport axes that connect to the ring road: Mohandisseen/Sixth of October City, Heliopolis and Nasr City/New Cairo, and Maadi/Moqattam/New Maadi. The erstwhile exclusive nineteenth-century Downtown hardly figures in their urban trajectories (cf. Battesti 2006).

This drive to create a globally appropriate and inviting Cairo entailed an obvious and spectacular convergence with other major cities in terms of spatial organization, built environments, and class-based cosmopolitan lifestyles

30 Dreams of a Global Cairo

and consumption patterns. It has resulted in the emergence of an exclusive, up-market Cairo that caters to its affluent citizens with conspicuously cosmopolitan products and spaces. It has also led to new forms of disjuncture and has augmented social segregation in the urban landscape. As Alan and Josephine Smart argue in their essay on urbanization and globalization, "Many interventions in cities have been seen as efforts to make them more hospitable to the professional middle-class as well as international investors and tourists, usually at the expense of the poor and minorities" (2003:273). Yousry et al. concur: "Most public and private investment has been used to upgrade Cairo's infrastructure and to improve the environment of those who are involved in globalization trends. The move towards globalization has been at the expense of the middle- and low-income groups on fixed earnings" (1998:305).

Picturing an Other Cairo

Egypt's neoliberal agenda entails significant reimaginations of the nation, its development, and its future. Who is to be the rightful heir of such new visions of the nation and who can, as a result, lay claim to its affections and resources? I first turn to advertising to explore some of the neoliberal imagery of the new, globally appropriate nation and its young urban professional protagonists. I then return to Cairo's urban landscape, where we can find the imprint of these new narratives in the form of a range of exclusive urban developments.

Watching television in spring 2002, I was struck by an unusual commercial. The images were beautiful and enticing and presented a stark contrast with the lower quality of most mainstream television. Though I no longer recall the text of the commercial, the images remain as a clear example of the mixture of dreams and denials that marks the longing for a global Cairo. The camera zooms in on rows of fit, light-skinned, straight-haired young men and women in business suits. They stare confidently into the camera toward the future from behind flat-screen monitors in the new Bibliotheca Alexandrina, a major prestige project of the Egyptian government that was largely funded by foreign donors. This sweeping commercial advertised the Future Generation Foundation, founded by president Hosni Mubarak's son, Gamal Mubarak, with the stated goal of developing Egypt's human resources in light of competition in the global market.[11]

The solemn yet luxurious and technologically advanced setting provided the backdrop for youthful, good-looking professionals, Egypt's *Jiil al-Mustaqbal*, Future Generation. Its images were seductive, but I was struck by the numerous exclusions it spelled out. This representation of Egypt's future generation reproduced most dominant lines of privilege within society. Their business suits spoke of Western professionalism, while their fair complexions functioned as important indicators of local elite backgrounds. This future generation did not feature *muhaggabaat* (veiled women). Not surprisingly, the *higaab* was not deemed suitable for Egypt's representative present and projected future. This exclusion mirrored official media policy, which staunchly portrayed modern Egypt as secular.[12] One might encounter a seductively veiled Bedouin girl in a music video or tourist advertisement, and television serials often featured a warm and inviting mother wearing an inconspicuous head covering. These were necessary, yet marginal, reminders of Egypt's exoticism and the comforts and safety of the private realm. Egypt's present and future were clearly located elsewhere, and featured different protagonists.

Portraying a message about Egypt as heading toward a bright, globally sound future, the commercial's subtext was too obvious to ignore: only certain people were to be part of the future generation that would take Egypt into the future. During an interview with Ahmed's *shilla*, a group of young lower-middle class men who had recently graduated from university, I asked who were getting all the good jobs. "*Shabaab il-musta'bal*" (the youth of the future) was their short but resolute answer.[13] These young men had few doubts as to their own situation and chances in life and were outspoken about the more general distribution of fortunes in contemporary Egyptian society. While a new Egypt was being fashioned in front of their eyes, they were bitterly aware that they were not included in its design. The commercial reflected their daily experiences and observations: the flashy new cars driven by people their age, advertisements for jobs for which they would not think of applying, and luxury goods in fancy new malls that might present a seductive promise but were clearly not within their reach. All this in a context in which, as one of the young men kept repeating, he could not even buy himself a new sweater. While this commercial obviously presented an image of Egypt's wished-for future, it also testified to the refusals, displacements, and silencing entailed in its creation.

Around the same time another commercial, advertising the national telecommunications company Telecom Egypt, spoke eloquently of the new national project in which the local is brought up-to-speed with the global (see figure). After a birds-eye view of Cairo and a shot of feluccas on the Nile (1), the commercial takes us into the heart of Cairo. To the rhythm of upbeat music, we embark on a visually exhilarating flight along reminders of the old glory of Downtown Cairo. A young, fashionably dressed woman talks on the phone in her Downtown apartment (2, 3). An equally smart young man, presumably her husband, talks on his mobile phone in an upscale coffee shop (4). This set-up of the commercial's main storyline is followed by a fast sequence of images that shows different uses and users of telecommunication, from videoconferencing between lavish, modern headquarters and a construction site (6) to an old *sha'bi* fruit seller who is shown using an old telephone (8).

This sequence is set within a nationalist framework. It includes images that do not have a clear relation to telecommunication, but are meant to evoke national sensibilities: supporters of the national football team (5), a young girl in a green, countryside setting, and a Nubian dance performance (7). Throughout, short sentences appear that remind the viewers of national unity: 'One Country,' 'One Voice,' 'One Soil,' 'One Family.' We then return to the young woman in her apartment, who receives a phone call from the man in the coffee shop. In the next shot we see them running toward each other on the pedestrian Imbaba bridge with the wide-open space of the Nile in the background. They meet and hold hands (9). The words 'One World' appear and the camera zooms out until we see the globe (10), which in turn transforms into a dot in the Telecom Egypt logo. The commercial ends with a female voice saying, "One network brings us all closer: Telecom Egypt."

The Telecom Egypt commercial was featured on the website of the Egyptian advertising agency that produced it, Bates Equity (www.batesequity.com). The site included a case description, which stated that the major problem faced by Telecom Egypt was its bad public image. According to the case description, the company was perceived as "old, unfriendly and of poor quality. The company embodies every public sector cliché." The commercial aimed to improve Telecom Egypt's standing in the market, attract investors, upgrade the brand image and establish strong ties between the brand and customers as the only company that "brings all Egyptians together." The site claimed that the campaign was a big success. It was chosen as the best campaign of Ramadan 2002 by *Business Monthly* and a track study showed that it had successfully projected Telecom Egypt's new image as "modern, pride of Egypt and the leader in communications."

The commercial invoked images of a modern, united nation that is conversant with global standards and connected to the world. It thus simultaneously emphasized the global and the national. In his discussion of Indian commercials, Mazzarella argues that the "promise of membership for Indians in a global 'ecumene' of world-class consumption was uttered in the same breath as the claim that globalization was in fact all about recognizing and acknowledging the cultural specificity of Indian desires" (2003:34–35, cf. Fernandes 2000a). In both cases entrance in the global 'ecumene' was significantly mediated by the nation. This Indian national modernity that is also global was intimated through Bombay's cityscape, which was figured as "a collective space of aspiration and transformation" (Mazarella 2003:50). The Egypt Telecom commercial similarly used Cairo's urban spaces to portray Egypt's up-to-date modernity. While nostalgic and exoticizing shots of the countryside and a folkloric dance performance symbolize spaces outside of Cairo, Egypt's modernity was located in Cairo's urban spaces. The imaging of modern Egypt through Cairo's urban spaces and its more affluent inhabitants is a standard feature of Egyptian media productions (see Abu-Lughod 2005). However, the specific ways in which these urban spaces were portrayed and the choice of protagonists speaks of the inclusions and exclusions in imaginations of a globally appropriate Cairo/Egypt. Even though different urban callers were featured to suggest national unity, the commercial focused on a young, fashionable, and affluent couple. The couple is easily locatable in Cairo's professional upper-middle class, the class that staffs Egypt's internationally oriented workspaces.

The choice for Cairo's downtown area seemed paradoxical, since it has increasingly become a predominantly (lower) middle class center, all but abandoned by the very same class portrayed in the commercial (cf. Battesti 2006). All the signs of the newly affluent classes are located elsewhere, in upper-middle class areas like Mohandisseen, Heliopolis, Maadi, and Zamalek. Yet these areas were apparently not imaginative enough and could not represent Cairo's stature and sought-after elegance. In contrast, the downtown area, with its turn-of-the-century French architecture, formed an ideal stage for a refurbished Cairo, that is, after the blemishes of actual everyday life had been removed. Shots that avoided the less suitable shops, traffic, inhabitants, and less-than-immaculate white façades presented Downtown Cairo as a rejuvenated, gentrified inner city, which intimates a European rather than American cosmopolitan locatedness.

Egypt Telecom Commercial
From left to right:
1. Fellucas on the Nile with the Imbaba bridge in the background
2. Woman calling at the balcony of a Downtown apartment
3. Inside the apartment
4. Man calling in coffee shop
5. Supporters of the national football team ('One Voice')
6. Videoconferencing between headquarters and construction site ('One Family')
7. Exotic touches of a Nubian performance ('One Soul')
8. Shots of people using the phone, in this case an old sha'bi fruit seller
9. After a phone call, the man and woman shown earlier run out to meet at the Imbaba bridge ('One World')
10. The camera zooms out from the bridge to the banks of the Nile and, eventually, the world

Stills from a commercial for Telecom Egypt, by Bates Equity
http://www.batesequity.com/ web/index.html
(accessed February 19, 2005)

The choice for the Imbaba bridge was even further removed from everyday realities. The pedestrian bridge where the eventual meeting takes place actually links two lower class areas on both sides of the Nile: Imbaba and Rod al-Farag. Affluent Cairenes like the couple portrayed in the commercial would never cross this bridge wedged between these two notoriously lower class areas. The image of the bridge seemed to speak to European rather than Cairene sensibilities. It evoked common Western gentrifications projects that invoke nostalgia for an industrial era left behind for a post-Fordist future. Yet, Egypt can hardly boast of such a turn-of-the-century industrial past. The Telecom Egypt commercial not only presented a desirable present and future for Cairo/Egypt, but even a fashionable sanitized industrial past.[14]

Whereas the urban reality of the metropolis of an estimated fifteen million has proven itself far from malleable, in the realm of imagination, a perfect, globally appropriate Cairo was fashioned. No impurities here, no cracks that showed what lies beneath. This new Cairo could measure up to the sophistication and elegance of old but rejuvenated Europe, while the new Egypt embodied global standards of professionalism and technological prowess. The commercials of Telecom Egypt and the Future Generation Foundation not only sold an image of their company/project, but also projected a vision of Egypt's present and future. The privatizing public sector company that was obliged to compete in global markets, and the state-affiliated NGO that aimed at facilitating Egypt's integration into that same global market, are emblematic of Egypt's new liberal age, as was the imagined Egypt they projected.

Egypt's refashioning parallels trends in other postcolonial nations that were once allies in the nonaligned movement. As Fernandes argues with respect to India, "If the tenets of Nehruvian development could be captured by symbols of dams and mass based factories, the markers of [Rajiv] Gandhi's India shifted to the possibility of commodities that would tap into the tastes and consumption practices of the urban middle classes" (2000a:614). In Egypt, the heroic images of the recaptured Suez Canal and the newly built Aswan Dam had been symbolic of the newly independent nation and the developmental state. After the demise of Nasserism such imagery changed. Sadat, in contrast, envisioned Egypt's future in terms of consumption and affluence, notably expressed in his assertion that "the goal of every Egyptian should be to have a car and a villa" (Ibrahim 1982:49, cf. Ghannam 2002:28ff.). The *infitaah*, iconic of Sadat's presidency, was associated with the unprecedented influx of foreign luxury consumer goods (see, e.g., Ibrahim 1982, Ayubi 1982).

Nasser-era celebrations of the urban professional middle class, symbolized by the engineer and the doctor, have made way for iconic images of young upper-middle class professionals in the hyper-modern offices of internationally oriented companies. As the ones who can match global standards and staff transnational workspaces, they are seen as the ideal proponents of the country's global ambitions. They fulfill a symbolic function similar to that of the Indian 'new middle class,' which, according to Fernandes, is constructed "as the social group who is able to negotiate India's new relationship with the global economy in both cultural and economic terms; in cultural terms by defining a new cultural standard that rests on the sociosymbolic practices of commodity consumption and in economic terms as the beneficiaries of the material benefits of India's 'new economy'" (2000b:91).

During Ramadan 2002, Egyptian TV channels featured numerous beautifully shot commercials portraying similar dreams of a clean, affluent, and globally appropriate Egypt. Many commercials spoke of harmonious and affluent family life, which could be had if one were to use a specific cooking oil or ghee in food preparation. Upper-middle class appearances and lifestyles featuring cosmopolitan standards and commodities had become central in such portrayals of the good life.[15] These commercials suggested inclusion through the simple act of buying products, from the attainable, yet to many foreign yogurt drinks, to the prohibitively priced apartments and villas in the gated communities surrounding Cairo. They not only addressed upper-middle class consumers with the financial means to engage in conspicuous consumption, but also less prosperous classes who might be enticed to aspire to such lifestyles. They suggested that an upper-middle class lifestyle could be attained through the purchase of consumer goods marked as upper-middle class. The elegance and affluence of up-market Cairo seemed almost within reach.

These commercials served as ambiguous invitations to exclusive and distinctive lifestyles that were only available to a small segment of the population, and as I will argue in the following chapters, were anchored in embodied privilege. Try to be this way, the invitation read, even if you will never make it, because this is Egypt's future. Emanuela Guano (2002) suggests that such a mixture of inclusion and exclusion is characteristic of neoliberal realities. The imagined Cairo and future Egypt were enticing and seductive. They offered a semblance of openness and inclusion in an exclusive, elegant promise, yet carried a subtext of displacement and denial. Their virtual erasure of popular claims to the city echoed and foreshadowed actual physical, social, and cultural displacements. The urban landscape allows us glimpses of some of the frictions that accompanied the creation of this affluent, conspicuously cosmopolitan Cairo.

Spatializing Exclusivity

Emanuela Guano's discussion (2002) of the hegemonic effects of recent urban development projects in Buenos Aires tells a story that could equally concern Cairo. Against the backdrop of a mounting economic crisis, many once solidly middle class inhabitants are reduced to poverty. Buenos Aires' middle class has been sharply divided between a minority of upper-middle class professionals who were able to profit from new service economy occupations, and an increasingly impoverished majority that suffered from the withering of state employment and public services. As a consequence, "a new Buenos Aires materialized to cater to the small upper middle class and, above all, the upper class that were reaping the fruits of neoliberalism" (Guano 2002:184). One of the features of this neoliberal landscape is an increasing spatial segregation that offers 'safe distance' from the growing population of slum dwellers. Guano argues that such spatial segregation is accompanied by a transnational spectacularism manifested in opulent shopping malls and a redeveloped waterfront. According to Guano, these spectacles of transnational consumption are part of a bid for neoliberal hegemony. While they obviously cater to the affluent upper-middle and upper classes, they also address a less affluent middle class public through a "simulacrum of inclusion" (Guano 2002:185).

Guano argues that Argentina's neoliberal reforms feed into longstanding narratives of exclusion from and desire for a First World that many middle class people felt to be rightfully theirs. The neoliberal promise to return Argentina to First World standards enthralled middle class inhabitants. While many were critical of the neoliberal program of the government, they also reveled in the new urban sites that were perceived as signs of a renewed inclusion into the First World. These visceral embodiments of a transnational modernity allowed for, and for most remained limited to, acts of imaginary consumption (Guano 2002:202–203). Like the Egyptian commercials discussed earlier, the power of malls and gentrified real estate lay in the suggestion of inclusion to an exclusive reality: elegant, fashionable and First World, as well as elite and restricted.

We can similarly read Cairo's transforming landscape as caught in such longing and desires for the reterritorialization of the First World. Social hierarchies have long been figured through degrees of familiarity with the 'outside' (barra), first France, now primarily the United States. Cosmopolitanism and being connected to the 'outside' have once again taken on marked significance, not only in the labor market where cosmopolitan capital provides access to relatively well-paid jobs, but also in social life, where such cosmopolitan capital signals upper-middle class belonging. Cairo's up-market circuits intimate a sense of transnational belonging and project a seamlessness and self-evidence that denies the existence of other, less elegant and comfortable realities. Like in Buenos Aires, they seem to tell a "story of transnational modernity whereby the privilege of the few strives to become the pride of all" (Guano 2002:203). Yet, unlike Guano's arguments with respect to Buenos Aires, these cosmopolitan spaces hardly address disenfranchised middle class Cairenes.

Attempts to seduce larger sections of the Cairene middle class to embrace the neoliberal program are piecemeal. The commercials discussed earlier offer conspicuous examples, as do the governmental exhortations to learn 'English' and 'computer' discussed in Chapter Three. While, for example, foreign fast-food restaurants and less exclusive malls (Abaza 2001) offer experiences of cosmopolitan consumption that are accessible to a less affluent public, most of these conspicuously cosmopolitan spaces are turned into themselves, located in up-market areas and exclusively meant for those who can afford to be part of an up-market cosmopolitan public. Cairo's polarized income distribution thereby produces increasingly differentiated lifestyles and spaces within a more and more class-segregated cityscape. The exclusive, spectacular global city primarily takes shape through new forms of social and spatial segregation.

Cairo has long harbored a wide range of economically and socially distinct areas, from the old upper class areas of Maadi, Heliopolis, and Zamelek to middle class areas like Shubra and Munira, which have increasingly become associated with a lower-middle class. Newer areas like Mohandisseen and Nasr City house an ascendant middle class, while the gated communities around Cairo have become a favorite destination for upper (middle) class Cairenes.[16] In the late 1990s, half of Cairo's population was estimated to live in 'ashwaa'iyyaat, unplanned or informal lower class areas that are marked by the large degree of informality of housing construction and the livelihoods of their inhabitants (Bayat and Denis 2000:197). Notwithstanding these important differences between such urban areas in socioeconomic and, as many Cairenes would insist, cultural terms, each area housed a heterogeneous population. Even an upper class area like Zamalek had lower class inhabitants and sha'bi shops and cafés, while an old sha'bi area like al-Hussein housed some very wealthy businessmen (Singerman 1997:11). Cairo in that sense resembles cities like Mumbai and Delhi, where, according to Fernandes, "distinctions [between wealthier and poorer neighborhoods] have historically been interrupted by the presence of squatters . . . and street entrepreneurs such as tailors, shoe repairmen and hawkers . . . who were generally located in the wealthier neighborhoods to provide services to their middle- and upper-class residents" (2004:2420). Fernandes argues that these spatial patterns are increasingly left

Al-Ghouriyya Street, Fatimid Cairo

behind for "urban aesthetics based on the middle-class desire for the management of urban space based on strict class-based separations" (ibid.). Bayat and Denis discern a similar tendency toward spatial segregation in the parallel growth of exclusive gated communities and *'ashwaa'iyyaat* on Cairo's peripheries (2000:199). As Denis argued recently, "the object of new urban policies is to struggle against combinations of incongruous elements, eliminate diversity, and criminalize density, mélange and proximity" (2006:67).

The most conspicuous spatial expressions of Egypt's new liberal age are the exclusive gated communities in the desert surrounding Cairo.[17] These gated communities — *compounds* in local parlance — promise lush green gardens and light, comfortable and elegant housing, varying from apartments to villas, amid the stillness of the desert. They provide an escape from the crowding and the pollution of the metropolis, the scarcity of affordable yet appropriate houses in 'respectable' areas, and importantly the intrusions of those belonging to lower 'social levels' (cf. Kuppinger 2004). First developed in the United States, such fortified suburban enclaves have become an increasingly common feature of urban development in cities around the world. The considerable body of literature on the subject signals a trend toward "the total segregation of spaces, the fortification of the middle and upper classes and the increasing neglect of older public spaces along with the lower class residents who populate them" (Kuppinger 2004:40, cf. Low 2001).

Cairene compounds were advertised as a socially homogeneous, clean, spacious, and green dreamland (Kuppinger 2004). The holiday resorts on the North Coast and Red Sea can be seen as the most direct predecessors of Cairo's compounds (see Cole and Altorki 1998). Built in the desert, these holiday resorts present spacious, completely controlled surroundings. While the owners are absent for most of the year, their villas and apartments are continually serviced by a range of personnel, most importantly the *ganayni* (gardener), who is responsible for the perpetually green and flower-filled gardens in the desert. Entrance is only for those carrying a carnet. In these resorts, one can choose to enjoy the sea in a bikini since those who do not know how to cope with respectable nudity are kept at bay. In these islands in the desert, affluent urbanites can realize their impossible dreams: they can keep out the dust, the noise, and the mass of people associated with these disagreeable realities of urban life (cf. Öncü 1997 on Istanbul). These are materializations of dreams destined never to come true in the huge metropolis.

Nostalgic stories have it that this is the way things used to be in elite neighborhoods like Zamalek and Heliopolis, that is, before the crowds intruded and elite privileges were eroded under Nasser (cf. Denis 1997). Though they are still marked as elite areas, they have become increasingly crowded, as villa after villa is torn down to make way for tall apartment blocks. They have partly followed the fate of the erstwhile elite Downtown. As Battesti argues: "From the mid-nineteenth century through the mid-twentieth centuries, downtown was frequented by a bourgeois elite parading through shopping arcades, gardens, and promenades in elegant dress under the shade of small parasols. But since then, downtown has changed into a dense and popular place of excursion for window-shopping and people-watching by another class of people" (2006:502). Holiday resorts and compounds present an escape from what Cairo has become for the elite: a place they can only to a limited extent control and form according to their ideas of taste, sophistication, and good life. They are insulated from their direct surroundings; gate control creates a perfectly peaceful and socially homogeneous green haven inside their walls. This is a clean, ordered Egypt inhabited by affluent people, without the otherwise so persistent reminders of Egypt's other realities. This is an Egypt that is not a Third World country. Needless to say, gates are the precondition of these sanctuaries.

Eric Denis argues that the spread of compounds signals the disappearance of the social mixture that was characteristic of Cairene life in the 1960s and 1970s. "Cairo's new liberal age in the 1990s echoes pre-1952 tendencies when chic and exclusive suburbs, such as Heliopolis, developed on new terrain away from a city which was too common and too difficult to reform" (Denis 1997:10). According to Teresa Caldeira, such fortified spaces represent a significant political shift, since these "new spaces structure public life in terms of real inequalities: differences are not to be dismissed, taken as irrelevant, left unattended, or disguised in order to sustain ideologies of universal equality or myths of peaceful cultural pluralism. The new urban environment enforces inequalities and separations" (2000:331). In the span of a few years, Cairo's built-up area is said to have doubled largely as a result of the spread of such compounds, as well as adjacent hotels, private hospitals, foreign schools, and amusement parks (Mitchell 2002:273). These compounds are perhaps the most complete expressions of widespread attempts to create the perfect surrounding for a clean, organized, classy, and exclusive life amid the chaos, crowdedness, and poverty of the metropolis.

Global Dreams?

Egypt's recent neoliberal reforms are commonly portrayed as largely 'negative' interventions: budget cuts, reduction of state intervention in the economy and society, and the erosion of the social contract established under Nasser. These 'negative' policies are, however, intimately connected to new narratives of national progress and concomitant investments. Upper-middle class professionals with cosmopolitan capital have become the protagonists of these new stories of national progress, with a globally appropriate Cairo as its natural home. These new national imaginations pervade the commercials of Telecom Egypt and the Future Generation Foundation, which portray a seamless, globally appropriate, even First World Cairo. Their visual messages gloss over actual urban practices and lives. They imbue Cairo with an inviting world-class aura, yet carry an unmistakable subtext of exclusivity and exclusion. Similar dreams and desires have materialized in Cairo's up-market circuits. The compounds in the desert around Cairo present the most perfect materializations of such dreams, devoid of persistent reminders of Egypt's other realities.

Such dreams of the global are related to economic globalization and neoliberal reforms that aim at integration into global networks, as well as to an attempt at global city formation. This striving for global city status is due both to the increased importance of cities in global economic networks and the related 'quest for the global' expressed in urban prestige projects. Moreover, as Guano (2002) argues, such projects are significantly informed by longstanding feelings of exclusion from and longing for First World affluence, sophistication, and membership. Sites like the exclusive compounds, the new Carrefour hypermarket, or the numerous up-market coffee shops intimate inclusion into such elitist First World consumption practices and lifestyles.

The virtual closures and displacements in the commercials have their counterparts in material forms of closure and displacement in the urban landscape. Neoliberal policies render the previous developmental Nasserite social contract increasingly obsolete. Dreams of national development that would include increasing numbers into the gathering speed of the nation have been abandoned. Large sectors of the population are relegated to the margins of narratives of national progress, and the urban areas they inhabit are largely left to their own devices. Meanwhile state and private sector projects have given rise to sites that claim global standards and could compete with First World locations in elegance and luxury. Such dreams of a global Cairo are reserved for a minority of the city's inhabitants. The search for the global has resulted in an increasingly divided urban landscape and disjunctive matrices of belonging.

Chapter 2

The Education of Class

The numerous private educational institutions that claim Western standards and may even award Western degrees are important signposts of Egypt's new liberal age, just as the high-rise office buildings along the Nile, the ring road around Cairo, or the immaculately clean shopping malls that offer Western designer clothes at unaffordable prices. The Western knowledge and degrees offered by these new schools make for sought after cultural capital and present crucial assets in the urban labor market. While Nasser-era policies were geared toward the creation of a broad, educated urban middle class, the policies and narratives of Egypt's new liberal era emphasize global standards and excellence, to which only a minority of the large urban middle class can aspire. Cosmopolitan capital has become a highly significant marker of social distinction and of the kind of social mobility one can expect. The increasingly dual nature of the educational system articulates, consolidates, and strengthens processes of segregation in Cairo's professional middle class. In this chapter I examine the intimate connections between education and class, and explore how changes in the educational system have contributed to new sociocultural divisions and distinctions in Cairo's professional middle class. I begin by sketching what it means to be middle class in Cairo.

Being Middle Class in Egypt

Pervasive combinations of class and culture, economic privilege and socio-cultural distinction mark Egypt's social hierarchies. Struggles over hierarchy and privilege have often taken the form of symbolic struggles over social and cultural worth (cf. Armbrust 1996; 1999). The terms middle class Cairenes use to talk about class reveal the intricate ways class and culture intertwine. *Tabaqa*, the Arabic word for class, is used in a more or less neutral way to refer to socioeconomic groupings. However, the most common term used to speak of social differentiation is *mustawa*, social or cultural level. *Mustawa* refers to loosely defined layers of social differentiation that invoke a combination of economic and cultural characteristics. A middle class professional in his late twenties, for example, explained the incidence of flirting and harassment, *mu'aksaat*, in terms of social/cultural level. He argued that *mu'aksaat* were much less frequent among what he reverently called people of a 'refined level,' *mustawa raqi*. He conflated a high-class position with a high level of cultural sophistication. His comment rehearsed common assumptions about the intricate connection between socioeconomic privilege and cultural superiority. In upper-middle class circles, the English word *class* is used in a similar way. 'Class' is employed to describe places, people, and things thought of as elegant and distinctive. Explicitly localized versus conspicuously cosmopolitan orientations, 'traditional' versus 'modern' dispositions provide central axes in the way such social–cultural hierarchies are construed.

As I argued in the Introduction, claims of cosmopolitan knowledge and connections to the 'outside' have long been prime markers of elite belonging, just as rootedness, locality, and authenticity serve to identify what are called 'the popular classes' *(ish-sha'b)*. The linguistic repertoire used to talk about 'popular' habits and lifestyles reflects this semantic universe.[18] *Baladi*, literally 'of the locality/country,' can be used to describe all things and people that are considered local, and often, lower class. The term can also have positive connotations indicating an old-fashioned quality of food products, or when pertaining to people, authenticity and steadfastness. The term, *sha'bi*, meaning 'popular' or 'of the masses,' similarly denotes things and people associated with the lower class—from *sha'bi* neighborhoods to people, tastes, and foods. *Sha'bi*, however, carries few of the positive associations of the term *baladi*.

Terms like *baladi* (local) and *sha'bi* (popular) are central to middle class conceptions of Egyptian society and Cairo's urban landscape. They invoke a landscape of explicitly localized vulgar, mass, and authentic tastes, set against appropriate, modern, and sophisticated lifestyles. These divisions are often taken to run between the professional middle class and lower class others. In his study on modernism and mass culture in Egypt, Walter Armbrust argues that ideals of education and being cultured are part of a dominant 'conservative modernism' in which the enlightened and modern, yet still authentic middle class is the main protagonist. The middle class is supposed to avoid the inadequate class cultures of both rich and poor. "The poor are suspect because of their 'failure' to adjust their lives to modern institutions, the wealthy for a rootless cosmopolitanism at the other end of the socioeconomic spectrum," Armbrust argues (1999:112). In this modernist discourse, a middle class protagonist, conversant with both tradition and modernity, typically engages in a coalition with less developed but steadfast Egyptians, and in the process, elevates them from their authentic, yet essentially backward state (Armbrust 1996:100; cf. Abu-Lughod 2005:60).

Armbrust insightfully sketches what it means to be middle class in Cairo.

[Middle class] does not correlate with a material standard of living. There are, however, certain attitudes and expectations commonly associated with a middle class ideal. Egyptians who have at least a high school education, and therefore basic literacy and familiarity with how modern institutions work, generally consider themselves middle class. Egyptians who think of themselves as middle class expect a lifestyle free from manual labor. In the media, the ideal of middle class is often associated with modernity, bureaucracy, and office work, and it is portrayed as having a degree of familiarity with an ideology of national identity that seeks to balance local Egyptian and classical Islamic cultural referents. (1999:111)

As Armbrust argues, middle class identification hinges on education. It is intimately connected to the Nasser era, which saw the democratization of education and the exponential growth of a state bureaucracy that provided office jobs to graduates of higher educational institutes. Under Nasser, new educational policies promised free access to education through university, and a guaranteed government position after graduation from a higher institute.[19] Education and an office job seemed within reach of all families who could support their children through university. Being educated became a widely shared aspiration. Enrollment at all levels of education tripled between 1952 and 1970 (Mina 2001:32).

The engineer became the hero of the Nasserite developmental project. Moore argues that in the course of the 1950s, the Nasserite regime increasingly relied on engineers to run the burgeoning state apparatus and public sector. The prestige of the engineering profession concomitantly soared. Even when industrialization stagnated and a surplus of engineers undermined the solidity of this professional career, its prestige remained (Moore 1994:43–44). A middle-aged woman from an affluent middle class family fondly remembered the Nasserite promise of educational access and social mobility. She rehearsed the commonly evoked image that "even the son of the *bawwaab* could become an engineer." The figure of the *bawwaab*, the doorman who lives with his (and at times her) family in the dark, musty rooms on the ground floor of middle or upper class apartment blocks, is often used to symbolize the lowest of the low. The image of the son of the *bawwaab* who becomes an engineer therefore represents the emergence of new avenues for social mobility and the existence of a sense of social justice in the Nasser era. With a keen sense of irony, she added, "he might become a brilliant engineer, but that does not mean that I would allow him to marry my daughter." Her comment indicates some of the tensions between the existence of new avenues for social mobility and the continued importance of family backgrounds and older social hierarchies. "Just imagine. . . . I would have to sit with his parents, the *bawwaab* and his wife, on an equal footing," she said.

In the 1960s seemingly everyone could dream of a middle class life, conceived of as a modern and, above all, clean *(nadiifa)* life. Cleanliness, *nadafa*, is an evocative term that can encompass anything from hygiene and order to the nonmanual and the 'social level' of a person. Such cleanliness is intimately tied to being or aspiring to be middle class. Being middle class implies a safe distance from menial and socially denigrated jobs and the expectation of a stable yet modest living standard. It first and foremost symbolizes the promise of being free from the grime and dust of lower class existence.

Hearing about my interest in Cairo's middle class, quite a few middle class intellectuals decried the death of Egypt's middle class. There was no longer a social middle, they said, only the poor and the wealthy remain. Such observations draw attention to the downward spiral of standards of living in which most middle class Cairenes were caught. Despite these observations, the category 'middle class' remains ethnographically salient in Egypt. If we reckon by locally significant taxonomies that link being middle class to educational achievement, the middle class has actually continued to grow. Levels of participation in higher education have continued to rise, even when, after the turn to economic liberalization in the mid-1970s, many of the policies to promote an educated middle class were gradually scaled down or abolished. While the country still has high illiteracy rates and large numbers drop out of the basic educational trajectory, Egypt has a high share of students in higher education, about twenty percent of the college-age population.[20] These growing numbers of educated professionals have, however, been confronted by falling chances of realizing their middle class expectations of a clean job and a modest yet comfortable middle class lifestyle (Amin 2000:36–37). While middle class remains a pertinent economic and sociocultural category in Cairo, large parts of the educated population have seen their standards of living decline. Recent university graduates have a hard time finding a job, let alone a decent, well-paying one that corresponds to their educational achievements. The professional middle class has become increasingly segmented in terms of individual wage-earning capacities, as well as cultural capital and lifestyle, the latter often inextricably tied to the former. Education has been instrumental in the articulation of this segmentation.

The Education of the Nation?

In Cairo schooling is a central repository for emotional and financial investments. It holds the promise of social mobility, not only in terms of careers and living standard, but also social status. The educational system is also a symbol of a certain state, society, and nation, at least in the Egypt that still remembers one of the ultimate symbols and achievements of the 1952 Revolution: free education for all through university. The Egyptian system provides six years basic education (*ibtidaa'iyya*), followed by three years preparatory education (*i'daadiyya*). Each educational phase is concluded by a general exam that determines access to the next level. Those with lower scores on their preparatory exams are assigned to vocational secondary education; those with high scores can continue general secondary education (*thanawiyya 'amma*), which, again depending on the scores at the concluding general exam, gives access to university (cf. UNDP 1999).

Public education was scarce at the beginning of the twentieth century, especially at the secondary level, and tuition fees limited access to more affluent families. Even though primary education had been declared compulsory and free of charge in 1923 and secondary education had become free of charge in 1950, democratization of education only took off during the 1950s and 1960s (Cochran 1986). Besides public secondary education, there were foreign private schools that taught most of the curriculum in a foreign language, mainly French or English. From 1934 onward, these foreign language schools were brought under the increasingly encompassing supervision of the ministry of education and had to adopt government curricula. They did, however, continue to teach a major part of the curriculum in foreign languages (ibid.).

After the 1952 Revolution, public education expanded dramatically. Though the quality of education differed considerably, a number of reputed state schools in Cairo and Alexandria came to represent the apex of learning in society. In the context of Nasser's Arab socialism, the educational system emphasized Arabic. European languages and curricula became a marginal presence in an educational system dominated by public (i.e., state) schools. However, private schools with their more exclusive population and European-language curricula remained a route to distinction for some. Against the backdrop of a worsening economy in the late 1970s, the government began to stimulate private investments in education. Simultaneously, as the educational quality of state education decreased, the predominance of state schools started to wane. While expenditure on public education was in decline, private education boomed (Nuwayr 2000). Due to the presence of thousands of Egyptian labor migrants in the Gulf, there was a large flow of remittances, giving considerable financial leverage to parts of the population. Domestically, the *infitaah* brought affluence to those who were able to profit from the increased leverage allowed to the private sector and the opening-up of the country to imports. A growing number of Cairene families was thus able to pay for private schooling.

While the choice for private over public education seems to have become common in more affluent circles first, particularly in Cairo it soon became a common aspiration in middle class circles. In 1999/2000, 20 percent of the Cairene *thanawiyya 'amma* students were in private schools, versus 8.5 percent nationwide.[21] Marwa's story illustrates this shift. Marwa was in her mid-twenties and had a well-paying job as a journalist at a French-language weekly. She herself comes from an economically modest background, yet attended a French language school. In the early 1970s her parents, both teachers with a modest income, were accused of showing off when they decided to send her older sister to a French Catholic school. By the time Marwa entered the same school in the early eighties, education at private language schools had already become a common pursuit among middle class families.

The French Catholic school trajectory was not uncommon in families with high qualifications but modest salaries. Considering their tight budget, Marwa's parents made a clever choice. Such schools were and still are among the cheapest language schools and generally enjoy a good reputation. Marwa's educational trajectory has led to a strong position in the labor market in the 1990s, when foreign companies entered the Egyptian market and Egyptian private companies similarly demanded people who had a private education and were fluent in foreign languages. The near-native French and reasonable English skills of these young graduates of modest middle class origins were in high demand.

In the 1950s and 1960s state education became the main route to social mobility, a secure career and middle class status. From the 1970s onward, the declining quality of the governmental educational system and the turn toward economic liberalization led to the rapid growth of private education from kindergarten to university and beyond. The educational system increasingly developed into a dual system in which overcrowded state schools provided education to a large majority of students, while the minority who could afford the tuition fees was educated in private schools, preferably in European languages (cf. Mina 2001:36–37). This trend has accelerated in the 1990s, with the establishment of four private universities, numerous private higher institutes, and a growing number of high schools that offer British and American diplomas. Preuniversity language school trajectories have become decisive for chances in Cairo's segmented labor market, and have become important markers of social distinction. The educational system that once offered social mobility and a secure future, a ticket out of limited family fortunes, and a predestined life trajectory now works to consolidate such family fates. While education remains a major route to social mobility, this social mobility has lost much of its earlier collective, inclusive character. This route to social advancement has been individualized and has come to rely strongly on one's family background (Abdel Moati 2002:334–36).

Privatization

The fate of the public education system and the consolidation of a parallel private one regularly stirred up heated debates inside and outside the media. These debates focused on the right to free education, the dismal quality of public schools, the fortunes parents were forced to spend on private lessons, and the incessant growth of private education, which highlights the de facto dual nature of the educational system.

The feeling that educational quality had been caught in a relentless downward spiral was widely shared. It concerned first and foremost public schools with their large classroom sizes, the double shifts, and at times underqualified teachers. I frequently heard stories about the erstwhile prestige and excellent facilities of a few select public schools that only admitted those with high scores on their primary or preparatory central exams. In the early years of the twenty-first century, these stories of excellence had given way to a general feeling that all government education was beyond redemption. In the late 1970s, Mostafa, from a lower-middle class family, could count the son of a minister among his classmates at a public high school. Such a mixed class presence in public schools has become virtually inconceivable in contemporary Cairo.

Attending public schools had become an anathema in middle class circles. Public schools have become imaginary repositories for inadequacy, suffering, and even vice for those able to avoid them.

However, feelings of decay also colored discussions about private schools. Though the quality of education in older private schools might similarly have declined, such feelings of decay seem to be primarily related to the fierce competition in the labor market and to the effectiveness of education as a mechanism of social distinction. The newest private schools located along the desert roads leading out of Cairo, pointedly called 'investment schools' to emphasize their 'for-profit' character, were the latest bid for excellence. They offered American or British standards of teaching and curricula, as well as Western or international diplomas, not to mention countless social and sports activities. With tuition fees reaching tens of thousands of Egyptian pounds, such schools could leave even upper-middle class families feeling underprivileged and unable to keep up. A thirty-eight-year-old professional from an affluent upper-middle class family said that while in her time attending a reputable language school had been a must, nowadays schools with an American or British system and degrees have become de rigueur. While the former schools largely work with state curricula and conclude with the standard general exam, the latter schools grant 'international' diplomas, like the IGCSE, that have limited validity in the national setting.

In contrast to public elementary and secondary education, Cairo's top state universities, Cairo University and Ain Shams University, remain sought after in middle class circles.[22] Graduates of the private American University in Cairo (AUC) generally occupied a stronger position in the labor market than those with public degrees; graduates with foreign degrees were even more sought after. Yet, since the tuition fees of private universities were beyond the reach of most families able to afford language schools, most pupils of private language schools, including most of my upper-middle class informants, continued their education at a public university.

Public university education remained strongly differentiated. The faculties of engineering, medicine, pharmacy, and political science and economy, as well as certain language departments, were considered to offer high quality and prestigious education. The general exam scores required for admittance to public universities had been raised year after year to limit enrollment at the overcrowded universities. Prestigious departments like medicine and engineering had come to require scores close to 100 percent. Central exam scores partially relied on the quality of education received and expenditure on private lessons. Admittance to these more prestigious colleges therefore strongly correlated with family income.

'AMR 'UKASHA, AL-WAFD, JULY 21, 2004

Finally you've succeeded in your central exams with high grades and you'll fulfill your father's wish. You'll study engineering and become an excellent unemployed person!! (The son is holding a certificate that says 99 percent.)

In the course of the 1990s this internal differentiation reached new heights after the top state universities opened 'language sections' in the faculties of law, commerce, and political science and economics, where the same curriculum is taught in English or French. Since they generally require a previous 'language education' and charge tuition fees, these language sections are highly selective. These are the relatively affordable public counterparts of private universities, with better educational facilities, a more select public, and a higher social standing than their crowded 'Arabic' counterparts. As Galal Amin argues, "A new divide is thus created within every college between those who can and those who cannot be integrated in the modern global system" (1999:17–18).

Lines of Relative Nobility

Private language schools were often assumed to produce a certain type of person. The choice of a particular school would thus be a choice for a specific mindset and should reflect the emphasis on certain values within the family. A young mother told me that even the Arabic teacher at her sons' private language school was a graduate of a private language school. Though graduates of state schools would seem better suited for the job on account of their reputedly superior knowledge of Arabic, the school insisted on employing a graduate of a private school because of the latter's 'social level.' According to this woman, "The school was afraid that a public school graduate might teach the children bad words and manners." Her words echo Bourdieu's observation that diplomas are not merely entitlements to a domain of expertise, but also 'patents of nobility' (Bourdieu 1984:142). In Cairo, names of primary and secondary schools are widely known signs of belonging and distinction. They function as important indicators not only of a person's educational achievement, but also of his or her 'social level' and concomitant 'cultural level.' In recent years, schools that offer British and North American diplomas have overshadowed the erstwhile prestige of older private language schools. The existence of yet more exclusive and expensive institutions and degrees has created new lines of 'true distinction.'

Economic privilege, cultural knowledge, family background, and social connections all contribute to divisions in Cairo's professional middle class. Bourdieu's notion of different forms of capital helps disaggregate these social hierarchies and sources of privilege and power. Bourdieu distinguishes three 'guises' of capital: "*economic capital*, which is immediately and directly convertible into money and may be institutionalised in the form of property rights; . . . *cultural capital*, which is convertible, on certain conditions, into economic capital and may be institutionalised in the form of educational qualifications; and . . . *social capital*, made up of social obligations ('connections'), which is convertible, in certain conditions, into economic capital and may be institutionalised in the form of a title of nobility" (1986:243).

Lines of segmentation that divide young middle class Cairenes rely on a combination of these forms of capital. As I argued in the Introduction, cosmopolitan orientations have again become highly significant markers of privileged class positions in Cairo. In the course of the 1990s cosmopolitan capital became the major form of cultural capital. Such cosmopolitan capital entails, as said, familiarity with, and mastery of, globally dominant cultural codes. Such cosmopolitan capital most clearly encompasses fluency in English, as well as Western diplomas or degrees from educational institutes associated with Western knowledge, for example, private language schools or the American University in Cairo. It also entails more informal knowledge of Western/global consumer culture. Such cosmopolitan capital overlaps with, and oftentimes doubles as, locally distinctive cultural capital, i.e., the kind of lifestyles, cultural knowledge, habits, and even appearance and body language that mark one as part of Cairo's elite or upper-middle class.

Private language schools were instrumental in the accruement of cosmopolitan capital. It is mainly through attending a prestigious language school that one could attain the near-native command of English crucial for employment in up-market companies. In such schools, students moreover acquired informal cultural capital such as familiarity with the upper-middle class vernacular, distinctive ways of dress and tastes, as well as the right comportment, choice of words, and self-confidence. A private language school education generally required significant financial investments. Such relative affluence was often connected to either prolonged periods of labor migration to the Gulf, successful careers in the upper ranks of the state apparatus, or successful private sector ventures inside Egypt. Comfortable family backgrounds provide professionals with diverse kinds of capital that conspire toward a comparatively secure career path in the internationally oriented upper segments of the urban economy (cf. Mina 2001:89, footnote ***). Persons from relatively affluent families could go on to find jobs as engineers, marketing specialists, business developers, or project managers in development organizations, or they might work in relatively well-paid secretarial or administrative positions in up-market companies. They are the exemplary *awlaad naas*, children of good families, their bodies and language speaking of the high capital investments made with respect to their futures.

The effectiveness of private schools is attested to by the success of friends and acquaintances from professional middle class families with modest incomes who had been educated at relatively inexpensive French Catholic schools. Lacking much of the privileged economic, social, and cultural capital that is imparted by more affluent family backgrounds, they nevertheless succeeded in attaining good positions in the labor market because of their fluency in French and English and familiarity with elite cultural codes and lifestyles. In the 1990s such fluency was still scarce, while many new jobs required such skills.

Private schools had become a crucial site for what Bourdieu calls 'reconversion strategies,' the strategic capital investments families make in order to retain or improve their class position (Bourdieu 1984:125ff.). Bourdieu argues that

> the reconversion of economic capital into educational capital is one
> of the strategies which enable the business bourgeoisie to maintain

the position of some or all of its heirs, by enabling them to extract some of the profits of industrial and commercial firms in the form of salaries, which are a more discreet—and no doubt more reliable—mode of appropriation than 'unearned' investment income. (1984:137)

His observations with respect to 1970s France are relevant to contemporary Cairo. Families that gained significant amounts of economic capital through private business ventures have commonly resorted to such reconversion strategies. These families constitute part of the clientele of the expensive new schools that offer foreign diplomas at school fees pegged to the dollar. Their reconversion strategies provide a central dynamic behind the expansive market of private educational institutes.

These 'new rich' reconversion strategies were a prime source of symbolic contestation for professional middle class families that had less economic but more cultural capital. The new affluence of such previously working class families has been a central concern of more established families that are confronted with declining incomes and the rising costs of middle class living standards. The universities and schools that offered the newest, most exclusive and by far most expensive degrees were the frequent target of derisive comments. On several occasions, middle class parents claimed that these degrees were worthless since they were merely bought with the financial muscle power of the new rich. These worthless diplomas were contrasted with their own children's 'real' diplomas, gained through dedication, talent, and hard work. Some also expressed their indignation at the lower social origins or lack of education of the parents.

The devaluing of new diplomas and graduates from less highly educated, nonprofessional families can be seen as a defense of the vestiges on which the social position of these professional families is founded. However, this symbolic struggle also draws on middle class ideals of education and culture, which are central to the longstanding national modernist discourse discussed earlier. Those who want to buy into such ideals and lifestyles without the hard work, discipline, and proper family backgrounds are scorned. The 'undeserved' riches and privileges of the nouveaux riches threaten to overturn the widely shared ideology of national progress and betterment through a combination of education and sophistication.

Strategies

Most middle class families could hardly afford to engage in this rat race for the best educational qualifications, but neither were they willing to give up on their children's futures. Mona's story exemplifies the intense efforts and strategizing of families caught in this dilemma. Mona was a fulltime mother and housewife in her early forties. Her father was a high-ranking civil servant, her grandfather an affluent trader. Mona attended an erstwhile prestigious private school and graduated from a well-regarded department of a public university. After working for a few years as a teacher, she decided to stay home and dedicate herself to the upbringing of her three children. The family is among the oldest residents of an old upper-middle class area. Mona herself lives in a newer, more mixed district. We often met at her elderly mother's house, which showed the signs of a decaying living standard since her husband died. Her mother told me stories about her youth, growing up in a state-of-the-art building among greater and lesser stars of Egyptian society. And about Mona's father, decency embodied in this hard-working and fair official. Now the fortunes of the family had somewhat turned. Though Mona seemed to be living comfortably, she could not match the social status or living standard of her parents and grandparents.

We frequently discussed the ins and outs of the education system in Egypt, a subject in which Mona had become expert. She emphasized the pains she takes to motivate her children and help them do well at school. For the education of their children, she and her husband chose an 'Arabic private school,' rather than one of the more prestigious 'language schools.' While most subjects are taught in Arabic, extra attention is paid to English. She explained that they would not have been able to pay for the private lessons if her children had attended a language school. Sending her children to public schools was not an option either. She mentioned wryly that the minister of education talked about raising the level of education to that of *barra*, the outside (read: the West), yet public schools had up to 80 pupils in a classroom. According to Mona, the only schools offering a level comparative to 'the outside' were "the language schools *illi bi-dollaar* [with tuition fees charged in dollars], and who has that kind of money?" Her children thus attended an 'Arabic private school' through the preparatory level. They then continued in a state high school. Many parents who similarly could not afford a language school preferred the educational trajectory Mona has chosen. They paid the more modest sums for Arabic private education through the preparatory level, after which their children would apply for a public secondary school.[23]

With its limited financial means, this family had to rely on its persistence and its professional background with its firm commitment to, and esteem for, advancement through education. Mona's children do not belong to the class in which futures are guaranteed by not only the best education, but also the important safety net of economic capital, which can buy a place in a private university irrespective of central exam results. In Mona's family all eyes were focused on Ahmed, the eldest son, who was entering his central exams. If he could not manage to attain a score close to 100 percent on his exams, he would have to choose one of the lesser colleges and with that, an unpromising future. Speculation about Ahmed's future was ongoing. His parents had decided that he should become a medical doctor but they had also begun to consider pharmacy, another top field, as a concession to the market-oriented *Zeitgeist*. Since many pharmacists eventually start their own businesses, pharmacy combines the advantages of a long exclusive study trajectory with the free market-promises of entrepreneurial wealth.

Many young parents who themselves experienced scarcity in the labor market were anxious about their children's future chances. The lucrative free market of schooling offered a range of options for parents who believed it is never too early to start working on their children's educational careers. Expensive kindergartens (KGs) employed qualified English, French, or German speaking staff, so that the toddlers were stimulated properly and became familiarized with 'languages' from the earliest possible moment.

A friend trained her one-year-old daughter in French. She paid the rather standard fee of LE500 a month for the French language crèche that should gain her daughter admission to a good French language school. Another friend wanted to get her six-year-old son a private teacher to playfully introduce him to English, his third language besides French and Arabic. At her German-language crèche, yet another friend's five-year-old niece was being prepared for the entrance IQ test that should gain her admission to the German School. The German School had gained the reputation of producing disciplined hard workers, even though, as several people told me, many families considered French schools more appropriate for women since they were assumed to produce a more feminine and delicate personality. The pressure for admissions to the German School had risen to such heights that even those with clear ties to Germany were no longer assured of admission. These stories are far from exceptional. They are emblematic of a larger trend in which only the best education is good enough in light of expected and feared cutthroat competition for the scarce pool of good jobs. As will be discussed in the following chapter, more and more qualified graduates 'with languages' enter an insecure and tight labor market.

Despite considerable differences in historical trajectories and present life standards, the three families discussed above were part of the upper segments of Cairo's professional middle class. But who knows whether they will be able to guarantee their children a similar position? They depended on their professional qualifications for their livelihood and had no businesses that could employ their children irrespective of their academic achievements or the condition of the labor market. They therefore invested heavily in their children's education, in the hope that this would provide them with an edge in an ever more competitive job market.

These worries about guaranteeing a decent standard of living for one's children seem far removed from the uncertainties faced by Hossam, a forty-year-old academically trained government employee. When he married, he still had a job in tourism and was making a good living, but after the Luxor attacks, the tourists stayed away and the sector went into a slump. He was offered a government job as one of the last beneficiaries of the increasingly watered-down governmental scheme of guaranteed employment.[24] He embraced the security of government employment despite the low rewards (with several bonuses he earned around LE400 per month). When we spoke, Hossam bitterly recalled that he and his wife had once considered enrolling their son in the American School. The additional financial burden brought on by his recent divorce obliged him to take his son out of the public language school that he once saw as a temporary compromise. He said he could no longer afford his son's private lessons and the occasional 'voluntary' presents for the teachers. Despite monthly help from his father, Hossam's income did not allow for more than the basics. He wondered about the prospects of his son's generation. If he can hardly make a living now, how would they? While we were discussing the importance of schools in determining a child's future, he sharply brought my analytic wanderings back to its real life drama. "But what if I know what to do to give my son a good future but simply can't afford to do so?"

Of 'Having a Language'

Language provides the most potent illustration of shifts in the constitution of distinctive cultural capital in the twentieth century. At the start of the twenty-first century, differential class membership and belonging was most markedly expressed through language. '*Ma'andush logha*' had become a common expression in contemporary Cairo. "He doesn't have a language" is the literal translation, which evokes associations of muteness and inability to communicate. It means that the person in question does not speak any language but Arabic, or more specifically, does not speak English. But it often implied much more: he will not be able to cope in present-day Cairo, or he can forget about his chances for a proper job. In her study of lower-middle class graduates in Cairo's labor market, Ghada Fakhry Barsoum quotes a young female graduate as saying, "If you do not know English, it is as if you do not know how to read and write" (1999:62). Such associations speak to the ways in which value is assigned to persons in Egypt's new liberal era. The 'possession' of foreign languages, particularly English, has come to denote a major split within society. It divides the educated middle class between those 'with' and those 'without' language; between those who attended *madaris loghaat*, language schools, can look forward to working in the upper segments of the labor market, and are generally born and bred in the 'better' families, and those who are none of these things, *illi maʿanduhumsh logha* (who do not have a language).

English functions as a sign of distinction not only between those 'with' and 'without' a language, but also between those with a differential command of English. The following scene illustrates the power of language skills in suggesting class belonging. One evening my friend Maha invited me to come along on an outing. We went to a dimly lit bar in Mohandisseen, which had already filled up with people lingering at the bar and groups of friends gathered around tables in the seating areas. Such bar visits were quite exceptional. Maha would mostly visit upscale coffee shops and restaurants, and avoided places that served alcohol, but she made an exception for this specific venue because she loved their karaoke nights. She knew a number of regulars, and like them, had a few favorite songs she could perform skillfully. We managed to get a table and ordered some nonalcoholic cocktails. We were soon joined by two other friends of Maha's, but were still waiting for Hisham. Hisham made a dashing entrance with a charming narrative performance in English that centered on his reasons for being late. As soon as Hisham had greeted us and sat down, one of the other men bombarded him with questions in an unusually aggressive way. Hassan interrogated Hisham about his life story and the origins of his language skills. Hisham was indeed surprisingly fluent in English, even for this multilingual milieu. He spoke not the lingua franca English with the usual Egyptian tongue, but an English that seemed to belong to a native speaker. His choice to speak English was moreover unusual in an environment where a mix of English and Arabic was the norm. It could easily be seen as pretentious.

I was surprised by Hassan's aggressive attitude. His attack on Hisham transgressed the rules of polite and cheerful conversation common in such upper-middle class circles. Maha later told me how upset she was. She said she knew that some people thought Hisham was somewhat showy, but said that he was really a very kind, friendly, and devout person. She did not understand why Hassan had reacted so aggressively to him and had so crassly broken the common rules of friendly social interaction. Whatever the precise reasons for his aggressive questioning, it significantly focused on the origins of Hisham's English. Such language skills and use constituted an important measure of social distinction. The kind of fluency in English that Hisham displayed was commonly taken to be a sure indicator of a high social and cultural level, and of elite origins. Hassan soon found out that Hisham had merely acquired his superior language skills in a British school in one of the Gulf states, and not, for example, by growing up in Europe or being of part-European descent. Hassan returned to being his amiable self and the evening continued as normal.

Throughout the twentieth century, knowledge of foreign languages has been a sign of distinction, indicating high social status and origins. It is the most salient component of the cosmopolitan capital that is instrumental to divisions in Cairo's professional middle class. Previously, elite repertoires focused on France and all things French. In the first half of the twentieth century, some elite families spoke French as their mother tongue. Upper class women were often educated in French Catholic schools, while men either enrolled in French or English language education (Baraka 1998). The Nasser period, with its Arabization policies, broke with this emphasis on European languages as a sign of superior learning and elite belonging. From the 1980s onward, such cosmopolitan capital has once more come to denote elite belonging.

The choice of foreign languages in upper and upper-middle class families shows a gendered division of labor with respect to linguistic capital (Abécassis et al. 1997). French has long been seen as the language of culture and sophistication, particularly suited for the education of sophisticated wives and mothers. Though in the course of the 1990s English had become the uncontested language of work and socializing in upper-middle class circles, many still considered a French education the most appropriate training for girls.

Everyday conversations in a wider middle class were still heavily inflected with French words—with Egyptian pronunciations and conjugations— that indicate sophistication and class. *Plage* was used for beach instead of the Arabic *shatt*; *merci* and *coiffeur* had become part of the Egyptian dialect. Whereas some French loanwords had become commonplace in wide sections of society, other words were specific to middle or upper-middle class circles and functioned as indicators of class membership. In lower-middle class circles the Arabic *ummi* and *abuuya* (my mother, father) was the common way to speak of one's parents. In upper-middle class circles, this was generally seen as unforgivably lower class and crude. Here, one used the Arabic conjugations of *mama* and *papa*: *mamti* and *babaaya*.

English has established a pervasive presence in Cairo. While the currency of French loanwords signals past elite orientations, English has increasingly become the dominant language of distinction in everyday life (cf. Amin 1999:21–22). At the start of the twenty-first century state television included an English-language channel, which broadcast in French in the slow daytime slot. English-language radio stations and English-language magazines catered to those with a modicum of knowledge of the language. English also signified modernity and sophistication to many Cairenes 'without a language,' as indicated by its iconic visual presence in Cairo's urban landscape. English shop names were ubiquitous and signs often boasted names written in Latin script. That they were frequently misspelled did not diminish their effectiveness as indicators of modernity and sophistication.

A discussion on SaharaSafaris' English-language listserv captured the importance of language in contemporary ideas regarding class and culture. It echoed earlier national ideologies that centered on the educated middle class, yet added a distinctly twenty-first century touch. In 2002 an upper-middle class professional started a debate about the dominance of English during group outings. He wrote:

> I noticed that most of the people on this trip spoke English more
> than they spoke Arabic. To be honest, I find this shameful. It's not
> that I do not say a single word of English when I speak, but I feel
> really ashamed that I do so. I mean we are—after all—Egyptians and
> should be proud of our mother tongue. We seem to be proud to say
> loudly that we do not read Arabic books. It's like we are saying it's way
> below our social level to read in such a common language and that we
> should differentiate ourselves from the rest of the Egyptian society.

Other contributors to this online discussion similarly urged their peers not to snub Arabic, and to resist the onslaught of English. One professional noted that the use of English in daily communication had simply become a fact of life. One contribution stood out on account of its elaborate discussion of the relation between language, cultural capital, and class. The author argued that knowledge of Arabic and European languages enables people like the SaharaSafaris members to play a pivotal role. Being Egyptian and speaking Arabic, they are endowed with the virtues of the Egyptian heritage: "charity, respect, honor, generosity." Yet they also know European languages and cultures, and are therefore conversant with the positive qualities of these 'other cultures'—"professionalism, hard work, punctuality"—and are able combine the 'cultural blessings' of both. The author situated herself and her upper-middle class audience as a possible vanguard that appreciates its cultural heritage yet is open to the accomplishments and virtues of the West. These comments resonate with modernist narratives about the educated middle class as a societal vanguard, though in this version it is their position as mediators between the nation and the West, the local and the global, that singles these professionals out as future leaders. They resonate with the discourses of Egypt's new liberal era, which similarly portray upper-middle class professionals with cosmopolitan capital as embodiments of Egypt's dreams of global standards and cosmopolitan savvy.

Despite the SaharaSafaris debate on the importance of language with respect to national identity, having a limited knowledge of 'Arabic' was generally seen as a fact of life within my upper-middle class circles. Haeri similarly notes that upper-middle class "speakers often comment on how 'bad' their 'Arabic' is and describe their knowledge of it as quite limited because of the kind of education they received" (1997:799). Such statements have to be understood within an Arabic language context and denote relative rather than absolute unfamiliarity with *fusha*. 'Not knowing Arabic' pertains to having a limited knowledge of *fusha*, classical and written Arabic, rather than *'ammiyya*, the common spoken language in Egypt. The actual extent of this unfamiliarity seemed to differ considerably among these professionals. Some had trouble reading or writing Arabic; others were actually quite comfortable in written Arabic. Rainer E. Hamel rightly argues that such distancing from Arabic has to be seen as a class strategy. The eagerly avowed lack of knowledge of classical Arabic can be seen as a procedure "for reproducing their own symbolic capital and reinforcing a dominant language ideology which produces a kind of 'declassement' of the official language" (Hamel 1998:354).

As Niloofar Haeri notes, upper- and upper-middle class occupations in Cairo's segmented labor market generally require bi- or multilinguism, rather then excellent knowledge of *fusha* (1997:800). Amin concurs: "Multinational firms naturally show a preference for employing those who can express themselves well in a European language and this gives a premium to these languages over Arabic. . . . [T]he national language comes gradually to be looked down upon, together with things or persons that are in one way or another associated with it, whether teachers, schools or consumer goods" (1999: 21). Fluency in English has become the mark of a certain kind of professional: one raised in language schools who works and socializes in upper-middle class environments in which a mix of Arabic and English is the norm. 'To have a language' has become a sign of inclusion into specific upper-middle class circles, as well as distance from less privileged Cairene realities.

Speaking a mix of colloquial Arabic and English had become part of a distinctive upper-middle class normalcy.[25] The hybrid vernacular of Arabic and English common in upper-middle class circles seems comparable to the 'Hinglish' spoken by their Indian counterparts (Fernandes 2000a). Like this colloquial mix of Arabic and English, 'Hinglish' involves the use of English words or short phrases within Hindi sentences and conversations. That such similarities exist is striking given the radically different local histories of English. While English had been introduced during Egypt's relatively short colonial period, it did not attain dominance or establish itself as a national language as it did in India. Even though English is taught in all schools, a fair degree of mastery of the language is limited to those who have attended private schools. Such familiarity is by and large exclusive to young Cairenes from affluent backgrounds who have followed upper-middle class educational and professional trajectories. English has become the provenance of a relatively privileged segment of urban society and functions as a highly effective marker of new lines of division and distinction.

Fernandes argues that "the scope of this particular form of hybridity in the formation of 'Hinglish' . . . transforms it from a cross-class to a specifically middle class phenomenon" (2000a:621). In Cairo, English has never been a cross-class phenomenon. The contemporary vernacular of English-Arabic is therefore even more class-specific than the Hinglish discussed by Fernandes, and functions even more as a gatekeeper and sign of privileged class belonging effectively. This English-Arabic vernacular is moreover largely particular to younger generations. Language schools have educated a generation drawn from diverse middle class and elite origins, and have given rise to a relatively broad stratum that is fluent in English and uses a class-specific mix of English and Arabic in work and leisure. Such social divisions based on language skills tend to reflect a number of other divisions: whether one has other forms of cosmopolitan capital, is familiar with and connected to the 'outside,' is eligible for up-market jobs, and can consume in up-market venues.

In light of the class-based character of multilingualism, Fernandes rightly criticizes overtly celebrative readings of the subversive potential of hybridity. She argues that such assumptions "[do] not interrogate the ideological and material conditions that constitute the production of conceptions of hybridity. . . . [H]ybridity in contemporary urban India is inextricably linked to the class-based cosmopolitanism of the urban middle classes" (Fernandes 2000a:622; see Friedman 2003 for a similar critique). I do not want to discount the creative and imaginative potential precipitated by the increased salience of different cultural global flows (Appadurai 1990). As Singerman and Amar (2006) and Ghannam (2002) argue, Cairo also harbors less privileged forms of cosmopolitanism, of world-making. Yet, "each form of 'cultural mixing' or hybridity . . . will be inscribed in its own specific geography of power" (Morley 2001:442). In Cairo, the ability to mix and blend depends on being familiar and comfortable with *barra*, an imagined First World abroad.

In the first years of the twenty-first century, Cairo has seen a boom of English-language magazines directed at an Egyptian audience. The emergence of such English-language magazines demonstrates the existence of a segment of the population that identifies itself with and through English. *Campus Magazine: The Voice of Our Generation* was founded in 2001 by a young Egyptian who wanted to create a magazine for young people in an "edgy language." *Campus* targets young upper-middle to upper class Cairenes, whom it dubs 'The New Generation.' As *Campus'* senior editor explained to me in an interview, *Campus'* target public consists of young Egyptian professionals between eighteen and thirty-five who are fluent in English, well educated, and travel, "mainly AUCians [students or graduates from the American University in Cairo] and people who have been living abroad." *The Paper*, a smaller and more recent edition, targeted the same public. The editor of both magazines explained that one has to use English to attract such people, "who would never read anything in Arabic." As the editors of *The Paper* emphasized, "If you have the choice between *Cleo* [an English-language lifestyle magazine] and *Kalaam in-Nas* [an Arabic-language equivalent], you would read *Cleo* first. It's easier and it just has more prestige and class." Though written in English, *Campus Magazine*'s frequent use of Egyptian slang firmly grounds the publication in upper (middle) class Cairo. Both *Campus* and *The Paper* make use of an Egyptian English that has become the thoroughly local, distinctive language of Cairo's young upper-middle class and elite.

These magazines portrayed their public—intermittently defined as the A- and B-classes, those educated in elite institutions or abroad, people who have traveled, the coffee shop public—as the future leaders of the country.[26] Such portrayals resonate with the narratives of new liberal Cairo discussed in Chapter One. Yet the editors of both magazines didn't consider this 'new generation' quite ready to take over. They decried its public's ignorance and complacency toward the country's troubles. They said that they wanted to wake this new generation up from its complacency, and encourage it to think about its societal role. The editors of *The Paper*, for example, said, "We are trying to get our readers to think and acquire general knowledge. The problem is that Egyptians do not read." And later, "Our generation is going to take over, and we have all these new things in the country. These changes should be accompanied by new mentalities." The senior editor of *Campus Magazine* similarly expressed a wish to create awareness among the future leaders of the country.

The magazine playfully teased its audience about its presumed ignorance. In its rubric 'Campus Spy' the magazine "sets out to test the general knowledge of our affluent Egyptian youth, the future of our country, with questions about geography and figures of recent Egyptian history," with the expected hilarious results.

Campus Magazine was distributed free of charge in a large number of upscale venues in upper-middle class areas: up-market coffee shops, clothing, book and gift stores, and gyms.[27] *The Paper* had a more limited circulation, but was similarly distributed free of charge in some Cairene coffee shops. These distribution networks indicate the intimate connection between 'the new generation' targeted by these magazines, and Cairo's upscale geographies. Moreover, *Campus Magazine* was entirely paid for by numerous advertisements of companies that were clearly interested in targeting this lucrative market segment.

While its target audience consisted of young upper-middle class to elite Cairenes, *Campus Magazine* was also seen as a new medium that could educate Cairo's less affluent young professionals. The editor said that *Campus* also reached less affluent Egyptian youths from Shubra, an old (lower-)middle class area, and students of Ain Shams University who, she said, considered the publication "cool." She argued that "they try to read our magazine because they want to better themselves. It gives them the opportunity to interact with us *in an indirect way* and learn from us" (my emphasis). Parallels with the commercials discussed in the previous chapter abound. Upper-middle class and elite professionals are portrayed as the role models of Egypt's new liberal era. Less well-off graduates are invited to emulate their ways, if only from a safe distance and without guarantees of an eventual inclusion in the former's privileged worlds.

Upper-Middle Class Contestations

New lines of segmentation in education and, as I discuss in the next chapter, in the labor market reconfigure older configurations of social stratification. While *Campus Magazine* and *The Paper* address a 'new generation' of upper-middle class professionals as a societal vanguard and processes of segmentation emphasize divisions between those with and those without cosmopolitan capital, older hierarchies and distinctions continue to permeate contestations over class membership. I end this chapter with an analysis of class belonging and social hierarchy among Cairo's upper-middle class professionals. To what extent have the stark changes in Cairo's political economy, and the concomitant shifts in valued cultural capital, influenced the way class standing and belonging are appraised?

Family backgrounds have long functioned as markers of true social standing and belonging. Despite the looming importance of cosmopolitan capital, such family backgrounds remained critical to social stratification in Cairo, indirectly, by way of the kinds of economic and cultural capital at one's disposal, and more directly in the form of social capital. Persons were often identified and classified by way of their family genealogy. They were, for example, seen as hailing from 'a big family' (a known family of good and long standing), or as *awlaad naas* (children of good, solidly middle or upper-middle class, families). Aristocratic hierarchies still lingered on in references to big families and their aristocratic titles. Even though aristocratic titles were abolished after 1952, it had once more become important to be able to claim a *bey* or *basha* in the family. Such family backgrounds provided an important measure of 'true' class belonging. Those who vied for a similar status without the family history to back up their claims could be dismissed as nouveau riche.

The figure of the nouveau riche has long been a major focus of contestations concerning true class membership. In my upper-middle class circles I heard frequent comments about the invasion of specific venues by nouveaux riches, which was taken to have lowered their 'level.' A friend regularly claimed that persons of whom she disapproved were likely from nouveaux riches backgrounds. As I discussed earlier, the educational strategies of newly affluent families regularly became the subject of scorn in older middle class families. The term nouveau riche (in upper-middle class circles the French term is mostly used, rather than the Arabic *il-aghniyya ig-gudaad*) gained currency after the *infitaah* policies of the mid-1970s and 1980s. When 'lower' strata gained wealth and indulged in conspicuous consumption, old values of civilization and educational achievement were felt to be dwarfed by money. More established middle and upper class families felt out-competed by these new elites. Solidly middle class dismay focused on their unsophisticated and showy ways. The nouveau riche became a prime character of the cinematic imagination of the 1980s (Armbrust 1999). Even if the figure of the nouveau riche seems to have lost some of the salience it had in the cinema of the 1980s and 1990s, nouveaux riches still appeared with frequency in popular television serials (see Abu-Lughod 2005:203), for example in the 2002 Ramadan serial *Ayna qalbi?* ('Where is my heart?').

E. Anne Beal argues that Jordanian contestations over true class membership were similarly fueled by the opening up of possibilities for labor migration to the Gulf states and domestically by the increased leverage for new commercial or industrial enterprises. Beal argues that these contestations were primarily couched in terms of a contrast between the 'restrained' lifestyles of the older elites and more conspicuous consumption of those with 'new money' (2000). In Egypt, such contestations similarly focused not so much on affluence per se (though the sources of wealth of the nouveaux riches were often discredited), but on the way one spent one's disposable income. The showy consumption seen as typical of the nouveaux riches was contrasted with the restrained sophistication of solidly middle class or elite families. Yet, education and social origins remained at least as important with respect to class belonging. The continued importance of social origins and educational attainment reflects the persistence of Egyptian modernist ideas regarding the importance of advancement through education, but also of family backgrounds and histories as markers of true class membership.

The professional upper-middle class is drawn from diverse origins, among others from families that would be considered nouveaux riches. Yet within my upper-middle class circles, the allegedly obvious contrast between the vulgarity of nouveaux riches and the sophistication of good families hardly seemed to hold. I found it almost impossible to distinguish the nouveaux riches from those of 'good' family backgrounds without specifically knowing their family histories. Depreciating references to the nouveaux riches continued to rehearse longstanding lines of social stratification and distinction and reiterate some of the central tenets of the Egyptian modernism discussed earlier. Yet, the combination of a comfortable family situation and private school attendance has contributed to the relatively homogeneous acquisition of upper-middle class cultural capital, particularly of the cosmopolitan capital and lifestyles that provide access to up-market Cairo. Mona Abaza argues that nouveau riche has become "a floating category" (2001:117). In upper-middle class circles it was indeed used in an almost random fashion to disqualify other upper-middle class professionals.

Cosmopolitan cultural capital, like fluency in foreign languages and familiarity with globally dominant cultural codes, has come to signify upper-middle class belonging. Such privileged capital was often assumed to imply good family backgrounds, which in the eyes of many remained key to 'real' class membership. These assumed correspondences allowed those with excellent mastery of upper-middle class codes to claim such social belonging, even in the absence of concomitant family backgrounds. Some of the intricacies of contestations of class belonging are exemplified in Nihal's story of Tareq.

I met Tareq on a SaharaSafaris trip. He was in his early thirties, tall and fair skinned. While he spoke a British English that was largely free of the usual Egyptian accent, he was also well versed in light-hearted Egyptian Arabic. He controlled gatherings with his well-placed jokes in that informal and playful language. His appearance seemed to radiate self-confidence. Among the most important qualities that lent such power to his appearance were his confident manner and his facile integration of Egyptian high-class and foreign repertoires. His light skin could indicate Turkish descent, which would signal a long membership in Egypt's absolute elite or, equally prestigious, a Western lineage.

Nihal was among the women charmed by Tareq's rather formidable presence. She started seeing Tareq on a regular basis after returning to Cairo, but their relationship did not turn out well. She told me that many of the details of Tareq's life were not as glamorous as they had seemed. He was not the *ibn naas* (son of a good family) we had imagined him to be, she reported gloatingly. His family lived in a mixed middle class neighborhood rather than one of the prestigious areas where most upper-middle class professionals lived. Tareq had told her that, in contrast to most upper-middle class professionals, he had always paid his own way through life. Even though he was now finishing a higher degree at an internationally accredited private institute, he had graduated from a public university. Nihal said that Tareq always took care to dress in distinctive ways, to have an impressive car and the latest laptop, even if he could not afford these symbols of prestige. He would tell her that appearance was all-important. His immaculate command of up-market repertoires, appearance, dress, attitudes, and language were crucial to his highly successful performance. He was a self-made man but did his utmost to hide it. There were many men like him, Nihal said, ambitious social climbers from modest middle class backgrounds who pretend to be otherwise.

Over the course of a year, Nihal kept me informed of new developments in Tareq's life. She eventually saw her misgivings about him confirmed when Tareq married a 'typical *muhaggaba*' (veiled woman) after a short engagement period. His marriage to a young woman with all the qualities of the ideal upper-middle class housewife symbolized the shallowness of his progressive performance and his interest in her as a professional woman. His marriage showed where his real roots lay, she concluded.

For all intents and purposes, Tareq actually did present an upper-middle class ideal: employed in a multinational, fluent in both local and global repertoires, hard working, full of male prowess, yet a real gentleman. He successfully implied that he was from an elite background by the self-confident way he carried himself. Yet, Nihal charged that Tareq bluffed to hide his more modest middle class background. In the end, his 'true' background showed itself in his partner choice. He was not the enlightened elite person he pretended to be, but merely one of the many outwardly progressive but in truth conservative male professionals who think it well to go out with and engage in intimate relationships with female colleagues and friends, but eventually choose to marry a typical housewife. Tareq's class act included ease and comfort in mixed-gender sociability, and progressive attitudes toward gender roles and imperatives of feminine modesty and chastity. However, in Nihal's eyes, his 'traditional' marriage showed his more modest social background.

Nihal's story about Tareq illustrates the complex politics of class membership in upper-middle class circles. Her analysis of Tareq's 'class act' exposes some of the logics of distinction in upper-middle class circles. Appearance and language skills were generally taken to be sure indicators of social level and concomitant family background. Privileged family backgrounds were often taken to imply a deeply rooted, authentic sophistication and a true adherence to cosmopolitan, 'progressive' attitudes with respect to gender. Successful presentations of the self played on these indicators. Nihal's story shows the efficacy of cultural capital as a mode of distinction and sign of a certain class belonging, but also highlights the fragility of such claims, since family background remained the arbiter of their validity.

Investments

After three decades of gradual liberalization and an ongoing erosion of public facilities and services, the realm of education showed multiple refractions of 'the private.' Privatization manifested itself in inexpensive, but low-quality private schools that offered meager alternatives to the increasingly notorious public schools. These schools were often 'investment opportunities' that targeted a large, but impoverished lower-middle class. At the other end of the spectrum, 'the private' resurfaced as conspicuous consumption of foreign diplomas in well-equipped new schools with swimming pools, located next to luxurious compounds along the highways in the desert. Meanwhile the nominally free public education system, emblematic of the Nasser-era developmentalist project, still turned out large numbers of graduates. The vast majority of these graduates found that their diplomas had lost much of their value. Yet, even in more privileged social segments the competition for qualifications and jobs had the feel of a rat race with everyone scampering for limited opportunities for decent futures. This rat race fuelled ever-greater investments in private schools and tutoring. Such investments signal an acknowledgment of the intricate connections between a dual school system and a segmented labor market. They speak of lines of relative nobility that keep moving up. They also express a stubborn insistence on being middle class. It is an insistence on a life free from the dust, an old promise that few can or want to forget.

This chapter examined a moment in a longer process of shifting social, economic, and cultural hierarchies, in which old and new divisions and distinctions merge in uncertain ways. While many Cairenes complain that "it is only money that matters these days," new forms of cultural capital have become highly effective in the creation and suggestion of difference. Private language schools are important sites for the acquisition of such formal and informal cultural capital. Much of this cultural capital could be termed cosmopolitan capital, since it entailed familiarity with, and mastery of, Western knowledge, as well as being conversant with globally dominant standards and fashions. Language had become the most potent marker of such cosmopolitan capital, not only in the labor market, but also in the distinctive lifestyles and transnational aspirations that characterize much of Cairo's upper-middle class. The emergence of magazines that address their Egyptian public in English most clearly illustrates the existence of a privileged, conspicuously cosmopolitan segment of urban society. The correspondences between these magazines and the narratives of Egypt's new liberal era are striking. Both present upper-middle class professionals as the new generation, a societal vanguard that will lead Egypt into a global era.

Chapter 3

The Logics of Reform

Stories of Cairo's Labor Market

I had met many young men and women who had experienced hardships in the labor market, heard numerous stories about the difficulties of finding even half-way decent jobs, and had sat with groups of youth in sidewalk cafés who seemed to have nothing else to do with their lives. Yet, it was a two-hour meeting with five young men in February 2003 that left an indelible impression on me.

I had asked a lower-middle class friend of mine to arrange an interview with a few other graduates who were similarly struggling with the harsh realities of Cairo's labor market. He contacted Ahmed, who had graduated in law a few years previously. At the time Ahmed worked long hours in a small law firm for a mere LE250 a month. Ahmed brought four young men along, who had met each other in the course of their studies at the Faculty of Commerce at Ain Shams University. These young men in their mid-twenties looked very proper, dressed in the lower-middle class style of casual dress one might expect to see on young accountants: wide fitting cotton pants, a shirt, and a patterned jersey. With the exception of Ahmed, the lawyer, they had graduated six months earlier and were presently unemployed. Though Ahmed often took the lead in the discussion, the contribution of one of his friends most evocatively expressed their shared predicament. "I was an excellent student and look at me now," he said again and again, pulling at his jersey. "I simply want to be able to buy a new sweater."

During most of the discussion, the five of them were in full agreement. One could speak for the others about their experiences in the labor market and the feeling of being cheated out of a promised fate. Their oftentimes hilarious stories contained a sense of despair and cynicism regarding the government and the shady practices of people they encountered in their search for a decent living, from the boss in a small copy shop to the tycoons who fled the country, leaving behind huge unpaid debts. After we finished our meeting they showered me with questions about the possibilities of working in Europe. They all wanted to leave, if only they could get the chance to do so. Yet they did not seem to have any idea what to expect or how to go about it.

The young men whom I call Ahmed's *shilla* are part of a large cohort of young, unemployed graduates. In the 1990s the ranks of the educated expanded, while diminished possibilities for labor migration and the return of labor migrants, as well as limited public sector hiring further decreased job opportunities that had already been insufficient for over two decades (Tourné 2003).[28] The swelling numbers of unemployed graduates captured the nation's imagination. These young unemployed graduates were unable to make the transition to adulthood, most notably married life. There were not enough affordable houses for newly married couples and no income to pay for the rent and provide for a family. These graduates, doubling as involuntary bachelors, were figured as a 'lost generation,' prone to vice and extremism (Tourné 2003). In contrast, upper-middle class professionals could find work as managers or professionals in the internationally oriented up-market segment of the urban economy, where wages were often five times higher than in comparable firms outside of this segment. Saad Eddin Ibrahim noted the beginnings of such segmentation in the early 1980s (1982:52–53, 1987:225). In the following decades it became an organizing feature of the Egyptian labor market. At the start of the twenty-first century, the relative share of the upper-middle class was approximately 15 to 20 percent of Cairo's professional middle class, and 5 to 7 percent of all Cairenes.[29]

The internationally oriented up-market segment consisted not only of multinationals, but also of large Egyptian corporations organized along the same lines as their multinational counterparts, for example, the mobile phone companies and the commercial banks. It also included agencies that provided business producer services to the former, NGOs with foreign funding, and private firms that provided services to an affluent clientele, for example, doctors in private clinics or architects (cf. Abdel Moati 2002:324–30 and Abdelrahman 2007). It is difficult to clearly delineate this up-market segment in terms of sector, company size, or ownership. It is comprised of companies in different sectors (though generally the 'global growth sectors' of ICT, consultancy, business producer services, development, and the like), with local *and* foreign ownership. Lines of segmentation also ran within companies and institutions, since most up-market companies also employed less privileged employees, like the 'office boys.' The wages of these low-ranking employees were generally similar to or only slightly higher than wages outside up-market pockets. Even governmental institutions increasingly displayed such segmentation. What most clearly distinguished up-market jobs was the kind of professional they were seen to require: professionals with cosmopolitan capital and skills, as well as specific social backgrounds.

Such privileged professionals could command concomitant wages. Whereas the oversupply of labor drove wages for educated personnel far below living wages, this segment functioned according to rather different scales. Wages tended to be three to five times higher than those paid in similar occupations in other sectors of the formal economy, but could also go up to twenty times. In 2002 a secretary in a small office would commonly earn around LE250, whereas an executive secretary in a large company might easily earn LE2,500, just as an engineer in a small business would usually earn LE500 to LE1,500 and an engineer in a multinational or local up-market construction company would expect to earn LE5,000.[30] Maha Abdelrahman reports that (internationally funded) NGOs were among the best paying employers. Low- to medium-level NGO salaries were equivalent to those of "highly qualified and experienced personnel [in the private sector], while only the upper-echelons of the public sector would ever reach the lower end of this scale" (2007:79).

In this chapter, I sketch the everyday dilemmas faced by recent university graduates of diverse social and educational backgrounds in the labor market. I rely on the narratives of professionals who could expect a secure career in a 'good company' and for whom government offices had become a distant and unattractive specter, as well as the stories of those professionals to whom such government jobs seemed rather attractive in light of a confusingly and frustratingly insecure and unrewarding private sector. I explore their highly divergent experiences, as well as the different logics and arsenal of common sense they used when faced with the question of jobs and careers. These young professionals were perforce experts at market analysis and career planning. With high unemployment and an economic landscape that was changing at a rapid pace, knowledge and connections could provide a vital edge. It is this knowledge, however partial and placed, that informs this chapter.

Their stories allow me to sketch how the new distinctions that I touched upon in the previous chapter materialized in Cairo's urban economy. I first examine some of the dilemmas of the less privileged graduates who were largely excluded from the domain of up-market companies and were likely targets of reform programs. Acquiring the cosmopolitan capital that was crucial with respect to up-market jobs had become a common pursuit, although the results of such remedial courses were far from clear. Next I turn to the up-market segment in which the new labor aristocracy with cosmopolitan capital was employed. I argue that at the start of the twenty-first century, even this up-market segment of the urban economy had begun to show cracks.

Remedial Courses

"We've become professionals in taking courses. I've had enough. I want to work! But there is no work at all these days." Fatma and Farida, both recent university graduates, were recounting their experiences in the labor market. Though both came from professional middle class backgrounds, they had not attended the private language schools that are crucial sites for the acquisition of the required fluency in foreign languages, as well as the more elusive informal embodied cultural capital that signals belonging in Cairo's upper-middle class. After taking a number of courses in *'ingiliizi wa computer'* [English and computer], they felt they were still left with nothing, no work in sight, and a whole generation trying, like them, to obtain the now ubiquitous English language and computer skills. "We need a revolution *ba'a*," Fatma concluded, barely joking. They clearly did not see many chances for even halfway acceptable jobs at a time when the private sector had begun firing people, small companies went bankrupt or simply disappeared shortly after they were established, and even the government was no longer employing people.

Only through *wasta* (one who deploys influence on another's behalf, i.e., connections; plural: *wasaayit*) could one find a decent job, they argued. The importance and ubiquitous nature of *wasta* in all kinds of social dealings was often taken as a sign of the contemporary pervasiveness of *il-fasaad*, corruption. One needed connections to gain admittance to reputable schools, to get things done in the bureaucracy, and for jobs in the government or the private sector. Within the workplace, *wasta* was crucial for promotions, bonuses, and lucrative deals, or, at times, simply getting paid or retaining one's position. For want of such good connections, what you need most is *sabr*, endurance, Fatma and Farida argued. Their stories intimated what such *sabr* might mean: doggedness in the quest for a job, and once found, resilience and resignation to endure the bad treatment, long working hours, and low pay.

In order to improve their chances in the labor market and simply to keep busy and have a reason to leave the house, Fatma and Farida had been searching out courses offered by governmental and semigovernmental institutions, chief among them the courses organized under the umbrella of the Social Fund for Development, which was set up to provide a safety net for those who would be negatively affected by Egypt's structural adjustment policies (Assaad and Rouchdy 1999:45ff., Elyachar 2002). The Social Fund offered vocational conversion courses to unemployed university graduates. These courses mainly targeted university graduates whose degrees had little currency in the labor market, for example, literature, business, social work, and law, that is all but the most highly regarded and sought-after degrees in medicine, engineering, politics and economy, and pharmacy. The participants received a small wage during the three-month study period. As Ahmed, the lawyer we met at the beginning of this chapter, scathingly remarked, these courses were actually referred to as job opportunities to give the impression that the government was successfully tackling the high unemployment rates. After completing a course, participants could apply for a loan to start a small project.

Beside this governmental offer, the Future Generation Foundation gave what were said to be high quality courses. This foundation was chaired by Gamal Mubarak, the president's son and a strong proponent of further economic liberalization and participation in the global market. 'Gamal' had become a strong political force in his own right, and had significantly tightened his grip on government policies in the course of 2003 and 2004.[31] Despite President Mubarak's insistent denials, Cairo has been rife with speculation about Gamal's position as the heir-apparent to the presidency. The Future Generation course for recent graduates, which taught English language, computer, and presentation skills, was meant to bring the future generation up to speed with the global economy. The Future Generation optimistically echoed IMF and World Bank policies that suggested that greater integration into the global market would eventually bring improved living standards for everyone. According to its mission statement, the foundation will "contribute to Egypt's economic growth and global competitiveness efforts" by "helping in upgrading local corporate culture. With a private sector driven economy, this will translate into greater fiscal well-being for the nation at large, a leading role in the regional economy, and a strong position on the global market."[32]

Many unemployed graduates looked to these remedial courses for salvation, hoping to miraculously transform from one of the countless unemployed with heavily devalued diplomas into the fast moving, fancily clad professionals advertised widely by the Future Generation commercial discussed in Chapter One. The question is whether its graduates could indeed find a job usefully employing their new skills, not to mention a job in a multinational or local up-market company. The labor market was not nearly as open and transparent as the Foundation's program seemed to suggest. Job prospects were inextricably bound up with family background and educational trajectories (cf. Barsoum 1999). Maha Abdelrahman concurs: "Since most NGO jobs require both a good knowledge of English and computer skills, only the most educated among the middle to upper-middle class will qualify and not the struggling members of the lower-middle classes who are excluded by their poor state education" (2007:82). While these remedial courses provide a modicum of the skills necessary for such jobs, they cannot replicate the level of those whose education at home and in private language schools intrinsically included such skills. Moreover, up-market jobs have many other implicit and informal requirements, chief among them a privileged family background and social circle. The middle class has become divided between *awlaad naas*, children of good families, who monopolize jobs in the up-market segments, and others who lack the right kinds of capital to aspire to such jobs. Lines of relative nobility had already been drawn and were constantly being raised due to increased competition over a limited number of good positions in the up-market segment of the economy.

Farida did not expect that she would be able to capture one of these prize jobs. The jobs she had had were all in small semiformal private companies and invariably came with starting salaries in the range of LE150 to LE250. Barsoum reports that female graduates saw a lack of recognition of their educational accomplishments and related social standing, as well as fears of sexual harassment in the small and informal offices, as the main problems of work in the private sector (Barsoum 1999:83ff.). Farida said she has given up on the careers she used to imagine for herself. If she accepts a job at all, she said, she would only do so to be able to pay for another course.

Entrepreneurial Spirits

At the start of the twenty-first century, university graduates continued to capture the national imagination, albeit no longer as the admirable protagonists of an educated, developing nation. They were rather portrayed as a source of problems, frustrations, and possible deviancy (Tourné 2003). This group, which most readily embodies the problems of the shift from the earlier Nasser era developmentalism to the contemporary neoliberal project, was targeted for reform. Instead of waiting for the government to provide them with a job and a modicum of middle class life, young graduates were expected to turn to the private sector. According to official government policy, not the civil servant but the entrepreneur should be their role model (Tourné 2003:19). This emphasis on self-help and the incitement to become an entrepreneur have become common exhortations in countries where international organizations and governments try to rewrite previous social contracts.

In a move away from large-scale development projects that centered on the state, international organizations have increasingly begun to rely on NGOs as 'partners in development.' Shifting the site and agent of development accords well with neoliberal precepts that advocate "a diminution of the state and a disengagement from the terrain of economic activity" (Elyachar 2002:496, cf. Abdelrahman 2004). Julia Elyachar labels these programs "anti-development development packages," since they are founded on a rejection of earlier development policies and are designed and marketed as the opposite of state-centered development. NGOs had become preferred partners in development. They were presented as the representatives of the community and 'civil society,' while the state, in contrast, was portrayed as anti-people (Elyachar 2002:495).

In the context of such anti-development philosophies, international organizations like the World Bank began hailing the informal sector, previously seen as the epitome of economic and cultural backwardness, as "the vanguard of entrepreneurial savvy in the global age" (Elyachar 2002:496). As Elyachar argues,

> key aspects of the practices whereby vast sectors of the urban poor
> have traditionally sustained themselves had been abstracted and
> modeled into an antidevelopment development package in programs
> geared towards the informal economy. . . . Yesterday's backward
> cultural practice becomes something to be admired and perhaps even
> taught to *recalcitrant downsized public sector workers and their children.*
> (2002:500, my emphasis)

The Egyptian government was quick to appropriate the mantra of microenterprise. Paradoxically, "The Egyptian state [thereby] appropriated an agenda that had begun as a way to bypass and overcome the corrupt essence of the Third World state" (Elyachar 2002:502).

Under the guidance and with the financial backing of international donors, a number of NGOs and semigovernmental bodies were established to offset some of the negative consequences of structural adjustment (Assaad and Rouchdy 1999, Elyachar 2002; 2003). The largest of them, the Social Fund for Development, was set up as a separate agency funded by foreign donors, yet the state had a strong say in its management and policies. The Fund directed as much as half of its funds to the aforementioned training programs and loans for unemployed graduates who wanted to start up a business (Assaad and Rouchdy 1999:64–66). Such microcredit programs were presented as a panacea for social problems. Egyptians, particularly the socially significant army of unemployed graduates, were expected to take their lives into their own hands, using the start-up capital provided by one of the funds for a small project. No independent evaluation of the efficacy of Social Fund loans to young graduates-turned-entrepreneurs had taken place. Despite the Fund's claims of success, Ragui Assaad and Malak Rouchdy seriously doubt that these loans have indeed brought any significant sustained job growth. "Unemployed graduates who have no labor market or entrepreneurial experience are very unlikely candidates for success in a highly competitive small business sector," they argue (1999:86). The high rate of defaults on these loans is an ominous sign (ibid.).[33]

Ahmed said he had considered applying for a loan of a few thousand Egyptian pounds, but found that he needed "half of the country to guarantee for me, while those people [referring to the business tycoons who defaulted on their loans] take three million and escape the country." Ahmed referred to the scandal of the lost billions in loans to big businessmen, which at the time had just reached another peak. Throughout the 1990s, the private sector had been 'stimulated' by substantive huge loans to a small number of big businessmen. These loans were furnished by public banks, often without proper collateral. These two kinds of loans were part of the same program of structural adjustment. The funds set up to provide a safety net for the onslaught of economic liberalization in the labor market were supposed to furnish small loans to the lesser gods of capitalism (Elyachar 2002); the parallel massive loans to private capitalists were meant to boost the private sector. The latter, however, mainly resulted in a temporary construction boom of luxury housing and resorts, as well as a high rate of defaults (Mitchell 2002).

In 2002 a popular Ramadan television serial addressed the issue of loan-defaulting businessmen, and more generally, elite affluence and corruption. *Amira fi 'Abdin* ('Amira in Abdin') told the story of a woman from a wealthy entrepreneurial family who is forced to leave her lavish villa with a swimming pool after her husband and son-in-law fled the country with a large sum of money they had borrowed from public banks. Amira then returns to her old apartment in Abdin, a *sha'bi* neighborhood in Cairo. While the police search for the escapees provides the backdrop, the serial focused on Amira's rediscovery of the good character and community spirit of Abdin's *sha'bi* and lower-middle class inhabitants. In line with euphemistic portrayals of Cairene realities, Abdin appears as a sober yet clean and comfortable place, and the apartments in Amira's building are all spacious, well maintained, and stylish.

While the serial addressed the burning issue of corrupt businessmen and their abuse of public funds, it focused on Amira's life after her 'return' to Abdin. The serial narrated the redemption of the leading upper class character by her rapprochement with the less affluent yet morally untainted and authentic Egyptian salt-of-the-earth. The serial could be read as a story of national healing, reestablishing the Egyptian modernist pact between the classes that, as I noted in Chapter Two, has long been a central tenet of Egyptian modernist discourse. It attempts to reintegrate the wealthy entrepreneurial elite that had been tainted by numerous scandals into the class-divided yet united nation. Significantly, however, it avoided addressing the larger underlying issue of socioeconomic disparity in Egypt's new liberal age.

Back to the Dust

"If the government passes you by, grovel in its dust," goes a well-worn Egyptian saying.[34] A government job, however base, is better than any other job. Government jobs had long promised a secure and relatively comfortable life. While a government job was a right for those with an intermediate and higher education during the Nasser period, the saying reflects an even older period, when government employment was highly coveted, yet difficult to attain (see, e.g., Abdel-Fadil 1980:9). As Fatma Farag notes, the saying seemed to have lost its salience with the advent of the open-door policies, the state's renunciation of its patronage role with respect to job provision and welfare arrangements, and a growing emphasis on the private sector.[35] In the early 1980s Waterbury declared the civil service to be "the employer of last resort" (1983:262). Yet, against the backdrop of demonstrations against the implementation of age limits for new government employees, Fatma Farag comments that these days, it is "back to the dust." Large numbers are once again competing for government employment.[36]

Government employment had again become attractive for those young graduates who seemed destined to linger in the lower regions of the middle class (cf. Tourné 2003). Several people told me that they would know when the government had advertised its job openings in the newspaper, because the streets in the Qasr al-Aini district where most government ministries were located would be flooded with young people carrying plastic file cases. Compared to the ill-paid, insecure employment in the private sector, government jobs seemed to offer a good alternative, despite the extremely low wages, which have declined to a fraction of what was already a modest real value in 1981 (Assaad 1997:92). Notwithstanding their often meager pay, government employment offered ironclad job security, insurance, pension schemes, and short working hours. The short and often flexible working hours allowed male employees to have one or several jobs after hours in addition to their government job. For women, government employment presented few obstacles to the household chores and familial responsibilities they were expected to shoulder. Government offices were moreover commonly perceived to be at least safe and respectable for women, in contrast to more capricious private sector settings.

Ahmed's *shilla* was similarly positive about government employment. In light of the insecurity they repeatedly experienced in their small private sector jobs—pay that came months late, if at all, getting fired on the spot—government employment seemed like a good option. After recounting numerous stories of insults and extremely poor wages in private sector jobs, Ahmed concluded: "With these kinds of jobs, you cannot do anything. Since you cannot save a single penny from your wages, you cannot even start thinking about marriage. You cannot start a business venture. With the little money you earn and the long working hours, you cannot even decide to give up on the future and simply live your life." The young men of Ahmed's *shilla* shared similar experiences from their six-month search for work, which had yet to yield tangible results. The small jobs they did manage to get were often so ill paid that, after subtracting the money spent on transport and food during the twelve-hour workday, there was little of their wage left.

Despite their poor position in the labor market and the limited prospects for change, many young graduates seemed hesitant to accept jobs far below their educational achievement. Dina, a graduate of a private four-year institute of business administration, regretfully told me about one of her experiences. She once accompanied a female friend with intermediate education to a very luxurious private hospital—"five stars, employing mostly foreign doctors!"—that was rumored to have some job openings. As it turned out, the hospital offered two kinds of jobs: men could work as handymen or security guards, women as housekeepers. Dina said she had not been looking for a job herself, but merely came along to support her friend. However, the manager that came to meet them ignored her friend and offered Dina a job as a housekeeper. She told him she had graduated from a private institute and could not possibly take the job. He assured her that they employed many graduates in similar jobs, but Dina insisted. "It's just impossible. I would feel shy. What if some of my fellow students would see me? What if I would be bossed around?" Her reaction is reminiscent of Walter Armbrust's (1999) description of what it means to be middle class in Egypt (see Chapter Two). Armbrust argues that the essence of being middle class lies in the ability to avoid socially degrading, menial work, where one is obliged to obey others. Morever, *sum'it il-bayt*, her family's reputation would be at stake, Dina continued. Though she argued that she wants to work and contribute to the tight family budget, she felt she did not have a "real need." She added that it might be different for young men. Even if many women work to suplement the family income, providing for the family was primarily perceived to be the husband's responsibility. Accepting a job in a low-status profession might be excused in light of a male graduate's need to 'open a house' (start a family) or his responsibilities for providing for his natal family. Such excuses did not hold for young women. The family who sent its educated daughter out to work in a menial and socially degraded occupation would be seen as either very needy, or irresponsible, immoral, and greedy.

Despite her clear arguments against accepting such a job, Dina still reminisced about the excellent working conditions and pay at the hospital. She depicted the hospital as the pinnacle of cleanliness, transparency, and fairness, with clear working hours and paid overtime, as well as insurance and allowances for transport and the mandatory uniform. The hospital's rule against employing family members of current employees struck her as a symbol of fairness and clarity. When I asked her what she planned to do instead, Dina said that she was waiting for her *wasta* to come through. One of her uncles was a state employee and promised to get her a position in his office in due time.

The issue of 'menial jobs' loomed large in conversations with lower-middle class graduates. Mohamed, one of the young men of Ahmed's *shilla*, pointed out that while they had studied hard in high school and university, a plumber earned more than them "without any diploma whatsoever." The figure of the plumber was one of the highly charged characters in middle-class social memory. In the late 1970s and 1980s numerous craftsmen found well-paid jobs in other Arab countries, which led to a shortage of skilled workers and rising fees. The construction boom that resulted from migrant remittances being invested in real estate exacerbated the shortage (Richards and Waterbury 1996:128). Professional middle class people had difficulties paying for these technical services and stories spread about simple craftsmen making fortunes, buying themselves a way into the world of the respectable middle classes by way of middle class houses, cars, and even wives. These stories were readily taken up in 1980s cinema. Exemplary is the story of Ali's educated middle class family, portrayed in *Hubb fi hadabit al-haram* ('Love at the Pyramids Plateau,' 1984). Ali's sister is courted by the neighborhood plumber who owns a new car and a luxurious apartment. The family's discussion about the proposed marriage is emblematic of the social changes that were underway in the early

1980s. When the mother comments that the uneducated suitor cannot match their family's standing, Ali cynically remarks: "No, he is not of our circles, he is of a much higher standing." His mother has to concede: "With your money, you become your bride's sultan."[37]

In the course of the 1990s the good fortune of craftsmen seemed to have worn off, with the construction sector in a slump and fewer chances of work in the Gulf, yet his figure still lingered in the collective imagination as a sign of all that went wrong with the struggling graduate. The plumber remained a symbol for the plight of the government employee who still looks to education as a guarantee of middle class status and life in a society where the value of a degree has been severely eroded and less educated others might have better prospects. Mohamed's comment about the plumber was met with general agreement. He seemed to be speaking for all those who entered their educational career with high hopes of moving up or at least reproducing their sober middle class status and standard of living, and now find themselves in a rather hopeless situation. Ahmed continued: "While we were at university, we still had hopes. They told us: 'If you work well, you'll do well in life.'" I asked them why they did not opt for such a technical profession. My question drew an immediate and sharp response. "I didn't study for all these years to do that. How are you going to marry once you do such a job?" Both Dina and Ahmed's *shilla* mentioned that besides personal expectations and vested social identities, marriage was a main reason for not accepting such jobs. Most people considered a comparable social and educational 'level' (or a slightly higher one for men) a crucial prerequisite in a match. Lack of such equivalence was generally believed to spell trouble in marital life.

However devalued the qualifications of many lower-middle class graduates in the labor market, their educational status remained an important aspect of their social identity and aspirations. Their status as graduates seemed to guarantee a modicum of respectability and a middle class aura, even if that was all it offered them for the moment. In *Distinction*, Pierre Bourdieu discusses the consequences of diploma inflation that resulted from the democratization of education in France. His comments under the heading 'The cheating of a generation' resonate with the disillusionment expressed by Ahmed's *shilla*.

> The collective disillusionment which results from the structural
> mismatch between aspiration and real probabilities, between the
> social identity the school system seems to promise, or the one it offers
> on a temporary basis, and the social identity that the labour market in
> fact offers is the source of the disaffection towards work, that refusal

of social finitude. . . . These young people, whose social identity and self-image have been undermined by a social system and an educational system that have fobbed them off with worthless paper, can find no other way of restoring their personal and social integrity than by a total refusal. (Bourdieu 1984:144)

Some graduates indeed chose to remain unemployed or underemployed rather than seeking employment in menial jobs that required one to leave behind the safe walls of the office, the guarantee of middle class respectability. However, in light of the absence of social security provisions, remaining unemployed was an option few could afford.

How Cairenes dealt with disillusionment upon entrance into the labor market depended on their family situation and, as I noted earlier, gender. A more comfortable family situation allowed unemployed graduates to fall back on their parents, and hold out for better job openings. Assaad argues that educated workers were generally much more likely than their uneducated counterparts to wait for a more regular job (2002:35). A more solidly middle class background also increased the social price of accepting socially degraded jobs, because of the greater social embarrassment involved. First generation graduates from more working-class families seemed to have less qualms about, and were obviously less able to avoid, accepting such jobs as a temporary solution. Mohamed, a law graduate, worked in one of Cairo's upscale coffee shops. When I spoke with him, he said that he had already been working for years in the job that he initially considered a temporary solution. Like Ahmed, he found that a law graduate needs at least ten years before being able to earn an even mediocre income. Because his family could not do more for him than they already had by putting him through university, he decided to acquiesce to a lower-level service job.

Even though further research is needed to explore such strategies, one of the options for unemployed or underemployed graduates like Ahmed and Mohamed were the low-level service jobs opened up by the growth of up-market consumption spaces. Their association with new forms of consumption and leisure, marked and marketed as Western or First World, elevated these jobs from their more lowly 'local' counterparts. The foreign titles, names and associations, and the higher standing of the public that is served, had a cleansing effect on jobs that were otherwise marked as lower class and seen as unacceptable for a university graduate. This elevation paralleled distinctions between, for example, administrative jobs in large multinational companies and those in smaller private sector companies or government bureaucracies, but was more ambiguous and did not generate a similar degree of incommensurability in wages and status. The upscale coffee shop, which I discuss in the following chapter, provides a prime example of such a 'cleansed' workspace. Several waiters in coffee shops stressed the importance of being able to talk with and understand upper-middle class patrons. The highly educated, yet lower-middle class graduate seems ideally suited for such jobs. The lower middle class graduate serving his more privileged colleagues from university might well be one of the most telling expressions of disjunctive fates within the educated middle class.

Higher education has long been the road to social respectability in Egypt's highly class-conscious society. A degree freed one from the obligation to work directly for others, in the worst case in people's houses. Providing personal services or working as a cleaner is generally associated with a distinctly low standing, which moreover obliges one to demonstrate deference and a submissive attitude. As Dina said, she would feel "shy" working as a hospital cleaner. She would be embarrassed if any of her old classmates were to witness her social downfall. Patients could boss her around as a servant, somebody with a lower status, not conscious of or not caring about her family background and the sacrifices her family made to provide her with a good education. Education still carried social value and continued to guarantee a minimum social standing. Irrespective of wages, a manual worker belonged to another class than the unemployed university graduate. While the latter still embodied the promise of a future middle class life, the former had settled for less. Yet, harsh realities obliged many to consider other options. I asked Ahmed in a later meeting whether it was true that he and his friends would not accept more menial jobs. "It depends on what I would earn," he said in a pragmatic tone of voice. Mohamed, the waiter, said he was not sure he would put his son through university. Ahmed similarly commented: "If you ask for somebody's hand, they will say, 'Okay, you are a graduate, but do you have a skill?'" It remains to be seen whether Mohamed and Ahmed will indeed choose to educate their children differently, since university education still accorded status and remained a shared dream among middle class Cairenes.

Embodying Excellence

The different shapes of the private sector in the stories and imaginations of graduates exemplify the realities of Cairo's segmented labor market. For the young men in Ahmed's *shilla*, and for Dina, Farida, and Fatma, the private sector stood for low wages, insecure employment, disrespect, abuse, and fears of harassment. More privileged graduates, significantly those 'with languages,' expected a job in the upper segments of the private sector. For them, the private sector represented the possibility of a well-paid job in which they may make use of their education, in a clean office with 'clean' people.

Governmental and international agencies portrayed the private sector as the engine of national affluence, economic growth, and job creation. In recent years the emphasis had shifted from the formal to the informal private sector, reflecting a growing awareness of the inability of the formal private sector to bring about promised job growth. 'Social capital' and the vitality of the informal sector were euphemistically celebrated as the major assets of Southern countries—repositories of resourcefulness and self-help—and had been given a pivotal role in development (Elyachar 2002; 2003, Fine 2000). It is not hard to see that such euphemisms are at least in part a façade for a lack of job growth and want of the promised redistribution of wealth. This shift is accompanied by a weakening of commitments to sound working conditions and the abolishment of protective labor legislation in the context of liberalization programs.[38] It justifies and even glorifies a scramble for the lowest standards in economic life: labor markets without labor protection or state responsibility for the provision of minimum standards.

The bifurcation of the educational system and the rise of a new segment of professional and managerial jobs in internationally oriented companies have led to increasingly tangible divisions between a privileged upper-middle class and other less fortunate middle class strata (cf. Abdel Moati 2002:338–39). Different forms of capital contribute toward the privileged social and occupational trajectories of young professionals working in this up-market segment of the urban economy. In the previous chapter I argued that schools were crucial in the articulation of divisions and distinctions in the professional middle class. The relative affluence of some families allowed them to send their children to private schools and provide them with the financial means to engage in up-market consumption practices, thereby helping their children secure up-market jobs and lifestyles. As Abdelrahman observes, there was a clear gender division with respect to jobs in the up-market sector. "The private sector in Egypt is well known to have a strong male bias, which results in women often being excluded from important positions," she argues. "Donor agencies, on the other hand, prefer to see women hired for their projects in Egypt, while the general consensus seems to be that women are more suited for development work because of their 'compassionate and nurturing disposition'" (Abdelrahman 2007:81). Many upper-middle class men would indeed find jobs as managers in a multinational or consultancy firm, while women found employment in one of the many NGOs with foreign funding.

Privileged educational and concomitant cultural capital, primarily in the form of cosmopolitan capital, was a crucial marker of upper-middle class trajectories. While the cosmopolitan capital imparted by private language schools was a crucial asset in the labor market, foreign or AUC degrees provided for an even stronger position in the labor market. Baher, for example, said that when he came back to Egypt after attaining an MBA degree abroad, he was offered a job in each of the five companies where he had presented himself. In none of the job interviews did the prospective employers feel the need to follow up on his specific qualifications, his motivations, or skills. After graduation, social capital became decisive. The *wasta* and good references provided for by privileged family backgrounds and social networks constituted valuable social capital. Though up-market jobs were also advertised in newspapers and the Internet increasingly played an important role in the mediation of jobs in this segment of the job market, many up-market jobs were mediated through class-specific social networks (cf. Abdelrahman 2007:81). *Wasta*—influential contacts that provide access to much coveted jobs—and *ma'rifa*—being part of networks that provide vital information about, for example, job openings— were crucial in the search for such up-market jobs.

Even if *wasta* was surely the most direct way in which family background became operational in the labor market, an applicant's social background also worked its magic in less tangible ways. Several people told me that up-market jobs relied as much on perceived 'social level' as on official qualifications. Presentation, language, and appearance were crucial in the job search of both men and women. A classy appearance and 'being presentable' were vital. Recruitment agents spoke of "a '*kashf hay'a*,' a trope borrowed from the army, where the army doctors physically examine new recruits to see if they are fit" (Barsoum 1999:65). Employers often took these qualities to be sure indicators of the 'social level' of a candidate. Based on interviews with recruitment agents, Barsoum argues that "the requirements of the ideal candidate constitute a full package." Family background could be taken as a sure sign of having a language and the proper appearance, just as a proper appearance or fluency in English was a sign of the *bint naas* (daughter of a good family) (Barsoum 1999:77). One particularly savvy woman with experience in a number of private companies told me that employers would routinely ask a job applicant to come back for further interviews to find out whether the applicant was able to afford several stylish outfits. Another woman told me that coming by car to an interview and dressing in expensive suits were preconditions for many up-market jobs. Many young graduates had to depend on family support for such symbolic assets. These stories suggest that apart from providing the right educational, cultural, and social capital, the family played an important role in furnishing one with the 'starting capital' needed to present oneself as an eligible candidate for up-market jobs.

Upper class or 'foreign' appearances presented significant embodied capital in the job market. Karim cynically remarked that he got his previous job because his former boss wanted fair-skinned people like himself for window dressing. Nihal similarly told me that her uncle, a successful surgeon who worked in a private hospital, was asked to appear in an advertisement for the hospital because of his European looks. I was told that employing professionals with a 'classy' appearance advertises a company's ability to employ high-class personnel and intimates a class standing necessary to attract an affluent clientele. The hiring of foreign staff points to similar dynamics. I heard a number of stories about foreigners who were employed in private schools, despite their lack of the required teaching qualifications. The presence of foreigners not only added to the school's prestige, but was also taken to indicate a higher level of proficiency and a truly cosmopolitan educational offer. According to a young woman, such a valuation of the foreign represents a typical Egyptian trait: *'udit il-khawaaga*. She told me that the term refers to an unqualified preference for everything foreign over local alternatives. "A foreigner always has the best views on things, even if he understands nothing at all," she added cynically.[39]

This concern for what Karim called 'window dressing' has a strong gender component. The presence of nonveiled women in an office was generally taken to signal modernity and a high class standing. The commercial for the Future Generation Foundation, discussed in Chapter One, significantly featured only nonveiled women. It represented common realities in Cairo's up-market companies. Up-market workplaces generally stood out because of the overwhelming presence of nonveiled women and the conspicuous absence of *muhaggabaat*. A woman's decision to take up the veil could seriously diminish her chances in up-market companies. Though the rising number of upper-middle class women who choose to wear the veil has had some effect on the previously solid associations of veiling with a lower class status and a lack of modernity, veiling was still considered problematic in many of these spaces, where intimations of an elite background and cosmopolitan belonging were of utmost importance. Dalia, for example, mentioned that at the commercial bank where she used to work, a female employee who decided to wear the veil was transferred to the back office. She was no longer allowed to represent the bank vis-à-vis its clients.

Cairo's segmented labor market valorizes specific forms of privileged cultural capital and social backgrounds, and thereby significantly reproduces and strengthens existing class divisions. In the process, earlier fluid divisions are substituted with solid lines of segmentation. These lines of segmentation divide those who can apply for up-market jobs from other middle class Cairenes who lack the necessary cosmopolitan and social capital to do so. As I discuss in the next chapter, these divisions are imprinted in the urban social landscape and contribute to the consolidation of increasingly distinct and distant social worlds in middle class Cairo.

"But I didn't go to a language school," said Tamer, a professional in his mid-twenties, when I discussed some of my research findings with him. "And I didn't get my jobs through *wasta*." His parents, both middle class professionals, moved back to Egypt after years of having worked in Saudi Arabia. At the time Tamer was past the age to enroll in a language school. Like Mona's children (see Chapter Two), he therefore attended a private 'Arabic' school and public secondary school. He said he was always eager to improve his language skills, which helped him in his search for better jobs. After his commerce studies at a public university, he started out working with ones of his relatives, earning LE400 per month. When he was able to take the place of a friend as an accountant at a private foreign institute, his salary rose to LE700. After a few years, he found another job through the Internet, working as an office manager at a five-star hotel. Shortly after he had started his new job, the management made it clear that he would be fired if his performance did not improve. In the end he managed to keep his job, but when I met him a year later he was again thinking of looking for another position. He wanted a job that would give him more opportunities to 'realize himself.'

Tamer's story defies clear-cut divisions between upper-middle class jobs and other jobs available to young graduates. He straddles the borders of Cairo's segmented labor market. Tamer said that in light of his middle class background, he cannot accept menial jobs and live in a *sha'bi* neighborhood and cope with a low living standard like a working class person might. "I can't accept work as a taxi driver or craftsman, or work for a mere LE500. But I can also not do everything I want to do. I want to live at a better level, have a better car. A peasant might not have these ambitions, but a middle class person needs both a certain standard of living and social level." He said he feels suspended between heaven and earth in what he saw as a typical middle class predicament.

Looking beyond the frayed and messy border areas where individual stories refute more general trends, lines of segmentation seemed rather robust. It is highly unlikely that young professionals from modest backgrounds like Ahmed and his friends, or even the securely middle class Tamer, will ever get prize jobs in the stock exchange, commercial banks, or development agencies.

The professionals employed in these upscale jobs belonged to what can be justly called a 'labor aristocracy.' Those eligible for such jobs were in the rule *awlaad naas*, children of good families, who possessed a combination of formal and informal privileged capitals as a result of their family and social background, economic affluence, proper 'language' education, and membership in more privileged circles. Their language, movements, and bodies spoke of another world: of the private clubs that provided the playing grounds for much of their childhood, and of the private language schools they attended. They spoke an embodied language of cultural competence and cosmopolitan savvy that could not easily be imitated or achieved by resolve. As a human resources consultant said: "Those educated in language schools will most likely have a different education, more westernized. They master a specific language. If I go to a company and they speak Arabic, I feel I am in a different world."

Cracks

Yet, at the beginning of the twenty-first century even the up-market segment of the labor market had begun to show cracks. In the mid-1990s the influx of foreign companies and the growth of private local ones gave rise to a relatively exclusive segment of the labor market for these *awlaad naas*. At the turn of the century, competition among applicants had grown fiercer, while many up-market companies were forced to downsize. In 2002 I heard numerous stories of people working in development organizations and marketing companies who did not receive their wages on time or were forced to accept permanent wage reductions. Many companies were 'letting go' of those employees they could easily fire, while some with more sturdy contracts were told that it was in their own best interest to leave, taking with them a reference letter and a sum of money. If they refused to leave, there were more informal ways of making sure they would eventually leave 'voluntarily.' Many upper-middle class professionals complained about their jobs, but few dared to speak out or take the even more radical step of quitting. Abdelrahman similarly reports that NGO jobs were often highly insecure, and that many NGO employees complained about long hours of unpaid overtime, but did not dare complain to their supervisors (2007).

Fernandes (2000b) discusses the harsh realities of restructuring and retrenchment that lie behind idealized portrayals of India's affluent new middle class. An initial period of high wages and apparently abundant chances for managerial staff in multinationals was followed by a period of retrenchment and restructuring that led to wage reductions, increased job insecurity, as well as casualization of much up-market employment. Fernandes attributes this overhaul not only to the economic slowdown that resulted from the Asian crisis, but also to the dampening of initial overblown expectations among multinationals, based on inflated estimates of the untapped middle class market in India. The retrenchment in Egypt's up-market sector can also partly be reduced to overly optimistic ideas about Egypt's market for luxury consumption goods and services. This holds especially true with respect to the downturn in the construction sector. Its large-scale investments in luxury housing projects did not reap the expected results. The market was flooded, while few people could actually afford such housing. The collapse of the market for luxury housing was at the heart of Egypt's post-2000 economic crisis (Denis 2006:68).

In response to retrenchments, Indian middle class professionals tried to improve their position in the labor market by earning new skills and credentials. In Cairo, the increased competition for a limited number of up-market jobs similarly resulted in a run on better qualifications and higher degrees. Many professionals I knew were studying for an extra degree, particularly MBAs, or were contemplating doing so. A large number of institutes, many affiliated with European or American universities, offered a range of packages to earn such credentials. These additional degrees required large investments for which one often had to rely on family support, yet had no guaranteed returns.

Heba's story about her brother's misfortune is indicative of the hard times that had befallen some middle class professionals. Heba's brother was trained as an engineer, like his father. He was in his late thirties and had a family to support. Heba emphasized her brother's fluency in English and his many contacts with foreigners to clarify his slot in the labor market. He was a clear candidate for any of the comparatively well-paying jobs in Cairo's upscale, internationally oriented economy. After his graduation in the early 1990s, when the building boom was at its peak, he immediately found a job as a civil engineer in a big contracting firm. After their father died, he tried to revive his father's small contracting firm, but he went bankrupt as a result of the suspension of payments by their biggest client: the government. He then took a job in a Lebanese company where he earned LE3,500 a month. When at the end of 2002 his request for a sizeable pay raise was refused, he quit. I asked around and found that, at the time, an engineer with his years of experience could indeed expect to earn LE5,000 a month. However, Heba's brother gambled and lost. After a few months without work he was forced to accept a job with a much lower pay and longer hours—one where, as Heba pointed out, overtime was not paid but coming late was sanctioned by wage deductions.

Whether upper-middle class professionals will look to government jobs in light of the tightening private sector labor market remains a moot point.

In 2002 salaries in the upper segment of the labor market started around LE1,500; the lifestyles of those who qualified for these jobs were concomitant. Even more prestigious government jobs generally paid far less than their private sector equivalents. During an interview about the labor market, a human resourses consultant in her early thirties expressed her surprise at the continued interest in government employment. "Some people of a somewhat lower class still look for government jobs, can you believe it?" The corporate lawyer similarly said she would never consider working in the government bureaucracy. Her secretary earns LE250 per month plus a 100 percent bonus, she said, more than the salary of a government employee with a degree. Like public schools, government offices had become a distant, less than pleasing reality, the government employee an outmoded character. Most people of her 'class' could not imagine working in such spaces.

In contrast to the bad reputation of most of the state bureaucracy, certain domains within the state apparatus did carry prestige, particularly those branches that carried out central state functions that could not be taken up by the private sector, such as foreign affairs, the judiciary, parts of the media, and the petrol sector. Though the pay tended to be less than in comparable private sector jobs, wages in these elite pockets far outstripped those of other government employees. These prestigious jobs moreover held good career opportunities. Besides, as an employee in the ministry of foreign affairs said, "It is not really seen as government, the level of the people is different." Still, several upper-middle class professionals who had chosen such privileged governmental careers told me that friends and colleagues with more lucrative private sector jobs pitied them. A graduate of a French language school said that many people with class backgrounds like hers would never think of applying for such government jobs. She herself worked as a journalist in a foreign language department of *al-Ahram*, the largest state media enterprise. She said she liked her job, which provided ample opportunities for lucrative side jobs to supplement the relatively modest pay of LE1,000 per month. Yet she said she was seen as stupid for burying herself in a government job while she could earn so much more 'outside.'

Besides these long-standing elite sectors within the government bureaucracy, new pockets of excellence with highly qualified and generally more privileged employees had been created where the government must offer quality services. Such pockets of excellence existed, among others, within media institutions, a number of ministries, and the Central Bank. Randa, an upper-middle class professional in her early thirties, used to work at the ministry of economics, in the minister's office. She told me that the floor they occupied at the ministry stood out from the rest of the building by its state-of-the-art furniture and excellent maintenance and facilities. It was not government, she said. "The ministry has two parts: the old part, where there is no work and people do not have a good education, and the other part, where they hire young, good people with fresh ideas to do the important jobs." The latter constituted the elite of the ministry and were paid out of separate funds furnished by the World Bank, at rates comparable to equivalent jobs in the private sector. When I asked her what kind of people they employed, she said: "People with a financial or economic background, perhaps with an extra degree. They all come from good families, are fluent in English, and have attended language schools. We have to maintain certain standards to avoid the spirit that is dominant in the government bureaucracy. They want people from comfortable families to deliver a certain presentable image." These pockets thus reproduced all the distinctions that set an upper-middle class labor aristocracy apart from professionals from more modest backgrounds and educational trajectories.

Similar discrepancies characterized Egypt's Central Bank. Alaa, a Central Bank employee in his mid-thirties, pulled out a pay sheet that detailed to the piaster how much money he had earned that month. It amounted to LE234, but with bonuses and incentives he usually received up to LE800. Alaa had been employed at the Bank for eight years. He comes from a modest lower-middle class background, attended public schools, and lived with his family in a poor neighborhood. He was lucky to get the job, he said. He was hired because he managed to obtain strong *wasta*. In the eight years he had been employed in the Central Bank, recruiting policies had changed drastically. In 2000 the Central Bank had halted recruitment. When they started hiring again at the end of 2002, they only recruited people 'with languages' and computer skills. Alaa's new colleagues, many of whom were young women, started with a base salary of around LE800. They were assigned air-conditioned offices with matching 'respectable' furniture and new computers, and there were plans to send them to the United States for further training. Alaa's office in contrast contained a jumble of furniture. At the time, air-conditioning had recently been installed. This good fortune had come about because an aunt of one of his colleagues worked in facility management and had taken pity on her nephew.

The differences in pay, career prospects, and work conditions within the Central Bank and other such governmental institutions echoed the segmentation within the private sector. Those eligible for such jobs were the same upper-middle class professionals who could expect careers in Cairo's private sector companies or NGOs. Yet as Alaa cynically remarked, "The people we get are still second choice. The ones with really good qualifications and *wasta* go to the more prestigious commercial banks with better pay."

Refusing Social Finitude

These stories about the labor market exemplify middle class negotiations and contestations of the social changes set in motion by Egypt's turn away from its Nasserist heritage, toward the neoliberal precepts of private sector agency and the global market. The effects of this economic and political reorientation differed markedly for differently positioned people. This chapter tells a specifically middle class story.[40] I have sketched the new lines of nobility that, in Egypt's new liberal age, entitle a minority of professionals to relatively rewarding private sector jobs at the upper end of the spectrum. These upper-middle class professionals are emblematic of Egypt's new liberal age; they are portrayed as a social vanguard able to live up to global standards. Others face a labor market that offers salaries far below a living wage since the supply of educated personnel far outnumbers the available jobs. The Nasserite middle class—a somewhat anachronistic but apt label for civil servants and lower-middle class graduates—has become emblematic of those segments of society that are in need of reform.

In spite of processes of disenfranchisement and enfranchisement that increasingly divide Cairo's professional middle class, old promises and expectations were not easily relinquished or forgotten. Macroeconomical analyses highlight the misallocation of educational resources that leads to degree inflation and 'human capital' gone to waste, yet personal stories illustrate the persistent investments in middle class professional identities and futures, as well as an unwillingness to relinquish established social rights. In light of internationally advocated neoliberal policies, large strata of the Cairene middle class should acquiesce to the artisan occupations, insecure employment, and a general financial austerity that supposedly befit a country like Egypt. Many resisted relegation to such 'Third World standards.' One could say that not a generation, but much of the Nasserite middle class refused its social finitude.

Many of these stories of schooling and the labor market breathe nostalgia. Gordon (2000) reports that in Cairo, nostalgia for the Nasser years had been growing. Since most Cairenes have not consciously lived these years, this was first and foremost nostalgia for a time that is not the present. As Joel Gordon argues, nostalgia for the Egypt of the 1950s and 1960s feeds on "political cynicism, uneven development, glaring social inequities, unfulfilled material expectations, and the vise of radical Islamist and state violence" (2000:177). It is, to quote Susan Buck-Morss' reading, "nostalgia for a world that was supposed to be," rather than for the more complex, and often less attractive realities these modernist dreams spurned (1995:23). This nostalgia is reinvigorated by the continual replaying of the now classical movies of the Nasser period, which reminded Cairenes of an Egypt that first and foremost existed in hopes and aspirations, rather than everyday realities. Zhang similarly argues that the pervasive Chinese nostalgia for the Mao era can best be understood as a critique of a present in which urban workers are displaced "onto the social and economic margins of an increasingly marketized society" (2002:325). As Zhang notes, "This selective process of remembering, forgetting, and reinterpreting the socialist past is an important component of social struggles in late socialist China" (2002:326). The same seems to be true with respect to Cairo. Buck-Morss argues that the collective desires that were expressed in such modernist dreams can provide powerful alternative stories, perhaps as much as religiously inspired dreams of a better society have done in the past decades.

It is telling that in Egypt's new liberal age, yet another nostalgia has taken hold in affluent circles. With respect to urban development, Eric Denis notes, "Today, a hybrid, Egyptianized version of the American dream predominates; but with a strong reference to the past and the khedival/colonial era itself (2006:54). Petra Kuppinger similarly discerns nostalgia for the comfortable, elegant, and elitist prerevolutionary times in advertisements for Royal Hills, a gated community on the outskirts of Cairo (2004:48). This nostalgia was also manifest in the publication of a bilingual magazine devoted to prerevolutionary Egypt, *Masr al-Mahrousa/Impressions of Egypt*, which mainly featured photo-articles of Egypt's lost elegance, and in the widespread passion for antebellum style furniture in privileged circles, a style that was sometimes scathingly called Louis Farouk. For some, not the Nasser period, but the prerevolution royal era of aristocratic lifestyles and privileges had become the object of longing, fantasies, and imitation, despite its common association with colonial rule and the disenfranchisement of the vast majority of the population.[41]

Chapter 4

Class and Cosmopolitan Belonging in Cairo's Coffee Shops

On a weekday in summer 2004 I had arranged to meet with Amal and Miriyam at the Retro Café in Mohandisseen for an interview about coffee shops. Like many of my upper-middle class friends and acquaintances, I had met Amal and Miriyam at a SaharaSafaris 'social.' That day we were to meet in one of the up-market coffee shops that had become an essential part of the daily routines of many upper-middle class professionals. These are *coffee shops*, always referred to in English, never to be confused with *'ahawi baladi*, the male-dominated sidewalk cafés for which Cairo is famous. Different coffee shops had become spatial orientation points, as well as social markers of a specific class belonging. A new and distinctive leisure culture had emerged in and around these coffee shops, centered on, but not exclusive to, young single affluent professionals like Amal and Miriyam. The spread of these coffee shops is a relatively recent phenomenon. Coffee shops started appearing in the mid-1990s in central affluent districts like Zamalek and Mohandisseen, as well as in outlying Heliopolis and Maadi. In 2002 and 2004, when I was doing research on middle class Cairo, new coffee shops opened regularly, crowding certain streets and turning formerly residential areas into lively hot spots.

This chapter examines the formation of upper-middle class spaces, lifestyles, and sociabilities in Cairo. I ask how the emergence of exclusive up-market spaces and lifestyles, set apart from the surrounding urban land-scape by conspicuously cosmopolitan references and comparatively steep prices, have effected belonging in Cairo's urban landscape. I first explore some central features of Cairo's upscale coffee shops. I ask how the 'First World' formula of the coffee shop has inserted itself in the highly contested domains of leisure and urban public life. I argue that these coffee shops have succeeded in creating a protected niche for mixed-gender socializing outside the purview of the family in a wider social landscape where such public mixed-gender socializing is more contentious. I then move on to ask what kinds of belonging are intimated and induced by upscale venues like the coffee shop. Coffee shops, I argue, reconfigure matrices of familiarity and ease, as well as discomfort and distance.

Caffè Latte

I found Amal sharing a table with our common friend, Miriyam. Randa, another friend of theirs, soon joined us. All three were professionals in their early thir-ties, employed in the internationally oriented segment of the economy. Like the other women at Retro, they were wearing tight cotton pants or jeans and equally tight shirts, which nonetheless heeded the red lines of public decency, covering everything but the arms and face. The small café with its art, earth tones, and modern wooden furniture was designed to give a contemporary, yet warm sense of comfort and home. Jazzy music, including global hits like the Buena Vista Social Club and Norah Jones, provided the finishing touch. Before we launched into our discussion, we chose some salads and sandwiches from Retro's extensive offer of "creative food" (Amal's term) and placed our order with one of the young waiters dressed in the Retro uniform: black jeans and a blue polo shirt that carried the name of the café.

Our discussion soon converged on the importance of coffee shops for women. "Coffee shops were able to gather girls from their houses and the club," Amal said. "Before, we did not have places where we could spend time after work." The overwhelming presence of women in most coffee shops indeed presented one of the striking features of coffee shop social life. In these upscale coffee shops both veiled and nonveiled women often constituted more than half of the customers. Many single professional women like Amal and Miriyam had taken to spending much of their time in coffee shops like the Retro Café. Half an hour into our discussion, two other friends joined our table, and a constant stream of friends and acquaintances arrived and was enthusiastically greeted. Retro's social life had swung into full gear now that the offices were out. Our conversation veered to the playful mix of tall tales and entertaining news typical of coffee shop socializing. The relatively small Retro Café had a large number of regular visitors, like Miriyam's *shilla*, who visited the coffee shop on a semidaily basis to meet up with friends and acquaintances. Amal knew the names of all the waiters and was friendly with the owner of the coffee shop. She explained that Retro was much like her second home.

Spectra Café was another popular venue, located only a few streets away, behind the well-known Mostafa Mahmoud Mosque in the heart of Mohandisseen. It was stylishly decorated with simple wooden furniture and was divided into two parts. The quiet front part offered seating to small groups; the back room offered space to larger groups in American diner style, with wooden benches that seated six people around a table. Television sets soundlessly screened music videos featured on one of the Arabic music channels, while similar Arabic and Western pop hits provided the musical background. I mostly visited Spectra in the daytime or early evening to meet a female friend or acquaintance. Despite the spaciousness of the coffee shop, we often had to wait outside for a table to free up. We would choose a table in the front part of the café and order a salad or sandwich. Spectra was reputed to serve good and relatively inexpensive food. The menu consisted of a wide range of burgers, salads, and sandwiches, including the ubiquitous Caesar salad and club sandwich. In the evenings, the back room filled up with a younger crowd that primarily came to socialize in mixed-gender *shilal*.

One evening I had an appointment with Tamer, the professional in his late twenties who featured in the previous chapter, to talk about coffee shops. When I arrived, I found him sitting in the back room with his sister, a female friend, and two male cousins. The space was already packed with young mixed-gender *shilal*. I greeted Tamer, who introduced me to the others. When I moved in next to one of his cousins, everyone turned silent. Tamer's sister came to me and asked me to move further away from my neighbor. He is a very religious person, she said, and did not feel comfortable with me sitting next to him. Like other coffee shop patrons, Tamer's cousin tried to devise a personal balance between a young professional lifestyle that included mixed-gender outings in upscale venues, and religious prescriptions, among others regarding mixed gender contact, that had become increasingly important to many young middle class Cairenes in the course of the 1990s.

After a while I was alone with Tamer and his female friend, and we had the chance to discuss the coffee shop phenomenon. Tamer explained that it used to be shameful for young people to hang out in cafés. "Now, even if dress codes have become more modest, there is more freedom," he argued, referring to the simultaneous popularity of the veil and the coffee shop among young

Costa Coffee, Zamalek

upper-middle class women. Tamer's comments concur with Abaza's observation that the "Islamization of public space in the 1990s coincides with survival strategies taking the form of a 'relaxation of norms' among youth, within an Islamic frame of reference" (2001:118). The public at Spectra confirmed these observations. Spectra attracted significantly more *muhaggabaat* than, for example, the Retro Café. Tamer's friend, who covered her hair with a scarf, gaily told me that the *higaab* (veil) was simply obligatory for Muslims.[42] Yet that did not mean that her lifestyle was that different from her female peers without *higaab*. She shortly after drew my attention to a music video that zoomed in on three long-legged, sexily clad girls who were dancing seductively to please their viewing audiences. "My favorite," she said.

In the course of my research I became familiar with Cairo's up-market leisure geographies. Whenever I would meet with upper-middle class professionals, I was directed to one of these up-market coffee shops. Some people liked the homey, but slightly kitschy interior of the different Roastery branches. Others preferred the fresh modernism of Cilantro, all stainless steel and metallic shine with cubist leather pillows in primary colors, or the stylish and hip but cozy Retro Café. The rapid growth of this segment of upscale venues has allowed for diversity and choice. Yet while each specific venue had its proponents and detractors, upscale coffee shops functioned as interchangeable spaces that were equally part of a larger up-market leisure scene.

The itineraries of upper-middle class professional friends and acquaintances generally included only such unambiguously up-market venues, while they, for example, excluded the growing number of less exclusive coffee shops in malls (see Abaza 2001). These coffee shops were unmistakably set apart from other venues and their immediate surroundings by their Western style, immaculate cleanliness, and the strikingly perfect maintenance of the interior, as well as the air-conditioning that generated a constant comfortable climate. These features seemed to be part of the implicit laws and minimum standards that must be observed in order to attract a certain clientele and maintain an upscale status. Well-trained, polite, young, and fashionable-looking staff and waiters were similarly of prime importance, as were style and suggestions of First World belonging, for example in the form of references to coffee shops in the United States or European coffee traditions. A strict selection of the sociocultural 'level' of clientele and a careful guarding of appropriate behavior was also prerequisite. Their mixed-gender sociabilities marked coffee shops as upper-middle class. This mixed-gender social life, however, required a highly select public. Personnel were instructed to watch out for breaches of propriety: a too intimate one-on-one between two lovers, a stolen kiss. If allowed to pass, this behavior would soon ruin the establishment's reputation and scare away other patrons.

Magazines like *Campus*, *The Paper*, but also *Al-Ahram Weekly*, regularly reported on new up-market venues and trends, as did glossy lifestyle magazines like *Enigma* ('The International Arab Magazine of the New Millennium'). They thereby publicized and, in a sense, constituted an up-market Cairo. Coffee shops, in turn, invariably stocked these and similar English-language publications, thereby confirming their belonging to this upscale, conspicuously cosmopolitan sub-city.

The hip Western styles of most coffee shops, the American menu that included Caffè lattes with or without flavor, Caesar salads and club sandwiches, and the prominent English on the menus of local establishments at first seemed out of place in Cairo's urban landscape. I found the casual and routine mixed-gender sociabilities of the coffee shop even more striking. My surprise was shared by Cairene friends who were not acquainted with these spaces. A restaurant review of the Retro Café by Nabil Shawkat in *Al-Ahram Weekly* (Issue 674, 22–28 January 2004) nicely illustrates the surprise of even seasoned well-off urbanites.

"Who are these kids, where do they come from?" asked my [intellectual] friend. . . . As the Egyptian intelligentsia cower downtown at increasingly overpriced, drab looking haunts . . . an altogether new genre of dining has hit the metropolis—one that peripatetic individuals used to seek out in Manhattan or Paris. Forget all that, a taxi ride to Mohandessin suffices. . . . Retro Café is a vision from Greenwich village, an up-market buddy of Central Perk, the coffee shop (does it really exist?) where the Friends of the famed TV show hang out. Only it is classier, in terms of ambiance and décor and food. All of the clientele were hip, each in his or her way—even the hijab-clad Amr Khaled nouveau devotees.

Note the references to Western spaces, which are inserted as signs of the author's cosmopolitan savvy and worldliness. The review declares that a form of First World sophistication, up to this moment unknown to Cairo, has finally arrived. Such longing for reterritorializations of the First World, which we had earlier seen in the case of Carrefour, is a common feature of upscale Cairo. Yet despite this sense of surprise, social life in coffee shops was largely marked by an aura of self-evidence and normalcy. Coffee shops and their exclusive public seemed to form the self-evident grounds for the social life of upper-middle class friends and acquaintances. Despite their recent appearance in Cairo's leisure geographies, coffee shop patrons acted as if their social lives had always been at home in these spaces.

Even if they largely rely on cosmopolitan referents for their distinctiveness and success, up-market coffee shops speak to class-specific Cairene desires and dilemmas. The originally American formula of the coffee shop has inserted itself in locally significant and highly contested domains of leisure, sociability, and urban public life, and has had an almost revolutionary effect on the social life of young affluent Cairenes. Upscale coffee shops have come to constitute an urban scene with conspicuously cosmopolitan styles that allows for new upper-middle class routines and sociabilities. In the following I explore how this transnational format has created spaces of cosmopolitan belonging that double as local class projects, and are negotiated within Cairene sensibilities regarding mixed-gender sociability.

From the Club to the Coffee Shop

Interviews with owners and staff suggest that the coffee shop concept was first introduced to Cairo by Cairenes from elite backgrounds who had been inspired by similar formulas in Europe or the United States. Coffee Roastery on Mecca Street, Mohandisseen, was claimed to be the first coffee shop of its kind. Shortly after its opening in the mid-1990s it began to draw large crowds. Several people told me that the coffee shop soon became so popular that one had to reserve in advance to secure a seat. The street in front of the coffee shop would be crowded with patrons who could not be seated inside. Following this initial success, the number of upscale coffee shops expanded rapidly in the late 1990s and has kept on growing since. Though in 2002 almost all of these coffee shops were locally owned, they were clearly modeled on American counterparts, including their food and beverages. They all offered a range of special coffees, as well as the ubiquitous club sandwich and Caesar salad.[43] At the start of the twenty-first century, such upscale coffee shops and restaurants like Chili's (TexMex) and Johnny Carino's (Italian-American food) had become preferred meeting places for young Cairenes who could afford their comparatively high prices.

Before the advent of coffee shops, the social lives of many of my upper-middle class acquaintances had revolved around the club. As Vincent Battesti argues, when in the 1950s popular classes began to make use of previously exclusively bourgeois spaces, like Downtown or the public gardens, "A desire to self-segregate caused the wealthier classes to . . . [leave] the gardens and [head] for their new members-only sporting clubs" (2006:502). Social and sports clubs formed the primary focus for the social life of middle and upper class families. In Nadi ig-Gezira, Nadi il-Maadi, and Nadi is-Seid, to name a few of the most illustrious and exclusive clubs, children would play a range of sports and hang around with age mates, while other members of the family socialized. These clubs have always welcomed a public made up of all ages and both genders. They were considered safe and respectable for women's socializing since they were marked by a family atmosphere and a high level of social control. They were moreover sealed off from the outside world by fences, while membership cards guaranteed social closure and a degree of social homogeneity.

Clubs were marked as family domain, even if some far corners would serve as hang out places for groups of young people. Nada, an upper-middle class professional in her early thirties, said that, when she entered university, she wanted to explore places other than the controlled spaces of the home, school, and the club. "In the club there will always be a friend of the family controlling you." She anyhow found the atmosphere at her family's club, Nadi il-Ahli, suffocating: "very middle class, lots of *muhaggabaat!*" Nada's annoyance with the overriding presence of *muhaggabaat* reflects ideas on class, rather than her own stance toward women wearing the *higaab*. Many of her friends and family members were *muhaggabaat*. At the beginning of the century more and more young upper-middle class women decided to take up the *higaab*. However, abstract associations of the *higaab* with a lower class public remained strong. "My parents gave me the club," Nada elaborated. "When I started working, I could leave the club behind and pay for entry in my own world." At the time of research, private clubs had stopped being prime places to spend leisure time for most young professionals carrying membership cards. Like Nada, many reported that they stopped frequenting the club when they entered university.

The shift from the family atmosphere of the club to the more generation-specific coffee shop reflects a number of important features of this new up-market leisure culture. Access to clubs is restricted to members. In order to become a member, one needs recommendations from sitting members and a considerable sum of money. In the 1970s a modest middle class income could procure membership in one of the moderately prestigious clubs. At the time of research, membership in these mid-range clubs had come to require large investments, while more prestigious clubs like Nadi is-Seid or Nadi ig-Gezira were out of reach of all but the wealthiest families. However, membership extends to all family members and can be transmitted to in-laws at relatively low cost. Club membership is thus first and foremost a family asset, comparable to the ownership of a furnished apartment or holiday home in one of the coastal resorts. Visits to a coffee shop do not rely on such family capital and require no major investment. Such visits instead depend on a steady cash flow, which corresponds with the comparatively high monthly incomes of many upper-middle class professionals. Coffee shops allow for a more individualized access based on financial means.

The shift from the club to the coffee shop entails a move to a more generation-specific public and space. Even though young people were not the only ones who visited coffee shops, they did make up the dominant public and thereby defined these spaces as their domain, in sharp contrast to the familial atmosphere of the clubs. The coffee shop moreover provided a meeting place for social relations that had outgrown those of the club. Friends from work or university might not be members of the same club, or might not be club members at all. The exclusive openness of coffee shops thus fit the composite nature of the upper-middle class, where not all shared family histories that would bring club membership.

Coffee Roastery and Cilantro, two of the biggest coffee shop chains, both started out as small outlets for specialty coffees and deli foods. By 2002 they had significantly modified their formulas to meet local preferences. Several branches across town provided comfortable and luxurious seating and had extensive menus of dishes and nonalcoholic drinks. Some differences remained. "We are different from coffee shops like Roastery's," one of the partners in the Cilantro chain explained. "They serve hot food. Our system relies on fresh, ready-to-go food on the shelf. It allows you freedom over your time, you can see and choose; you are in control. No one bugs you about what you want. It gives an independent feel."

With their increased emphasis on food, many coffee shops have moved closer to restaurants. The editor of *Campus Magazine* was clearly not amused by this 'degeneration' of the 'original' coffee shop formula: "A few years ago, there was only one coffee shop, Harris Café. It was exciting, European. But Egyptians have turned it into something else, smoking *shiisha* [water pipe] and eating, eating, eating. They do not get the idea of reading in a coffee shop or simply chilling out." Karim, a professional in his late twenties, observed a similar discrepancy, though he was less judgmental about Cairene trends. "Coffee shops in Canada are like McDonalds [i.e., a routine and unremarkable, foremost functional visit]," he said. "In Egypt, we changed them to our form. Here, going to a coffee shop is an outing." Coffee shops were still set apart from proper restaurants by the fact that eating was optional and the atmosphere and seating arrangements were largely informal. The partner in the Cilantro chain considered such informality a defining feature of their coffee shops. "We don't want people to consider going to Cilantro as an outing," he said. "It is a second living room; read, work, do anything you like." Ismail, the owner of the Retro Café, was of the same opinion. What for many patrons defined the coffee shop was indeed its café-like character. One could meet up with friends to have a drink without being obliged to eat, as one would in restaurants.

Several people pointed out that frequenting a coffee shop was much less expensive than going to restaurants or five-star hotels. As Karim put it, "Drinking a coffee in a coffee shop is one of the best ways to spend LE10 in Cairo. And who does not have LE10 in Egypt?" When I insisted that not everyone in Egypt could afford to pay LE10 for a coffee, Karim specified: "Well, of course not *ibn il-muwazzaf* [the son of a civil servant]." His comments rehearse the new lines of segmentation that run through Cairo's professional middle class. He implicitly designates a more affluent upper-middle class legitimate inhabitants of upscale Cairo, and sets it apart from the larger, increasingly impoverished state-educated and state-employed middle class. The comparatively 'soft prices' (a term used by a waiter in a coffee shop) indeed allowed many upper-middle class professionals to include the coffee shop in their semidaily routines and were instrumental in establishing the coffee shop as a primary space for upper-middle class social life.

Global Flows, Local Spaces

Coffee shops have taken up new positions within local geographies of leisure around the world. The taste for cappuccino has become a potent global sign, signifying gentrified tastes in highly diverse local taxonomies of cultural distinction. They borrow much of their signifying potential, prestige, and distinctiveness to their embeddedness in global flows (cf. Appadurai 1990; Guano 2002). Yet the kind of spaces coffee shops constitute within local geographies of leisure and the distinction conferred by the taste for caffè latte are eminently local matters.

All coffee shops laid claim to a sense of First World belonging. Their design and menu were modeled on American counterparts. Most coffee shops carried English names. English was also prominent on the menus, ranging from a simple English list (with typos) to a menu exclusively in English, describing the food and beverages in baroque terms. On the Cilantro menu, for example, caffè latte was described as "espresso soothed by a generous pour of steamed milk and topped with a whisper of foamed milk." The use of English and the claims of direct or indirect links to American counterparts bestowed a sense of cosmopolitanism and exclusivity on a venue, its food and beverages, and its clientele. In line with the menu, the common language used in coffee shops was the upper-middle class mix of Arabic and English characteristic of young upper-middle class professionals. It blended in nicely with the cosmopolitan decor and menu.

PETER ALFRID (2008)

Coffee shop patrons at Costa, Zamalek

These choices point to the exclusive clientele coffee shop owners wished to reach. The partner in the Cilantro chain said that Cilantro targets people who have experienced similar venues and products abroad, "business executives, people who work in banks." Yet such routines had made their way into a wider constituency. Just as English (and a mix of English and Arabic) had become a local class language, cosmopolitan routines like having a caffè latte and a Caesar salad in a coffee shop had been taken up by a less exclusive public and become part of a class- and generation-specific everyday. Going to coffee shops or a restaurant like Chili's had become an intimate, bodily experience that indicated an upper-middle class belonging. Whereas some would not be able to go a day without a good cappuccino, others would regularly compare the seductive qualities of chocolate pies on offer at different coffee shops.

Coffee shops reshape bodily experiences of need and pleasure. They thereby also redraw mappings of enjoyment and relaxation and the urban itineraries that are based on such mappings. *Fuul* and *ta'miyya*, the daily breakfast of a vast majority of Egyptians, may then become 'oriental breakfast,' as someone put it in an invitation to the SaharaSafaris e-mail list. Michael D. Smith (1996) argues that a taste for the specialty coffees in American coffee shops constitutes a new form of easily accessible cultural capital. In Cairo, coffee shops in contrast introduced one major opposition: one between foreign food and drinks, and local ones. The person who has developed a taste for anything from a cappuccino to a double espresso stands in contrast to those people who keep to their *'ahwa mazbuut* or *ziyaada* (Turkish coffee with exact or extra sugar). Distinction lies in this case not in the knowledge of and taste for the specifics of specialty coffees, but in the cosmopolitan referents of food and drinks, the venue, and its clientele.

As said, cosmopolitan repertoires like those employed in coffee shops have a long history in Cairo. In earlier times Europe, and particularly France, was the measure of all things elegant. Many of the shops catering to the upper and upper-middle classes of the time carried French names and sold the latest French products and fashions. At the turn-of-the-century, Cairo's exclusive department stores were modeled after the Parisian *grands magasins* (Abaza 2001). Much like contemporary coffee shops, exclusive establishments like Groppi or L'Americain long conveyed a sense of cosmopolitan belonging and local distinction that focused on Parisian styles and fashions. France has ceased to be the measure of sophistication and cosmopolitanism. "Nowadays," as a coffee shop manager said, "Middle Eastern youth want an American style." Emanuela Guano (2002) observes a similar shift from an orientation toward French styles, consumption goods, and architecture to American ones, with

Buenos Aires changing from the 'Paris of Latin America' to the local version of Los Angeles or Miami. This shift clearly reflects the increased dominance of the United States in the international arena and the prevalence of North American mass culture in global cultural flows. Coffee shops can, however, also be seen as the leisure equivalent of the up-market workspaces of many coffee shop patrons. These up-market workspaces are tied into global economic networks and aim to function according to 'global' standards, which are similarly largely modeled after American formulas. English has replaced French as the language of the elite and *café au lait* has been overtaken by caffè latte, American style.

Coffee shops conveyed a sense of cosmopolitan belonging through food, drinks, and leisure culture. While sipping a vanilla-flavored caffè latte, one could reach into other sources of imagined worlds that were mediated through the global cultural flows of advertisements, films, and music videos (Appadurai 1990), as well as by potential experiences abroad, and feel part of a transnational community of young coffee shop-going, caffè-latte-drinking people. Yet, the prominence of English in names and menus, and the social life in upscale coffee shops signaled the creation of divisions as much as communalities. While creating a sense of cosmopolitan belonging, upscale coffee shops and their patrons also distanced themselves from the surrounding spaces and the majority of Cairenes who 'do not have a language,' i.e., do not speak English.

New Sociabilities

Even though coffee shops paid tribute to overseas connections, Cairo's coffee shop leisure culture differed significantly from social life in their Western counterparts. Coffee shops in Western settings are generally marked for limited activities and times of the day. Cairene coffee shops, in contrast, hosted a more encompassing leisure culture, including outings comparable to Western nighttime leisure. I would regularly visit coffee shops for personal chats with one or two friends, but would also join larger groups for outings on Thursday or Friday evening. On Thursday evenings particular coffee shops became as crowded as popular bars in Western cities on Saturday night. *Shilal* of young people socialized, showed off the latest fashions, and engaged in endemic but subtle flirting. These gatherings mostly ran until ten or eleven in the evening, when many single women were expected at home.

Cairo's coffee shops had by and large succeeded at introducing a First World feel, while avoiding more damning associations of immoral Western nighttime leisure. The coffee shop formula that was pioneered by the Seattle-based Starbucks Company (M.D. Smith 1996) is ideally suited for the Cairene context. This 'First World' formula is part of global flows of distinctive cultural consumption, yet is not associated with 'immoral' spaces of alcohol and subterranean sexuality like bars or nightclubs. The fact that none of the coffee shops or equivalent up-market restaurants like Chili's and TGI Friday's sold alcohol is crucial in this respect. The absence of alcohol contributes significantly to the coffee shop's aura of respectability and its appeal to a broad upper-middle class public. As Mona Abaza notes, "The younger generation, through meeting in coffee houses, seems to have gained some previously unknown liberties. While the 1970s witnessed a growing policing and segregation of public space, which coincided with the ascendance of Islamism, the 1990s witnessed a growing availability of such reshaped spaces" (Abaza 2001:118). Maha Abdelrahman explores the rise of a world of consumption goods and services that are tailored to Islamic lifestyles and offer "practicing Muslims the opportunity to express their piety without necessarily having to abandon a consumerist life style which allows them to exhibit their affluence and enjoy the luxuries of middle-class consumerist culture prevalent in Egypt" (2005:4; for an exploration of similar issues in Istanbul see, Navaro Yashin 2002). Abdelrahman argues that this "new wave of Islamic consumerism" fits with the new generation of preachers like Amr Khaled, whose teachings focus on reconciling 'religion' and (affluent and comfortable) 'life'" (Abdelrahman 2005). While they are not marked as Islamic, coffee shops do negotiate religious prescriptions and desires for conspicuous consumption, and are, for many patrons, part of their own reconciliation of 'religion' and the 'world.'

When I asked people about the reasons for the popularity of coffee shops and the increased acceptability of such mixed-gender public leisure, most mentioned media influences. Many considered influences from abroad (*barra*, in this case the West) central to the 'greater freedom' of coffee shop social life. The media were seen as instrumental in this respect, particularly the increasingly numerous and popular Arabic satellite channels. 'The dish' shattered the government monopoly on television programming, and more generally, its politically significant control of information flows. It opened a window on a more globally up-to-date visual and music culture, as well as a globalized range of consumption goods and desires. The influence of these global cultural flows has been significant, but, as said, this has been the case at different moments in twentieth-century Egypt. I argue that the early twenty-first-century popularity of the coffee shop and the mixed-gender leisure culture of young affluent Cairenes should primarily be understood against the background of the socioeconomic changes of the last decades, and the particular urban social configurations that were brought into being in this context.

Many of the women and men who frequented up-market coffee shops belonged to the new sub-class of upper-middle class professionals whose cosmopolitan capital and social references enabled them to earn relatively high salaries. Having embarked on a professional career, many had grown used to spending much of their time outside the familial sphere. Their social networks had outgrown specific neighborhoods, the school, and the club. These professionals inhabited class-specific workspaces where casual mixed-gender relations, a mix of English and Arabic, and cosmopolitan references were the norm. The coffee shop can be seen as the leisure equivalent of these workspaces. Like other coffee shop entrepreneurs, the owner of the Retro Café argued that coffee shops cater to 'new professionals' rather than families. He linked coffee shops to the new up-market workspaces, which he described as "*modern giddan*" (very modern) and very different from the "Eastern atmosphere" of the family.

Perhaps most crucial with respect to the development of this mixed-gender leisure culture is the long liminal period of partial adulthood and independence that many single upper-middle class professionals experienced. A rise in marital age and a trend of frequent and early divorce in upper-middle class circles had created a situation in which many upper-middle class women and men lived for prolonged periods with their parents, while they *did* have a large degree of financial and personal independence. They did not yet have responsibilities toward husband, wife, or children, but neither did they have their own space to entertain guests or more generally conduct a social life away from family supervision. For many of these young Cairenes, the home could therefore only partially function as a space for the unfolding of a personal life that corresponded with their adult status in work and social life. As a result, much of their personal social life played itself out in public spaces, specifically in up-market venues like coffee shops or restaurants. A single professional in his late twenties jokingly explained why he had to stay home on the first day of the *'iid* celebrations, despite his travel plans. His mother had begun to complain that he acted as if his home were a hotel, he said.

Only more affluent Cairenes could afford to spend time at such relatively expensive venues as upscale coffee shops. Yet young men and women of other strata also engaged in mixed-gender socializing in public spaces. Unemployment, low wages, and a lack of suitable housing have made marriage a difficult accomplishment for most lower and lower-middle class youth. This is one of the causes of the rising marital age in the last two decades (Rashad and Osman 2003; Osman and Shahd 2003; Singerman and Ibrahim 2003). Like their more affluent counterparts, many therefore experience a liminal period of extended adolescence or partial adulthood while living at their parents' home. At the same time, there seems to be a partial relaxation of restrictions on public mixed-gender socializing, allowing engaged couples somewhat more room to meet and get to know each other—with or without cognizance of the family (cf. Abaza 2001).

Walking the city one could not help but notice the importance and frequency of public mixed-gender socializing among less affluent youth. Romantic couples were a pervasive presence in Cairo's public spaces. Most striking was the ubiquitous presence of 'limited income' couples in public parks and on the banks of the Nile. This colonization of public space for romantic and intimate encounters seems ironic in light of the extensive vice laws proscribing intimacy in public, which express the state's always incomplete attempts to enforce the private marital home as the single legal and proper space for intimacy.

In the last ten years Cairo has seen the rise of a large number of shopping malls, some of which target a broad middle class public. In an article exploring the significance of malls in the reshaping of public space, Mona Abaza argues that Cairene malls provide new spaces for "social interaction, for shaping lifestyles and needs for consumption, a space for youth and the new professionals. . . . Malls are ideal places for mixing, for flirting" (2001:118–19). These malls created protected and respectable urban spaces for mixed-gender socializing under the innocuous heading of shopping. However, the upper-middle class professionals I knew did not use malls as their regular meeting spaces. They preferred the more exclusive and specifically young, upper-middle class coffee shop environs. Concerns and dilemmas that were by and large shared by a majority of young Cairenes thus found class-specific expressions in Cairo's increasingly segmented cityscape. In contrast to their less affluent counterparts, upper-middle class professionals possessed the capital to create prestigious, 'respectable,' and comfortable solutions for these dilemmas within the urban landscape.

Contested Modernities of Leisure

Coffee shops were emblematic for an emerging upper-middle class presence in Cairo's landscape. They had carved out public spaces for new upper-middle class lifestyles and modes of sociability. The daily nature of visits and the considerable degree of acceptance within a broad upper-middle class distinguished coffee shops from other leisure spaces. While an explicitly mixed-gender public has long been one of the hallmarks of middle class and elite leisure venues, such venues were often defined as family spaces or tended to serve a more exclusive public. Moreover, such leisure was often conceived of as a special outing rather than everyday routine. Conversely, coffee shops particularly stood out on account of the casual, everyday character of women's public socializing.

Walter Armbrust (1999) argues that the mixed-gender character of elite leisure practices—the mingling of women and men in public spaces—has provided the focus for class contestations throughout the twentieth century. The presence of women in public leisure spaces has been a major marker of cosmopolitan or 'westernized' elite practices, which have long been taken to indicate modernity and sophistication, and have legitimized elite status and prerogatives (cf. Abaza 2001). In "Bourgeois Leisure and Egyptian Media Fantasies" (1999), Armbrust argues that the mixed-gender character of elite leisure practices—the mingling of women and men in public spaces—has long been a focal point for contestations revolving around authenticity versus westernization, and sophistication versus immorality.

> [T]he beach, with its controversial mixing of partially dressed
> men and women in public . . . presents a zone of danger that media
> representing it share, symbolized by their treatment of women as the
> most contentious issue in East/West polemics. Beach representations
> always pointedly include women. If they did not, there would be
> nothing to say or represent, nothing to register the zone of social
> experimentation that they mark out and share. (Armbrust 1999:107)

Armbrust moreover notes that contestations surrounding leisure practices display a strong emphasis on class. He argues that middle class Egyptians should avoid both the pitfalls of lower class backwardness and the moral looseness and rootlessness associated with the wealthy.

> Leisure is not for the poor, and it is not healthy when the extremely
> wealthy indulge in it. The presumed decadence of both the poor
> and the rich brackets middle class identity. The poor are suspect
> because of their 'failure' to adjust their lives to modern institutions,
> the wealthy for a rootless cosmopolitanism at the other end of the
> socioeconomic spectrum. This failure 'to get with the program'
> is marked by presumed backwardness, and for the rich, by an
> inauthenticity tainted with foreignness. To be middle class is to
> refuse both extremes. (Armbrust 1999:112)

According to Armbrust, the terms of contestation over class, morality, and authenticity have remained remarkably constant throughout the twentieth century. Yet what specific forms these contestations have taken in the course of the volatile twentieth century remains unclear. To what extent was Nasser-era modernism able to pry notions of the modern away from damning images of the West and conceptions of rootless cosmopolitanism and to successfully recreate the modern as a field for a large progressive and authentic middle class? What role was assigned to mixed-gender sociability in this 'modern'?

State-produced films of the Nasser period give the impression of a successful localization of the modern, in which easy mixed-gender sociabilities in public spaces such as the university, club, and the beach played a key role (see Armbrust 1996, Gordon 2002). I heard frequent comments on the comparatively liberal atmosphere of the 1960s and 1970s, the era before increased religious mobilization. These were times when, as I was often told, women did not wear the *higaab*, but the *mini-jiip* (miniskirt). The iconic *mini-jiip* notwithstanding, it remains unclear what kinds of public mixed-gender socializing actually took place. The now classical films that portray an Egyptian modern were part and parcel of a modernist program. The question remains to what extent they represented practices that were indeed common in large sections of the middle class. And what were the reverberations of Islamic movements and the subsequent increase in religiosity? How did religious mobilization influence mixed-gender leisure and women's use of public space? Given the paucity of detailed sociocultural histories of Cairo's middle class, I can merely indicate that the new coffee shop leisure culture must be placed in this complex field of contestation over gendered norms of propriety, religiosity, and Western influence. Coffee shops and their affluent mixed-gender publics can be seen as the latest manifestation of distinctive cosmopolitan practices and lifestyles, negotiated within social and religious matrices of propriety. As before, contestations of these distinctive leisure practices significantly focused on the moral fiber of the women who took part in such forms of leisure.

Unchaperoned mixed-gender socializing and the presence of single women in leisure venues were often surrounded by suspicions and restrictions. Such concerns tie into broadly shared notions of marriage as the single legitimate context for nonfunctional mixed-gender contact, as well as the perceived need to control young single women's movement and (sexual) behavior in order to guard both her own and the family's reputation, and safeguard her marriage prospects (see MacLeod 1991, Ghannam 2002). Familial responsibility and accountability for a single woman's behavior generally did not cease when she became a financially independent adult. Supervision of marriageable women was taken to be a fundamental part of the familial responsibility of keeping a daughter from going astray and protecting her reputation. Curfews were the most common form of family supervision, which, as a number of women argued, were primarily enforced to protect the reputation of the family in front of the neighbors.

The spaces of the coffee shop stood in implicit tension to the familial space of the home, particularly with respect to mixed-gender socializing. A number of professionals pointed out that they would not be able to meet friends of the other sex at home. "If there is a sister at home, you cannot bring your male friends over," Karim said. Tamer elaborated: "The family would not like to have visits of boys and girls. *'Ayb, haraam* (shameful, forbidden). In a coffee shop, it is possible. The family would criticize things that have become normal in the coffee shop. At my previous workplace, there was no shyness *(kusuuf)*; men and women would interact freely. Most people were openminded and didn't have any problems. In the street such behavior would not be possible. In other places it depends on the girl's appearance and the place itself." Tamer's comment sketches out the divergent spaces that many single professionals inhabited, and the distinct social rules and norms prevalent in these spaces. It also illustrates the crucial role of coffee shops in framing upper-middle class public mixed-gender socializing as normal and respectable. The familial space of the home often did not allow for the casual mixed-gender sociabilities that had become the norm in coffee shops.

While some people would bring friends home to meet their parents, most maintained a separation between their 'public social' and 'familial' lives. As Baher said, "You have to be selective whom you bring home." He argued that the mobile phone has played an important role in this respect. The possibility of privately receiving or making phone calls facilitates the division between family and personal social life. Exceptions notwithstanding, most of my upper-middle class acquaintances went to great lengths to separate the familial world of the home from their work and social life. Family lives were rarely discussed in coffee shop meetings, even though almost all unmarried professionals still lived with and financially relied on their parents. These other moments and lives were only vaguely present in the coffee shop, for example in the form of curfews that recalled the family's supervision, or the whispered comments about somebody's financial worth or illustrious family connections.

The issue of greeting is emblematic for the complex renegotiation of mixed-gender sociabilities in coffee shops. Among men, greetings with a hug and kisses had become less common. There was a shift away from such physical intimacy between men; among women, it remained the norm. Bodily intimacy between men and women had its own limits, which differed from person to person. Whereas some would routinely greet friends from the other sex with a hug and kisses, others would decline to shake hands for religious reasons and, particularly in the case of women, out of concern for propriety and their sexual reputation. One day I visited the opening of a photography exhibit of a number of SaharaSafaris members. When I as usual greeted an acquaintance in his mid-twenties with two kisses on the cheek, I met with an unusually stiff response. Somewhat embarrassed, he introduced me to his parents, who had come along to see the opening. With his parents present our usual way of greeting had become inappropriate, an act he may have had to answer for later, after the family had returned home. His discomfort illustrated the discrepancy between the public social lives and home lives of many young professionals. Changes in greeting practices speak to the redrawing of lines of mixed-gender sociability in up-market coffee shops. They, however, also indicate the limits of easy bodily contact between men and women. Such mixed-gender intimacies were largely limited to spaces of the coffee shop, and even there, were considered problematic in their own right in light of religious and social prescriptions.

Upscale coffee shops constituted experimental spaces for a new class presence. In the spaces of the coffee shop certain selves and sociabilities could be lived far from familial intervention, intimacy could be experienced and professional identities remained intact. The spaces of the coffee shop however also prescribed certain normative modes of sociability and public performances, which may or may not concur with personal views and practices outside of these specific spaces. Coffee shops patrons usually appeared to be completely familiar and at ease with the cosmopolitan setting and the mixed-gender company. They all seemed equally lighthearted and appeared to hold similar moderately liberal views. Conversations would often reflect an innocuous middle ground and tended to bar aspects of the life of those present that were either too 'liberal' or too 'conservative,' particularly in larger mixed-gender groups. These conversations would generally avoid contentious issues like alcohol, clubbing, and premarital sexual relationships, while they simultaneously projected a certain general progressiveness toward mixed-gender socializing. Such normative performances were particularly common in groups of young single men and women, in part because such social meetings were routinely evaluated in light of possibilities for the almost universally sought after marriage. Coffee shops appeared to provide a safe middle ground, where young upper-middle class professionals from diverse family backgrounds and convictions could meet and interact within the common framework of a cosmopolitan, yet respectable normalcy.

Many people argued that, despite appearances, such progressive yet respectable attitudes were not shared by all present. A number of my male coffee shop companions would occasionally frequent bars, a fact that was rarely mentioned in such meetings. Conversely, many of my single female friends in their late twenties and early thirties distrusted the progressive attitudes that many of their male friends and acquaintances adopted. They suspected that these men would not live up to the progressive views they displayed in the setting of the coffee shop. Egyptian men might portray themselves as progressive, they argued, go out with female colleagues and friends, and even engage in more intimate relationships with women who similarly had careers and a social life outside the home. Yet they were convinced that, irrespective of their public performance, most if not all men eventually preferred a young, inexperienced wife who would be content to take care of her family and stay home attending to her husband's and children's needs. Maha, single, in her late twenties, regularly discussed the fine lines she treaded to safeguard her sexual reputation and respectability. Yes to frequent phone and e-mail contacts with possible dates, but no meetings with a man alone until they had formalized their relationship through plans for an engagement. At the time, she was involved in a drawn-out flirtation with a man she thought might make a suitable husband and repeatedly brought me along as a chaperone. Before and after such meetings, and during quick time-outs in the bathroom, we discussed the thorny issues of female respectability and marriage. In his presence she made arduous attempts at impression management. She would, for example, comment negatively on some forms of conduct he might consider inappropriate for women, like wearing a bathing suit, and would let her body speak the language of modesty. Like other upper-middle class women, she was afraid that he would eventually prefer a veiled woman who would agree to stay home in order to concentrate on her role as mother and wife, a model of modesty and home-making. Their mutual exploration indeed ended in disagreement over women's employment. When he became outspoken about his preference for a housewife, Maha finally gave up her attempts to appear as his ideal future wife.

Cairene men generally have more leverage concerning their social and sexual behavior. As Karin Werner (1997) argues in her study of Cairene university students, men can switch from being the seductive or harassing male stranger, to the loving boyfriend, the strict fiancé, husband, or brother, depending on their relation to the woman in question. They might be seductive lovers who, once caution has given way to love and the loss of chastity or even virginity,

Mr. Ayman Abdel Baki and Ms. Tina Antaki.

Mr. Tamer El Leithy, Mr. Tarek Ganainy, Mr. Mohamed Abdel Haq, Mr. Adham Kamal.

Ms. Ira., Mr. Tarek Ganainy, Ms. Lubna El Kafrawy, Ms. Picko El Akkad.

Mr. Mohamed Abdel Haq, Mr. Sherif Khalifa, Mr. Helmi, Mr. Mohamed El Kholi.

Mr. Ayman Abbas and Mr. Mohamed Abdel Haq.

Mr. Mohamed Kurdi, Mr. Mohamed Abdel Haq, Mr. Rasheed Kamel, Mr. Sherif Rashad.

From Coffee to Dining

Café Mo, Cairo's newest hangout is a fabulous blend of coffee shops and restaurants. The first of its kind in Cairo, this cosy venue boasts a fine selection of coffees and an extensive menu with mouth-watering dishes, in an atmosphere of warm earth colours and dark wood. Café Mo is proving to be Cairo's number one choice.

Ms. Nevine Abbas, Mr. Ayman Abbas, Ms. Iman Maghawry, Ms. Radwa Maghawry, Ms. Dina Maghawry, Ms. Picko El Akkad.

Mr. Mohamed El Seweedy and Mr. Tamer El Leithy amongst friends.

Mr. Ahmed Badawi, Ms. Ghada Raafat, Mrs. Ameera Abdel Haq, Ms. Sherin Saeed and friends.

Photo feature on Café Mo in *Enigma*, February 2003.
The section 'Out and About' reads: "From Coffee to Dining. Café Mo, Cairo's newest hangout is a fabulous blend of coffee shops and restaurants. The first of its kind in Cairo, this cosy venue boasts a fine selection of coffees and an extensive menu with mouth-watering dishes, in an atmosphere of warm earth colours and dark wood. Café Mo is proving to be Cairo's number one choice."

declare the object of their unremitting love unfit for marriage. Women have less room to maneuver. Their lifestyle choices and everyday routines mark them as women who have made particular moral choices. As I argue in the next chapter, their urban itineraries can be read as negotiations of the contradictory exigencies of public visibility and sexual propriety and respectability.

Up-market coffee shops, restaurants, and bars were taken to differ along axes of price and smartness, as well as the expected and allowed attitudes of their patrons and their 'social level.' While they need not to go together, high prices, modishness, and permissiveness were generally assumed to combine in high-end places like Café Mo. Such rankings corresponded to perceived class differences with respect to such practices. Tamer echoed a common view when he located such attitudes along Cairo's class-segmented map. "In Heliopolis it is normal to have a boyfriend," he said. "They are more influenced by the outside, they are more *free*. In Mohandisseen, half and half; in other areas, no way." Or, as Maha explained, "the lower and upper classes do not have problems [with sexual relationships], not like us." These comments resonate with Armbrust's arguments about the specific nature of middle class leisure, discussed earlier. Being middle class in Cairo entailed avoiding the perceived lack of sophistication and cosmopolitan savvy of the lower classes, as well as what was seen as the licentiousness of the elites. Middle class people navigated between allegiance to 'modernity' and the specter of rootless cosmopolitanism (Armbrust 1999:112). Female propriety and respectability presented an important focus for the negotiation of these distinctive leisure practices.

Whereas female coffee shop patrons I knew would condone most coffee shops that were clearly up-market and classy, they did monitor these spaces for possible breaches of propriety and respectability. In spring 2002 the recently opened Retro Café drew much attention in my upper-middle class circles. It was praised for its coziness and unique ambiance, which owed much to its homey interior and the personal touches of the owner. Whereas other coffee shops and restaurants created islands of privacy where already existing *shilal* could socialize, the design of this particular coffee shop included a long table and a comfortable common sitting area, which were intended to allow for more chance encounters. Maha told me that she had stopped visiting Retro after a few visits. "This place gathers girls looking for relationships. Did you see how they crawl up to each other?" she said. For the most part, Retro's public seemed to consist of young well-to-do professionals who displayed rather casual attitudes toward mixed-gender socializing. While Retro should have been comfortable for Maha in class terms, the public was a bit too *free* for her taste. Continuing to frequent this place would put her in an awkward situation. Would people think that she, by virtue of her presence, was also *that* outgoing and easy, and, by implication, not very respectable?

The public mixed-gender sociabilities that unfolded in up-market coffee shops were remarkable in Cairo's public geographies, yet they had been rapidly incorporated in the daily routines of many upper-middle class professionals. The cosmopolitan, mixed-gender spaces of coffee shops had an embryonic presence in socializing practices, work and study spaces, as well as in imaginations of and desire for a First World. For many, coffee shops finally provided a public space for mixed-gender sociabilities away from the family, yet within the bounds of respectability. Commenting on what she called the "coffee shop frenzy," the editor of *Campus Magazine* insightfully noted that "the coffee shop answered a lot of questions about outings."

Exclusivity and Closure

Social closure was a precondition for the privileged upper-middle class lifestyles and performances that unfolded in Cairo's upscale coffee shops. The mixed-gender sociabilities and performances of professional upper-middle class identities often appeared to be effortless and self-evident. This class-specific sense of normalcy and self-evidence relied on the exclusion of other Cairene realities outside of the coffee shop, as well as the more familiar but possibly equally disjunctive other realities of family lives. Upper-middle class socializing was largely confined to the spaces of those coffee shops that were clearly marked for an affluent public of a certain 'cultural level.' It was sheltered from other judgments and modes of sociability by strong class markers, high prices, and a door policy.

The upscale coffee shops frequented by upper-middle class professionals were in principle open to any consumer willing to pay over LE5 for a cup of coffee. Some argued that these 'soft prices' made coffee shops accessible to 'everyone,' in contrast to more expensive restaurants and hotels. However, to be a coffee shop patron one needed both the economic capital that allows one to consume in these spaces, as well as a more general familiarity with local forms of cosmopolitan consumption and embodied upper-middle class styles, including the elusive body language that signals belonging, ease, and the right to be there. In coffee shops high prices and/or a minimum charge kept out those who did not belong to this 'comfortable' class. Economic controls were often augmented by an entry policy. One coffee shop manager clearly considered such selectivity of utmost importance. "We have a door policy because we don't want *unqualified guests*," he said. He explained that by 'unqualified' he meant not dressed well, or appearing to be a 'troublemaker,' who makes noise and flirts. 'Being among like-minded people' was one of the main attractions of coffee shops and 'exclusivity' was crucial to their standing and success. The spaces of the coffee shop were thus characterized by a combination of openness and exclusion. They were public in the sense that they represented open societal spaces, while their class markers and access requirements resulted in less-than-public, closed, class-specific spaces.

The fear of attracting those of a lower social level was not only based on the importance of guarding the class markers of a place, but was also stirred by the conviction that these others might not abide by the implicit rules of gendered sociability. Overwhelmed by the availability of young women, men might flirt or harass. Conversely, some women might come with the aim of picking up wealthy male customers. These fears echo assumptions about less exclusive leisure spaces with a mixed-gender public, which were thought to be marketplaces for easy relationships. Mixed-gender sociabilities were assumed to be normal and respectable only for a certain class of people. Accordingly, venues were judged on the 'level' of their public.

Most upscale coffee shops seemed rather effective in keeping out those 'who did not belong.' This social closure created a semblance of community and social control. In such a place one would be afraid to overstep the boundaries of hegemonic sociality. As Miriyam and Amal noted, "The atmosphere forces a certain attitude. People will shy back from crossing certain boundaries." Such social closure created a class-specific normalcy, comprised of young upper-middle class codes regarding mixed-gender behavior. Those coffee shops that succeed in reaching and limiting themselves to a 'classy' public thereby became safe spaces for women. In such venues a select company could engage in subtle, civilized flirting that was not likely to be seen as harassment, since it involved people 'of a certain level.' The class markers of a venue framed a woman's presence as normal and respectable. In such classy venues going out and sitting in a place in mixed-gender company or even alone, wearing a skirt, a *body* (body-tight shirt), or a *cut* (a sleeveless shirt) was framed as part of a distinctive and respectable, class-specific lifestyle. The presence of these women conversely marked a particular establishment as up-market, exclusive, and *class*.

It is not surprising that the coffee shop has replaced the private social and sports club—the previous stronghold of upper-middle and upper class socializing—as the focus of suitable and respectable social life. Coffee shops reproduce the club's spatial and social closure, albeit in ways suited to Cairo's young professional upper-middle class. In contrast to club membership, access to the space of the coffee shop is individualized and rests on the financial means to consume, as well as a familiarity and liking for this specifically 'young' and cosmopolitan leisure culture. The coffee shop's mechanisms of inclusion and exclusion are adapted to new divisions and distinctions within Cairene society. The spaces of the coffee shop helped create a relatively homogeneous, young, and affluent cosmopolitan upper-middle class.

Geographies of Belonging

In Cairo's divided landscape, spaces are crucial markers of identity. Names of neighborhoods like working class Shubra or elite Zamalek and Maadi stand in as signs of a class-specific belonging (cf. de Koning 2001). Eating certain food in certain places—Caesar salad in a coffee shop or a *ta'miyya* sandwich at a *sha'bi* restaurant—constitutes a visceral way of belonging, as well as an obvious sign of class positioning and distinction. Coffee shops were located only in those areas that were assumed to have an upper-middle and elite public ready for such tastes and forms of leisure. As one of the owners of the Cilantro chain put it, "Our formula is espresso-based and offers only healthy food. With respect to both, places outside Cairo are generations behind. We choose locations where you have people who appreciate our offer: those who work in offices, banks. We target highly paid executives." Until 2005, the Downtown Cilantro branch was the only upscale coffee shop in the downtown area, an area that had been all but abandoned by young affluent Cairenes. The American University was the single reason for its odd presence. Most coffee shops were located in upscale areas like Mohandisseen, Maadi, and Heliopolis. Located next door to Cilantro was a shop selling car parts, and next to that an *'ahwa baladi*, one of the numerous 'traditional' sidewalk cafés that have an almost exclusively male clientele. Cilantro, in contrast, harbored an affluent mixed-gender public enjoying cappuccinos or caffè lattes with brownies rather than the *'ahwa mazbuut* (Turkish coffee with sugar) served next door. Cilantro represented an upscale island in Downtown Cairo that was closed to the young passersby, their keen sense of cosmopolitan fashion notwithstanding. Certain areas in Cairo had thus been educated to appreciate certain tastes and leisure practices, while it was taken for granted that the rest of Cairo, not to mention spaces outside of the capital, were not ready for such forms of leisure.

Cairenes have a rich linguistic repertoire of expressions for distinction and merit, as well as lowliness and vulgarity. As I noted in Chapter Two, *sha'bi* (popular, lower class) and *baladi* (local, authentic, lower class) are basic, yet ambiguous signposts in Egyptian readings of society. They intimate divisions between what are seen as local and traditional working class, and cosmopolitan and modern upper-middle class and elite worlds. Though these terms

Cilantro coffee shop, Downtown Cairo

remain crucial to imaginations of Egyptian society, I was struck by the currency of the term *bii'a*. When I asked Nada's *shilla* about the meaning of *bii'a*, they explained that *bii'a* literally means 'environment,' but was commonly used to talk about anything "low class." Nada added that *bii'a* was mostly used for people who tried to pretend they were from higher social backgrounds by (unsuccessfully) adopting classy looks or attitudes. *Bii'a* was not used for people and places that were obviously poor, but for those who lacked an upper-middle class sense of style and were considered to be of a lower 'social level.' Vulgar would be the best way to translate the term. Unlike *sha'bi* and *baladi*, *bii'a* does not refer to the lower classes or their presumed habits, but to a 'failed' middle class.[44] The shift from *baladi* to *bii'a* reflects the relocation of symbolic struggle from the borders between the 'educated middle classes' and the 'crude lower classes' to divisions within the middle class itself. The clear and confident class-cum-culture differentiations captured by the dichotomy of *baladi* versus *chic* or *class* had been replaced by more fickle distinctions in a highly charged continuum of tastes and styles.

Space was a crucial arena for these contestations. Persons from slightly lower middle class backgrounds who shared some of the same urban spaces provided the most immediate class other, while many of Cairo's other spaces, products, and people became an ever-present yet largely unknown, and almost unreal outside. These other spaces lent themselves to projections of all kinds of disliked features, ways of life, and people—vulgarity, poverty, bacteria, dirt, as well as a dangerous unknown on which all kinds of fears could be projected. Asef Bayat and Eric Denis (2000) argue that the *'ashwaa'iyyaat*, the informal areas that house half of Cairo's inhabitants, have been portrayed as a Pandora's box of dangers, as sites that harbor immorality, lawlessness, poverty, and violence. This other Cairo also became a target for feelings of compassion, religious duty, and inspired charity. A number of upper-middle class professionals tried to put their skills and social network to good use in a charitable project aimed at helping poor women gain an independent source of income. During Ramadan, others joined in the distribution of basic consumption goods and foodstuffs among deserving poor families in the medieval quarters of Cairo. They came back with stories of deserving, noble poor, as well as scheming families who merely posed at being poor in order to receive another charity package. Denis rightly sees the burgeoning of such charity as an exponent of Egypt's new liberal age. He argues that "charity again becomes an urban bourgeois value and a way of self-presentation essential to the image of a good citizen and a good Muslim." He considers the invented tradition of charity tables in the month of Ramadan "an emblematic figure of the rapport between the bourgeoisie and the urban people. . . . Charity is imposed as the only relation to the poor and their only vehicle for social uplift, with the police as the last rampart. There are no other modalities allowed for the redistribution of the fruits of liberalization" (Denis 2006:57).

The return of this unprivileged Cairo in the form of an exotic 'local' is as emblematic of the social cleavages that run through Cairo's cityscape. *Baladi* products and people were recycled to represent exotic authenticity. These stylistic elements were common in more exclusive up-market places that catered to a mixed public of expatriates and elite Egyptians. The exclusivity of the venues allowed them to safely introduce explicitly localized elements such as the *mashrabiyya* (lattice-like wooden screen), low seating arrangements, and 'oriental food,' without any concomitant confusion over the distinctively up-market status of the venue and the level of its clientele. These places exemplified a local orientalism made possible by sufficient distance from the less pleasant realities of the existing 'oriental' setting. A similar local orientalism was, for example, apparent in Cairo's gated communities, where, as Denis argues, "Arab and Muslim values . . . are present architecturally, but made into folkloric consumer symbols. Islam and Arabness are referenced in a way closer to the iconography of Disney's Aladdin and Sinbad rather than to the culture of austerity, modesty and self-discipline identified with contemporary Islamic populism and militance" (2006:53).[45]

Fear, disgust, concern, and compassion could all be part of attitudes toward the spaces outside the bounds of upscale Cairo. These diverse attitudes all implied unfamiliarity and distance. Such unfamiliarity seemed rather realistic and speaks of the social closure and exclusivity of up-market circuits. Yet, it could also be used to signal distance from other Cairene realities realities. During one coffee shop outing with some of Nada's colleagues, a woman in her thirties made a point of recounting her accidental one-time venture into Dar es-Salaam. She said that en route to the center by car, she had lost her way and ended up in the crowded streets of this informal, working class area. It was only logical that she had been afraid, she said, but even the man who accompanied her had become nervous and wanted to get back to the main road as soon as possible. Nada told me afterward of her annoyance with the story and storyteller. She has an aunt who lives in Dar es-Salaam and felt one could not be safer than in such a crowded neighborhood. She thought it typical that this woman came up with and elaborately performed such a story to make clear that she was far removed from such base realities. On another coffee shop occasion I overheard someone say that he was from Shubra. I asked him whether he was really from Shubra. He replied with an indignant air that he was only joking. His body language conveyed a message that was at least as clear: Can you imagine, me being from Shubra? I felt that my question had been rather innocent. While the once affluent Shubra had become crowded and somewhat dilapidated, it housed a heterogeneous population. However, I had misunderstood the jest of his comment, and more generally, had not fully grasped the importance of such spatial markers and distinctions in upper-middle class circles.

The emergence of an up-market Cairo has redrawn and consolidated social segregation in the urban landscape. Many upper-middle class Cairenes had come to inhabit the Cairo's up-market circuits alongside the city's elites, while less affluent middle class strata appeared increasingly distant, old-fashioned, or *bii'a*. Such spatial arrangements strengthened emerging social–cultural divisions in Cairo's professional middle class. The borders of up-market spaces and publics became the focus of class contestations, expressed most frequently in depreciative comments on the encroachment of *bii'a* or nouveau riche, while Cairo's poorer spaces and inhabitants came to function as a constitutive outside of the world upper-middle class Cairenes inhabited. This segmentation of the urban landscape has produced disjunctive matrices of belonging.

Configurations of Closeness and Distance

Saskia Sassen (2001) argues that the global touches ground and takes material form in global cities where the control functions for a dispersed production process are situated, thereby reconfiguring axes of centrality and matrices of closeness and distance. Such processes of global city formation give rise to a new geography "that explodes conventional notions of context and traditional hierarchies of space. They do so, in part, through *the unbundling of national territory*" (Sassen 2000:225, my emphasis). According to Sassen (2000, 2001), central business districts in major cities around the world are more closely connected than any particular central business district with its more immediate surroundings. More generally, the 'global spaces' produced by a city's position in global economic networks have stronger links with similar urban spaces outside the national boundaries than with the less global spaces next door (cf. Smart and Smart 2003).

When we extend Sassen's insights beyond networks of global finance and business producer services, we might identify numerous networks and concomitant matrices of connection and disconnection. A unitary concept of space is imploded in favor of an erratic, disjunctive crisscross of connections, not unlike the concept of disjunctive flows of images, ideas, capital, and people proposed by Arjun Appadurai (1990). Such a reading concurs with Doreen Massey's proposal to see place as "formed out of the particular set of social relations which interact at a particular location" (1994:168). Flows and networks create diverse and overlapping configurations of closeness and distance in local sociocultural landscapes. In Cairo diverse global flows come together in the formation of up-market circuits of production and consumption, which carve new lines of segmentation and segregation in the cityscape. Since they are instrumental to, and emblematic of, a new urban upper-middle class presence, coffee shops can be said to be central to such processes of remapping.

Benedict Anderson's seminal work on the imagined character of communities offers one way to explore the sociocultural aspects of such remapping. As Anderson argues, national imagined communities were forged through such media as newspapers, which created a (proto)national community of readers. He singles out the rise of print capitalism, and in particular, the growth of a newspaper reading public as one of the prime mechanisms for the imagination of national communities in the eighteenth and nineteenth centuries. I propose to understand the impact of Cairo's coffee shops in a similar fashion. I therefore want to revisit Anderson's arguments briefly.

> The significance of th[e] mass ceremony [of reading the newspaper] . . . is paradoxical. It is performed in silent privacy. . . . Yet each communicant is well aware that the ceremony he performs is being replicated simultaneously by thousands (or millions) of others of

whose existence he is confident, yet of whose identity he has not the slightest notion. . . . At the same time, the newspaper reader, observing exact replicas of his own paper being consumed by his subway, barbershop, or residential neighbours, is continually reassured that the imagined world is visibly rooted in everyday life. . . . [F]iction seeps quietly and continuously into reality, creating that remarkable confidence of community in anonymity which is the hallmark of modern nations. (Anderson 1991:35–36)

Anderson argues that the very private reading of the newspaper with the knowledge of others doing so at approximately the same time suggests simultaneity and communality, both of which are crucial to the imagination of national communities. But that communal reading in anonymity is not enough. The imagined community is grounded in daily life through the observation of others carrying similar symbolic goods or performing similar symbolic acts, which act as proof of the reality of the community.

These two mechanisms crucial to the imagination of community—simultaneity in anonymity and verification in everyday life—can be usefully transposed onto Cairo's coffee shops. Anderson's analysis concerns the rise of national communities and the entrenchment of the imagination of sovereign, territorially bound nations through national media, institutions, and symbols. In the case of Cairo's coffee shops, we might, in line with Sassen's arguments, map out a multitude of partial imagined communities, overlapping and intersecting, of short and longer span. Coffee shops like Retro, Beano's, and Tabasco allow for the imagination of certain modes of belonging that are inflected by First World fashions and experiences and suggest membership in a cosmopolitan space that is local, Cairene, and Egyptian, yet part of wider First World circuits and publics. Some had traveled abroad and taken part in overseas leisure cultures. Yet, such travel was not necessary for a thorough familiarity with these cosmopolitan spaces and routines. As the editors of *The Paper* noted, "Go to a coffee shop and you will see two girls who do not look Egyptian and speak English, yet are Egyptians who have never traveled abroad."

Emanuela Guano argues that Buenos Aires' neoliberal landscape speaks to longstanding narratives of "the self and its relation to an elsewhere—its exclusion from and desire for a First World to which most of the middle classes of Buenos Aires felt an entitlement" (Guano 2002:184). In Cairo, a similar longing for First World experiences and inclusion was expressed in the initial excitement about new First World sites like Carrefour. The phrase 'Now in Egypt,' which was often used to market goods and services with cosmopolitan referents or a foreign origin, evokes a similar combination of exclusion of and desire for First World sophistication. "It is as if you are not in Egypt," a woman in her thirties once told me while enthusiastically recommending a bar in Mohandisseen. She was from a more affluent background than most people I knew and had lived in and frequently visited Europe. The bar could indeed have been situated in hip London, Paris, or New York, with its minimalist interior design, blue leather benches, soft lights, and range of alcoholic cocktails on offer. While the occasional bar or café still aroused such feelings of surprise and delight at the presence of a new First World venue in all too familiar Cairo, the opposite had actually become commonplace. Places like the upscale coffee shops, the up-market supermarkets that cater to cosmopolitan preferences, and exclusive malls hardly elicited awe or excitement.

The conspicuous cosmopolitanism of up-market Cairo speaks of a sense of transnational cosmopolitan belonging. Upper-middle class conceptions of a comfortable life often relate more to assumed First World standards and routines than those that mark the lives of less privileged urbanites. For upper-middle class Cairenes, the contradiction between being in Cairo and enjoying such 'First World' lifestyles had largely ceased to exist. The paradoxical post-colonial combination of a sense of exclusion from, and longing for First World sophistication and belonging had been largely resolved by Cairo's "reterritorialization of the metropole" (Guano 2002a:182). I would argue that coffee shops are prime places where, for young affluent Cairenes, such convergences were both normalized and secured. Take the words of the owner of the Retro Café. He argued that a coffee shop could not have a 'local' menu. "The classes of the coffee shop want the things they see outside. If you choose a local décor, it will not be a coffee shop. These people want the other, more successful life, and find it here." Coffee shops offer visceral experiences of a reterritorialized First World in Egypt. They allow for the imagination of a local cosmopolitan community characterized by a normalized and self-evident affluence and ease that is simultaneously connected to *barra*, abroad.

Though this *barra* (literally: outside) is an imagined geographical trope, it reflects Egypt's historical trajectory and has to be situated in the context of past and present global structures of hegemony, inequality, and exclusion, as well as the domestic inequalities that tie into these global structures. Whereas the United States acts as a trendsetter in realms of work, education, and consumption, close by Europe is the most important tourist destination and source of transnational friendships and family connections. The Gulf states have been a common destination for upper-middle class professionals since the 1970s. Many visited or lived in the Gulf with their parents, and at the time of research the Emirates were seen as an attractive destination for labor migration. Discussions about working in Abu Dhabi and Dubai not only touched on the cleanliness and organization that presented such a contrast with Cairo's chaos, density, and pollution, but also on the extensive first-class consumption opportunities. People's extensive knowledge of 'Western' consumption goods and leisure venues owed much to such experiences in the Gulf (cf. Vignal and Denis 2006:119–20).

As Benedict Anderson argues, imagined communities are created through an intermingling of fiction and reality, where daily life provides proof of the actual existence of community. Coffee shops provide ample material for such verification, since they welcome a relatively exclusive public with cosmopolitan capital in oftentimes conspicuously cosmopolitan settings. The socially segregated everyday life of many of my upper-middle class acquaintances similarly helped confirm the normalcy of upper-middle class lifestyles, wishes, and expectations. This local, class-specific cosmopolitan normalcy and sense of belonging originated in and was continually confirmed by commonalities of class and lifestyle.

This class-based cosmopolitan belonging was firmly rooted in material, social, and cultural configurations of social distinction and segregation. Being close, familiar with cosmopolitan lifestyles, and distant, disconnected from anything *sha'bi*, is part of a local class structure in which cosmopolitan capital presents a form of highly valued cultural capital that opens doors to the best professional jobs and social circles, and confirms that one belongs to a Cairo of relative affluence, ease, and cosmopolitan elegance. The same skills and cultural expertise that allow one to participate in the social life of the coffee shop—the English-Arabic vernacular, the sexy and fashionable clothes or the more modest but equally stylish dress of some *muhaggabaat*, and the casual mixed-gender socializing—are also those that firmly define a person as a candidate for up-market jobs and networks. Being a coffee shop patron thus meant inhabiting an up-market Cairo of multinational companies, Metro supermarkets, and prestigious social clubs and compounds, where a decent living was measured along cosmopolitan standards that were at once local and global. As Anthony D. King argues, this 'global' mostly refers to consumption practices and lifestyles that are common to privileged First World spaces and lifestyles across the globe, rather than to the actually existing complex 'First World' realities with their social inequalities and intricate lines of privilege (2004:133). New cosmopolitan lifestyles and matrices of belonging come into being through an intricate convergence of local distinctive class cultures and transnational economic and cultural flows that reflect the realities of a highly unequal world.

The spaces of the coffee shop provided an everyday, visceral confirmation of such cosmopolitan belonging, which was significantly secured through social closure. The exclusivity of the coffee shops and clientele were guarded through financial and cultural barriers, which guaranteed the undisturbed performance of upper-middle class sociabilities and secured the normalcy of Cairene upper-middle class life. The space of the coffee shop was thus founded on, and simultaneously created new forms of social segregation. I have argued that this local, yet cosmopolitan affluent community of coffee shop-going professionals redraws maps of familiarity and belonging. Communalities of cosmopolitan belonging came with their counterparts of distance. Following Saskia Sassen's lead on the unbundling and rebundling of space resulting from global circuits of finance, labor, technology, and capital, we could say that the class-based cosmopolitan belonging of the coffee shop gave rise to new configurations of closeness and distance, slicing up and segmenting Cairo's social landscape.

Does such segmentation of the social landscape also lead to the unbundling of the national community in a political sense, as John Clammer suggests in his discussion of the new middle classes in Southeast Asia (2003:411)? I do not think there is a straightforward answer to that question. While class-based forms of cosmopolitan belonging did not seem to contradict feelings of national belonging, I would argue that they did significantly reconfigure loyalties and familiarity within the abstract space of the nation, as well as the more concrete spaces of the city. Affluent Cairenes could opt out of national or public spaces and institutions that were increasingly underfunded, derelict, and clearly not up-to-speed with First World standards and fashions, and withdraw into their exclusive private counterparts. Consequently, different class-based worlds existed side-by-side in a divided cityscape. Denis argues that the social mixture of 1960s and 1970s has rapidly given way to increased segregation in Cairo's new liberal age (1997:10). Contemporary Cairo has highly segmented life worlds, spanning the fields of work, consumption, housing, and leisure. Upper-middle class cosmopolitan belonging that is embedded in an urban geography marked by social segregation has contributed to a slicing of urban space and the social realities that inhabit the city. This is a city where some cannot even begin to imagine what it means to survive on a few hundred Egyptian pounds a month and where the fact that this is the lot of most Cairenes is for many not a major concern.

The Space of Class

Cairo's new upscale coffee shops have created a protected niche for nonfamilial mixed-gender sociabilities within contentious public geographies of leisure. They have been able to wrest such mixed-gender sociabilities away from associations with immorality and loose sexual behavior that cling to less exclusive mixed-gender spaces outside of the redemptive familial sphere. These up-market spaces bring together a wide range of upper-middle class performances and desires, while they contribute toward the creation of distinctive upper-middle class lifestyles and practices.

Up-market circuits comprised of private schools, universities, and hospitals, as well as shopping and residential areas and leisure venues like the coffee shop, have been crucial to the elaboration of new divisions within Cairo's middle class. They have carved out public spaces for new upper-middle class lifestyles and modes of sociability and simultaneously inscribed the urban landscape with the new divisions in the middle class that were the subject of the previous chapters. A certain segment of the middle class meets and mingles in the spaces of the coffee shop that largely exclude other segments of that class. These upscale spaces not only intimate cosmopolitan belonging, but also distance from other local realities. The lines of exclusion and inclusion in the narrative and project of Egypt's new liberal era thus find their counterpart not only in the urban labor market, but also in social segmentation and segregation in Cairo's urban landscape. Cosmopolitan references and ambitions are crucial markers in both cases. Global flows feed into local social hierarchies and come to inform new lines of division and forms of sociocultural distinction. These are imprinted in the urban landscape in the form of exclusive spaces with a large degree of social closure.

One of the hallmarks of these conspicuously cosmopolitan spaces and the privileged sociabilities they harbor was their mixed-gender character, which constituted a seemingly self-evident up-market norm and comfortable class normalcy. However, as I argue in the next chapter, such upper-middle class gendered performances were fragile. This fragility became apparent in concerns over the possible presence of others who might not abide by upper-middle class standards of respectable mixed-gender socializing. It is shown in full force when, in the course of the next chapter, we move from the coffee shop into the less class-specific spaces of the street.

Chapter 5

Of Taxi Drivers, Prostitutes, and Professional Women

Gender, Public Space, and Social Segregation

> A taxi driver kidnaps, robs, rapes, kills women and then cuts their
> bodies into pieces, puts the parts in several plastic bags and scatters
> them around Heliopolis and Nasr City.
>   This horror story has been spreading like wildfire amongst
> Cairenes over the past two weeks. Fortunately, it appears to be
> nothing more than a rumour. The Interior Ministry has issued a
> statement, published in most newspapers, which says the 'rumours of
> a serial killer raping and killing women are completely groundless.'
> *Al-Ahram Weekly*, 21–27 February 2002

In early spring 2002 a persistent story went around about a serial killer operating from a taxi in and around Heliopolis, one of Cairo's old upper-middle
class districts. The purported killer was said to kidnap, rape, and murder
young 'well-dressed' women and mutilate their bodies. I received several
e-mails describing these crimes in horrific detail. These e-mails included witness statements of policemen and a victim's mother who had talked to her
daughter on her cell phone just before the fatal moment. The story became
big enough for the government to react. It vehemently denied the factuality

of the stories in national newspapers. Despite these remonstrations—or rather partially because of them—rumors kept spreading through e-mail. After some two months, the e-mails stopped coming and the story died down. I heard and read several accounts of the 'real' story behind the rumor. The rumor was apparently based on a single incident that had nothing to do with serial killing. The killer had been caught and the case closed. However, a young man had been inspired by the incident and started sending e-mails reporting new cases.[46]

The rumor of the taxi killer provides a good starting point for exploring Cairo's class-divided landscape against the background of neoliberal policies. Luise White argues that "rumors can be a source of local history that reveals the passionate contradictions and anxieties of specific places with specific histories" (White 2000:83). This particular rumor indicates some of the tensions that accompany new class configurations and their expressions in Cairo's urban landscape. I am particularly interested in the complex ways in which it knits together issues of gender, class, and public space. Why was the alleged perpetrator a (male) taxi driver, we might ask. Why did he supposedly single out young upper-middle class women? And why did the rumor show such tenacity, despite the government's widely published denials?

This chapter examines the micropolitics of space in liberalizing Cairo at the start of the twenty-first century. I explore everyday negotiations of new class formations in Egypt's new liberal era by following female upper-middle class professionals—the supposed victims of the rumor—as they inhabit and traverse Cairo's diverse public spaces. I discuss how these female upper-middle class professionals in their late twenties and early thirties negotiated two types of public spaces. First I return to the controlled spaces of the up-market coffee shops discussed in the previous chapter. In these socially closed spaces the management of a respectable public presence took center stage. I then discuss the open and less class-specific spaces of the street and transport, which were marked by constant efforts at shielding the pure, properly sexualized upper-middle class female body.

Through my participation in upper-middle class circles, I learned about the logics and rules that guide young professionals as they move through the urban landscape. I also draw on some my own spatial experiences to understand that mixture of metropolitan anonymity, ascribed social identity, and urban social life that shapes interactions in Cairo's public spaces. I found that upper-middle class trajectories were crucially determined by class-based inequalities and distinctions, especially class-specific elaborations of masculinity and femininity. In the following I analyze how young upper-middle class women negotiated Cairo's cityscape and discuss the sociospatial logics that ascribe social identities to specific women in a range of public spaces.

I use public and private to denote the spaces of the home versus more open, societal urban spaces. I take the term public space to indicate a tendency toward accessibility, rather than a clearly defined and bounded domain. We can thus think of publicness as a complex set of characteristics. Places can be public in some senses, while in other respects they resemble private spaces. Coffee shops, for example, are public when compared to the private spaces of the home. Compared to the 'public' spaces of work, where access is mostly restricted to employees, coffee shops constitute a relatively open space, nominally accessible to anyone who can afford to pay. They are, however, privately owned, protected from view, and have numerous explicit and implicit entrance requirements. In this sense, they differ considerably from open public spaces like streets or parks.

In her excellent reading of the gendered uses of space in a working class area of Cairo, Farha Ghannam argues that we need to go "beyond emphasizing the gendered character of public space to examine which, when, why, and by whom certain publics are closed or opened to age and gender groups" (2002:92). Notions of public and private space intersect with ideas about proper social forms, permitted and prohibited forms of intimacy. These complex configurations of space defy straightforward equations of public with male and private with female space. Different public spaces have differing rules of access and expected behavior, and carry differential symbolic significance. For example, the functional spaces of work and study constituted less contentious public arenas for mixed-gender contact than leisure spaces like the coffee shop. This was echoed, for example, in the greater acceptability of having 'colleagues' of the other sex, rather than friends or acquaintances.

To walk the city with these upper-middle class women allows me to bring out some of the logics implicit in urban life, to map the knowledge and the specific cartographies that movement through the city presupposes. My analysis of city life through movement resonates with the methodology proposed by Michel de Certeau in *The Practice of Everyday Life* (1984). De Certeau argues that movement through the city can be analyzed in terms of the spatial strategies of the powerful, which operate from an 'own' space, and the ephemeral spatial tactics of the powerless, which can only momentarily materialize in what he calls pedestrian speech acts (1984:37). His reflections on space and power resonate with the urban trajectories discussed in this chapter. However, lines between the powerful and powerless, between those who can develop spatial strategies and those who have to rely on momentary tactics, are not as clear as de Certeau seems to suggest. The urban trajectories of Cairo's young upper-middle class women defy clear dichotomies of elite versus dominated, and dominant strategies versus momentary spatial tactics, and thereby allow for a more complex understanding of the workings of power in everyday micropolitics of space.

The urban itineraries discussed here can be read as the footsteps of the social segregation that has increasingly come to mark Cairo's cityscape after more than a decade of neoliberal policies. They demonstrate the centrality of gender in the elaboration of class in contemporary Cairo. I argue that the public presence of women is central to the elaboration of a new upper-middle class culture, and in turn becomes the focus of class conflicts. In Egypt's new liberal era female upper-middle class bodies have once again become a central arena for the elaboration and contestation of social inequality.

Female, Professional, and Upper-Middle Class

In Cairo I made the acquaintance of a number of high-powered upper-middle class women in their late twenties and early thirties who routinely moved around the city from home to work to gym to coffee shop to cinema to concert before they returned home to sleep, wake up early and once again cross half the city to reach work. They were all professionals from middle to upper-middle class families, who had been educated in language schools and had found high-end jobs in media establishments, NGOs, or marketing departments of multinationals. Most were not yet married, and lived with their parents, but spent much of their time in the diverse up-market spaces of work and leisure that have mushroomed in Cairo since the mid-1990s. Some would dress in tight cotton pants or jeans and equally tight shirts. Others would have similar looks, but wore a head scarf and long sleeve tops, while again others had adopted fashionable Islamic looks, wearing smart flowing robes and matching scarves. In all cases, the style and quality of their clothes would intimate their comfortable class position. While moving across the city, they were in constant contact with friends over their mobile phones, coordinating where and when to meet, relatively indifferent to the surprisingly vast distances covered in order to socialize. They also remained connected to their families by frequent mobile phone contacts, reassuring those at home of their safety and good conduct, and informing them of their whereabouts.

These young professionals were among the most visible exponents of Egypt's new liberal age: young, classy women, relatively fluent in English, who were employed in the internationally oriented segment of Cairo's economy and claimed knowledge of global trends and cosmopolitan fashions. Their presence in both professional and social public life had become normalized, even critical to upper-middle class lifestyles, which were marked by the mixed-gender character of contacts and places. Their presence was a crucial part of a claim not only to the elite status of such work and leisure spaces, but also their modernity and global suitability. As Shilpa Phadke argues with respect to a strikingly similar setting in Mumbai, "middle class women as consumers and professionals are welcomed [in] the new spaces of consumption

ANOUK DE KONING (2004)

Two women on Gama'it id-Duwal Street

(shopping malls and coffee shops) where the presence of a certain kind of woman is a marker of the modernity of the city and its claim to global status" (2007:1514). The highly mobile and rather public lifestyles of female professionals were valued cultural capital in parts of the upper-middle class. Their negotiations of space and their public performances were part of an elite class project that, on account of its continuing referencing of 'the outside,' could be called conspicuously cosmopolitan.

What constitutes the ideal upper-middle class marriageable woman was the subject of heated debates. While conspicuously cosmopolitan lifestyles were common among marriageable upper-middle class women, class-specific forms of religiosity and modesty provided different, but equally attractive gendered models (see Mahmood 2005). These two models were hardly mutually exclusive. Many women I knew tried to create their own blend of professionalism and public lifestyles, and religiously inspired definitions of virtuous femininity, amid much wondering about, and somewhat tense discussions of, men's preferences.

Since the 1980s Egypt has seen an increased religiosity among large sections of the population. The increased religiosity in Egyptian society has certainly influenced upper-middle class lifestyles, albeit in highly class-specific ways (cf. Macleod 1991). It has impacted notions of gendered propriety and modesty and has contributed to the rise of more religiously inspired ideas regarding the ideal wife, which are partially at odds with the public lifestyles described here. Women's adoption of the veil was often taken as one of the clearest expressions of the strengthened role of religion and religious identifications in Cairo's social life. The new veiling had been particularly prominent among lower and lower-middle class women, and less so among their upper-middle class counterparts (cf. McLeod 1991). The veil was perceived as a sign of a low sociocultural level, and particularly young, marriageable women from more affluent families were discouraged from wearing the *higaab*, let alone a *khimaar* or *niqaab*. Yet in the late nineties many young professional upper-middle class women also started taking up the veil.[47] Some women who donned the *higaab* stated that by doing so they were trying to come closer to God *(yi'arrabu min rabbina)* and start on a road toward self-improvement. Others merely mentioned that it was a religious obligation to cover one's hair. In my experience, the choice to veil was not necessarily framed in terms of good versus evil, or moral versus immoral. It was often framed as a choice for a more religiously inspired lifestyle over a 'worldlier' one.

Though further research is needed to outline the diverse class dynamics behind this 'delayed' upper-middle class veiling, many people pointed to the influence of Amr Khaled, the wildly popular lay preacher who drew large middle and upper-middle class audiences to his weekly lectures and his religious programs on satellite television. Amr Khaled has been characterized as 'the preacher of the affluent,' since he specifically addressed upper-middle class publics and their lifestyle choices in an attempt to show them how to combine '*id-dunya wid-diin*' (the world and religion), as I was told by one of his fans (cf. Bayat 2002; Tammam and Haenni 2003). He was remarkably successful among young upper-middle and upper class women and devoted a large part of his lessons to 'female' concerns—the *higaab* being a central theme. In the summer of 2002 he was banned from preaching in Egypt. Though the precise reasons for this ban remain unclear, his extraordinary success in this affluent and influential segment of society seems to have been an important rationale.

The women whose trajectories inform this chapter differed regarding their participation in religious activities and their choices with respect to the *higaab*. They were part of an upper-middle class mainstream that was consciously seeking a balance between an active public life, respectability, and to differing degrees, religious prescriptions. Regardless of their choice regarding veiling, respectability and reputation were crucial issues for all these women. Central to their concerns was their reputation as sexually pure and unavailable, other than in marriage.

Dilemmas of Public Visibility

Upper-middle class women negotiated their being in public against the background of longstanding dilemmas of female public presence and visibility. As I argued in the previous chapter, specific forms of women's public visibility have a checkered history in twentieth-century Cairo. They have been a central arena for contestations over modernity and authenticity (see Abu-Lughod 1998; Ahmed 1992). The presence of women in public leisure spaces has been a major marker of cosmopolitan or 'westernized' elite practices (see Armbrust 1999; Abaza 2001). In Cairo, such cosmopolitan referencing has never been an unproblematic marker of elite class membership and sophistication; it could also be taken as a sign of alienation and rootless Westernization, evoking associations with moral looseness. Being visible could thus be part of a claim to a cosmopolitan elite belonging that hinges on a particular public female presence, but it could also be taken to indicate moral and sexual looseness. These two interpretive possibilities continued to haunt interactions in public space, and elicited continual efforts at managing interpretations of public presence. How was this female public presence and visibility negotiated and how were the oftentimes contradictory exigencies of public visibility, propriety, and respectability managed among young upper-middle class women at the start of the twenty-first century?

Though spending much time in public leisure spaces was an important aspect of the daily routines of the upper-middle class women I came to know, such outings were largely restricted to unambiguously classy places with a large degree of social closure. The trajectories of these women were invariably based on class maps: places that were safe for women were classy places. Cairo's upscale coffee shops played a crucial role in the establishment of a young, upper-middle class presence in the urban landscape. While intimating a sense of First World inclusion, these upscale coffee shops also heeded religious sensibilities and gendered notions of propriety. They provided upper-middle class professionals with new opportunities for socializing, finding partners, and other forms of networking and self-presentation. In contrast, the possibility of visiting *'ahawi baladi* was resolutely dismissed by all women I asked, though some made an exception for the cafés that were part of the Downtown intellectual scene. As Marwa, a single woman in her mid-thirties, put it: "The *'ahwa* is a public place, but for a particular cultural level. It is only for men. People will refuse a girl sitting in a *'ahwa*. In our places [upscale coffee shops], we are not strange. They are used to seeing women sitting alone. If you go sit in a normal *'ahwa*, everybody will look, and then someone will say something, someone will flirt."

As I argued in the previous chapter, upscale coffee shops had created a protected niche for nonfamilial mixed-gender sociabilities in contentious public geographies of leisure. They had wrested such mixed-gender sociabilities away from associations with immorality and loose sexual behavior that cling to less exclusive mixed-gender spaces outside of the redemptive familial sphere. Yet, reading between the lines of the social lives that played out in Cairo's upscale coffee shops one could discern a continuous concern and anxiety over the possibly problematic status of public mixed-gender sociabilities. Critiques of cosmopolitan lifestyles and practices often centered on sexual norms and female propriety, which, as a consequence, were a focus of anxiety for many young female coffee shop patrons who were eager to find a suitable marriage partner. The sexual reputation of a young woman was of vital importance for her and her family's reputation and her chances of marriage. These reputations were the stock subject of whispered gossip and constant concern. Especially in mixed-gender groups, discussions would quite often subtly touch on issues of respectability and virtue. Many marriageable women seemed eager to confirm their respectability in the face of possible criticism of their presence in such public venues, or of their appearance and lifestyle.

Compared to their male colleagues and friends, these women had comparatively little room to juggle lifestyles and moral standards. They bore the brunt of the imperatives of (sexual) respectability (cf. Werner 1997). Their presence in public spaces like the coffee shop marked them as women who had chosen a more public lifestyle, which could raise questions regarding their respectability. As Miriyam put it, "Girls who know both the home and the outside world will be stronger. Men might ask: 'How did she get her experience?' But that's pure hypocrisy. Why should she be pure and he impure?" Karim similarly criticized such double standards. He argued, "There are guys who will go with girls to coffee shops but want to marry a girl who doesn't know the coffee shop. I do not see why her respectability has to depend on her outings." Their comments resonate with Farha Ghannam's analysis of gender and public space among the inhabitants of iz-Zawiyya il-Hamra, a lower class neighborhood in Cairo. According to Ghannam, "the attempts to control women's access to the workplace . . . are not limited to the desire to control the female body and female sexuality. There is also a strong desire to control women's minds, the knowledge they have access to, and the kind of solidarities they may form" (2002:90). Miriyam's comments however also allude to skepticism toward women who do not remain within clearly demarcated borders of female propriety and respectability. Even minor 'transgressions,' in this case 'having experience,' suggested the possibility of more serious ones like premarital sex.

These contestations regarding female respectability must be located in the safe space of the coffee shop, with its considerable degree of acceptance of women's public lifestyles. The rather exclusive context of the coffee shop helped frame a woman's appearance and comportment as upper-middle class and thereby guaranteed a certain interpretation of her presence. In order to provide such a class framing, coffee shops needed to secure an unambiguously classy clientele.

The Safe Space of the Coffee Shop

Social closure was a crucial feature of coffee shops that wanted to appeal to a mixed-gender upper-middle class public. Even though internal and external borders were heavily guarded, there was a continuous anxiety about the possible presence of unsuitable others in these spaces. Unsupervised meetings of unmarried men and women could only claim respectability when the class standing of those involved was beyond question. The presence of unsuitable others would put such a class standing, and thereby the respectability of the mixed-gender social life, in question. These others were also thought unable to abide by the implicit rules of gendered sociability that guided social life in upscale coffee shops. They were expected to overstep the carefully crafted red lines of respectable mixed-gender socializing by harassing patrons or engaging in prostitution. Take for example Amal's remarks on different publics one would find at a number of upscale leisure venues. "There are some places where a girl can sit on her own, here [Retro Café], Cilantro. These places are more westernized. You have to see what kind of people you find in a place. For example, Maroush[48] is just trash. The *shiisha* [water pipe] gathers low class people and upper class boys who want to pick up girls. People are always looking at you."

'Social level,' a concept of social differentiation that combines notions of class and culture, was a central criterion in judging whether a certain woman was able to indulge in respectable casual mixed-gender contact and play with features that otherwise suggested a lack of respectability. These assumptions implied that women (and men) from a high social level knew how to conduct mixed-gender interactions properly, since it constituted part of their cosmopolitan, yet respectable class normalcy. Similarly, wearing 'naked' (*'iryaan*) clothes did not necessarily indicate a lack of respectability as long as the good origins of the wearer were beyond doubt. These clothes were then framed as part of respectable class-specific norms and lifestyles, as much as the stylish clothing of upper-middle class *muhaggabaat*. Their class markers protected these young women from being associated with girls from other social 'levels' who wear similar clothes and might be perceived as being *saay'a* (a bum, of the streets; in a more positive sense, streetwise) or even *illit il-adab* (literally: impolite; often a polite way of speaking about anything from loose morals to prostitution). Again the parallel with similar spaces in liberalizing Mumbai is striking. As Phadke notes, "As long as they dress class-appropriately, the presence of couples and even their displays of affection are not looked on in askance but in fact constitute part of the message these spaces are striving to convey: that these are global spaces with global rules where one can leave behind the city and its parochial cultural contexts" (2007:1514).

These logics are apparent in Tamer's discussion of coffee shops. The 'style of people' frequenting a particular venue was crucial to his judgment. This middle class professional in his late twenties remembered a one-time visit to a 'cheap' open-air coffee shop in Maadi, an outlying elite district of Cairo. "The style of people was not that great, I did not feel comfortable. When I go out, I do not want to encounter some rancid girl, some *bii'a* [vulgar person] that disgusts me. The atmosphere was definitely not *classy*. This is an even bigger problem for girls. I can't take my fiancée to some of the places I visit with my male friends. The places I visit with her have to have people of a 'clean' level, where everyone minds their own business and nobody looks at you in a non-respectable way or laughs really loud." The coffee shops located on Gamaa'it id-Duwal Street, a major shopping street and thoroughfare in Mohandisseen, were clear examples of the places he would never visit with his fiancée, he said. "In these coffee shops most of the girls are prostitutes. I can't go there with my fiancée. Others will think that she is not my fiancée, but my girlfriend. She will be seen as one of those girls." Karim, a professional in his early thirties, concurred: "You have to keep a place comfortable for women. It has to be closed, clean, and part of the staff needs to be female. You need to keep a certain standard of people coming in. If a woman finds a man who harasses her, or a woman who looks like a prostitute, she will not come again because people might say that she could be one of them."

Nihal's account of her visit to a disco that was not clearly marked as upper-middle class illustrates how the presence of questionable others can impact a woman's sense of herself. This upper-middle class professional in her early thirties told me she felt embarrassed as soon as she entered. She estimated many of the women present to be *easy* with regards to sexual morals and suspected that some might be prostitutes. Even though she was accompanied by a male friend, and despite her self-identification as a proper upper-middle class woman, she felt she was included in this group of loose women as a result of her mere presence, and felt tainted by the experience. Other women told me similar stories, imbued with similar feelings. Some stressed the social repercussions of being seen in a certain place, others emphasized their sense of embarrassment or even defilement by being identified as less than respectable. This sense of embarrassment and defilement could be elicited by anything from personal misgivings to subtle signs of others present, from benevolent teasing and flirting to concrete interventions. What struck me is the extent to which such (imagined) social identifications came to influence women's own perceptions of their sexualized bodies and selves.

As these stories indicate, these women's public presence was haunted by the specter of prostitution. Elizabeth Wilson's discussion of the 'public woman' in nineteenth-century European cities is instructive in this regard. "[T]he prostitute was a 'public woman,' but the problem in the nineteenth-century urban life was whether every woman in the new, disordered world of the city, the public sphere of pavements, cafés and theatres, was not a public woman and thus a prostitute. The very presence of unattended—unowned—women constituted a threat both to male power and a temptation to male 'frailty'" (Wilson 2001:74). A similar ambiguity, reflecting a fraught relation

'Ahwa baladi, Bab al-Luq

Trianon coffee shop, Mohandisseen

between morality and visibility, continues to provide the central backdrop to women's negotiations of public space in numerous settings, among others in contemporary Cairo. It pervaded the ambiguous views of young upper-middle class women who moved—apparently unowned—through public space. The core of this ambiguity consisted of the contrastive possible interpretations of a young woman's presence in public. Did her presence indicate a disreputable sexual openness or was it part of a more respectable lifestyle and everyday routine? Susan Ossman notes a similar ambiguous relation between morality and visibility in Casablanca's public spaces. "One of the problems posed by the new public encounters between young men and women is the lack of adequate paradigms for flirting practices," she argues. "In the past, openly seductive women in public spaces were prostitutes, and this idea continues to color many people's condemnation of those engaged in the drague [public flirting]" (Ossman 1994:163). Public visibility could suggest (immoral) availability, and had to therefore be carefully managed. As Rachel Newcomb argues with respect to women in Fez, Morocco, "in public spaces women must maintain a careful balance between visibility and propriety, advertising their beauty while creating a sense of separation between themselves and the words and gazes of unrelated men" (2006:299).

The management of women's visibility was an important feature of the design of coffee shops, as Karim pointed out. "The 'ahwa does not have a door," he said. "Coffee shops, in contrast, are closed. Not every passerby will see you when you sit there; you do not get influenced by other people. My girlfriend would not like to sit in a place where she would be seen and would have to hear comments. She would refuse to sit in the street. She prefers a safely closed place." Protecting women from view is an old theme in Cairo's leisure architecture. Many older restaurants have a second floor where families or mixed-gender groups can sit hidden from view. Most coffee shops were similarly designed to block views from the street. Karim's story about the Fashion Café, another coffee shop on Gamaa'it id-Duwal Street, illustrates the importance of such management of visibility. The owner of the Fashion Café had wanted to create a café with large windows that opened up to the street, "like cafés on the Parisian boulevards." The idea proved fatal in the Cairene context. Karim said that the crowd that began to frequent the café consisted largely of men who came to meet girls. "People came who could create problems, who came to flirt/harass (yi'aksu). Female patrons stopped coming, and another type of women started to come."

While concerns regarding visual protection most obviously focused on the gaze of passersby, they also extended to the gaze of patrons of a doubtful social level or social origins. As the recurrent references to 'a certain standard of our people' and 'our kind of people,' as well as the frequent negative mention of less classy others indicate, it was a specific gaze that was viewed as problematic and even harmful: the invasive look of undeserving men directed at respectable and classy women. The impact of such a gaze is illustrated by a comment Amal once made. She emphatically stated that she would not 'go in the water' (swim in a bathing suit) if she did not feel sure of the 'social level' of the others present. "They might be *bii'a* and *eat you with their looks*" (my emphasis). As I argue more extensively below, the undeserving male gaze was experienced as a defilement of physically and symbolically pure and respectable female bodies.

The essential question was who could be seen by whom. A look might be part of an appropriate and desired visibility, or might be harmful and defiling, depending on 'social level.' In contrast to the unwanted gaze of men of a lower class, those of classy others were invited, even desired. Yet, being seen was hardly ever discussed, except in comments about the shallowness, vanity, opportunism, and lack of respectability of those others who made it their priority to be seen in the latest, hippest place or who wanted to be seen in order to find a partner. The desire to be seen was apparently too contentious, and could evoke accusations of shallowness and, in the case of women, charges of disrespectability.

The anxiously guarded spaces of the coffee shop allowed for the performance of upper-middle class gendered identities—the leisurely socializing of mixed-gender *shilal* and the public routines of single career women. This mixed-gender sociability in turn marked these establishments as upper-middle class. With respect to the appearance of feminized consumer spaces in late nineteenth-century New York, Liz Bondi and Mona Domosh argue that certain parts of the city became associated with bourgeois definitions of femininity. These spaces, in turn, reinforced the bourgeois identities of women shoppers. "Definitions of femininity became interwoven with delineations of certain spaces within the city," they conclude (1998:279–80). Cairo's upscale coffee shops fulfill a function similar to that of nineteenth-century shopping districts. As long as its class framing was beyond question and disreputable others were kept out, the space of the coffee shop by and large prescribed the interpretation of these women's public lifestyles and sexy appearances as normal and respectable. In the streets, where up-market norms were not hegemonic and a clear class framing was absent, such (self-)representations could well be overturned. The same fashionable *cut* (sleeveless top) would seem out of place, but could also be taken as a sign of disrepute and easy morals, an open invitation to comments and even harassment.

Into the Urban Jungle

One day I was walking on one of the busy Downtown shopping streets, when a passerby angrily commented, "*Mish haraam 'aleeki kida?*" (Shouldn't you be ashamed of yourself?). It took me a moment to recover from the shock. While I had grown used to *mu'aksaat* (flirts/harassment) when walking in the streets, I had never before been reprimanded in such a way. I quickly went over my clothes: a knee-length skirt and a somewhat tight t-shirt with short sleeves; nothing out of the ordinary. The anonymous middle-aged man had gone and I could not demand an explanation. I looked around and saw myself surrounded by numerous examples of sexy and 'naked' clothing in the shop windows.

Still baffled, I continued on my way home and called Nada to ask her opinion. She was far from surprised. At first she suggested he was merely flirting. When I insisted that it had sounded more like a reprimand, she said, "Then he must have thought you were not properly dressed. He must have taken you for an Egyptian." I told her that I had heard that such 'interventions' used to be common in the early 1990s, at the height of religious mobilization, when people would accost others in the street and admonish them to better their lives and live up to religious prescriptions. I had, however, never experienced anything like it and had thought such interventions were a thing of the past. Upon getting out of a minibus, a fellow woman traveler would occasionally pull down a shirt that had moved up, baring part of my waist. Such small gestures invariably reminded me of the bottom lines of decency for women in public and often left me slightly embarrassed because of my inattention to such important details. Yet, these benign, caring gestures seemed far from the man's angry reprimand. "Well, there is a first time for everything," said Nada philosophically. "That was a fanatic man from another time."

It is difficult to capture and mediate the intensity and bodily felt character of interactions in Cairo's public spaces, or the intense self-awareness of many women when they move through public space. Gillian Rose argues that women are constituted as explicitly embodied, located subjects. Most men, in contrast, enjoy a masculine illusion of freedom from the body and its inevitable locatedness. These differential forms of subjectivication give rise to specific experiences of space, Rose argues. "The threatening masculine look materially inscribes its power onto women's bodies by constituting feminine subjects through an intense self-awareness about being seen and about taking up space. . . . [I]t is a space which constitutes women as embodied objects to be looked at" (Rose 1993:145–46). As I noted earlier, class and sociospatial context importantly classify this gaze and the way it is experienced and interpreted. The gaze of affluent young men in a coffee shop would be interpreted quite differently from the more diffuse, yet omnipresent male gaze in the street. Conversely, a woman with a clearly elite appearance would experience a rather different gaze in both contexts than a more middle class woman. While I take up the themes of the male gaze and female embodiment that Rose articulates, I explore the specific dynamics of 'the gaze' in the Cairene context and ask what these particulars can tell us about the constitution of female upper-middle class bodies and gendered identities.[49] The gaze figured as an active polluting and defiling agent that physically impacts the female body. It was, moreover, able to impute a bad reputation and suggest a lack of respectability. These threats were crucially connected to the presence of non-upper-middle class others, those who were perceived to be of a lower 'social' or 'cultural level,' and were therefore seen as unable to grasp, and likely to defile the subtly negotiated respectable public presence of young upper-middle class women.

In the case of the coffee shop, 'public space' took on a prescriptive quality. 'Being in public' was first and foremost a matter of representation, of the management of a respectable public presence. Public space could, however, also denote a less scripted social space where rules are unsure, interactions not scripted, and the others one might encounter unknown (cf. Kaviraj 1997; Mitchell 1995). These different modalities of public space also entailed different forms of the gaze—the one sought after, the other feared. Streets evoked such a sense of an unpredictable urban jungle harboring manifold threats and pollutants. The sense of a dangerous urban jungle focused primarily on the sexualized threats it presented to the female body. Anxieties about the propriety of being in public were displaced by, or perhaps translated into, fears of pollution and defilement of the highly fragile and vulnerable upper-middle class female body.

In contrast to the closed coffee shops, Cairo's streets were largely characterized by male entitlement.[50] The street was a space for men to inhabit, a space where they could spend time, observe and interact with passersby, comment, and flirt. Unaccompanied young women, in contrast, had a liminal and ambiguous status as marginalized, and potentially illegitimate and disreputable, passersby (cf. Ghannam 2002). They were supposed to be on their way somewhere, have a clear destination, and not linger for too long. Hanging around in the streets, especially on their own, was taken as an open invitation for men to make contact. Indicative of their liminal presence in these kind of public spaces were the efforts of my friends to carefully plan their schedules and meetings to avoid time gaps during which they would have to spend time waiting alone in a public space. Waiting alone in open public spaces was tantamount to inviting sexual innuendos, and thus opened women up not only to physical defilement, but also the symbolic tarnishing of being seen as open for sexualized contact. This male prerogative to judge, comment, and accost women in the street was only partially staved off by the high-class status of my female acquaintances.

Women's strategies in crossing the city depended on social maps of Cairo that indicated what to expect in certain places, and marked these places with a sense of ease and tension, safety and danger. They negotiated the different everyday spatial regimes that frame social interaction in Cairo's public spaces. Such spatial regimes are made up of ideas and norms regarding comportment, propriety, and identity, which ascribe social identities to specific persons in specific spatial contexts and times of the day.

A young woman's presence was subject to constant observation and judgments. Such judgments were based on looks, class markers, and signs of modesty such as the *higaab* or loose fitting clothing. As Anne J. Secor (2002) argues with respect to Istanbul, specific attires allow for certain interpretations and interventions in public space and are therefore crucial with respect to the micropolitics of interaction in public spaces. Different styles of women's dress were central to and iconic of different styles of femininity. Yet, each of these styles had to be negotiated across diverse spaces with differing interpretations of a woman's presence. How the tight, yet not too revealing jeans and top, or the fashionable matching headscarf and loose fitting dress would be interpreted depended on the sociospatial context. Depending on the trajectory, these women would choose to dress in specific ways: not too tight, not too revealing, not too much makeup for more popular or mixed areas. They would put on a defensive attitude: eyes focused straight ahead, signaling detachment from the surroundings in an attempt to erect an invisible shield around them.

The importance of such spatial framing of a woman's public presence became clear on one of my trips to Heliopolis. I had made an appointment to meet someone in front of Merryland, a large park with restaurants and cafés. The park is a clear landmark and seemed an easy meeting point. Something went wrong and I ended up waiting in the street by myself. Several men in cars stopped and stared at me. My premonitions were validated when one of them pulled out a large wad of notes and waved them at me. I realized that I had clearly chosen the wrong landmark. Even my rather prudish outfit (long black pants and a simple blouse, hardly any makeup) did not shield me from the overriding framing of this place as a pick-up site for prostitutes. Since prostitution is illegal, prostitutes do not usually stand out from the general female public. One would have to identify a woman as a prostitute by her contextual appearance in a certain space/time, like the girls in the lobby of a five-star hotel whom Maha pointed out to me, with slightly too much makeup, their clothes a tad too tight.

The male prerogative to judge, comment, or accost women in public space was most readily expressed in the frequent *muʾaksaat* (flirts/harassment) women encountered when traversing the city. The following excerpt is part of an article on harassment in the streets of Cairo that appeared in the English-language *Community Times*, a monthly magazine that targeted a local upper-middle class public.

> Sexual harassment on Egyptian streets; women simply cannot walk in this country without being pestered by male voyeurs. . . . Some of the language used on the streets to harass women is shockingly obscene and sometimes violent, with vulgar anatomical references becoming the pathetic norm. A friend of mine gags every time she recalls a male passer-by who bestowed her with a list of the various sexual acts he would like to practice on her. Another colleague has had to endure the *trauma of having a stranger on the street brush his hand against her hips.* . . . Male harassers place the blame on women for evoking their own dirty sexual fantasies. . . . [Yet] the problem is not in women's attire, as demonstrated by veiled women far from being exempted from harassment in the streets.
>
> Shaima'a Bakeer, *Community Times*, June 2004 (my emphasis)

The female author articulates a common enough feeling regarding sexual harassment in the streets of Cairo. She expresses her frustration with the way her passage through public space is hampered by unsavory comments and unwanted physical contact. In my experience *muʾaksaat* varied from highly creative pranks to blunt sexual harassment, while the standard '*ya 'asal*' (hey, honey) merely functioned as a persistent reminder of a constantly observant male gaze (cf. Ghannam 2002:100). Such *muʾaksaat*, though not class specific per se, were mainly attributed to men who linger in the street, and had significant lower class connotations.

My upper-middle class friends instructed me that a middle class woman should staunchly ignore *muʾaksaat*, however playful, if she wants to safeguard her respectability. A couple of men who engaged in the occasional flirting concurred. *Muʾaksaat* are contacts that have no other aim than flirting, they argued, no other meaning than a sexual one. Polite middle class women should not respond, not even to defend themselves or chastise the man who dared to harass them, not to give him a chance to start a more prolonged interaction. To engage in conversation or respond to *mu'aksaat* was seen as tantamount to a certain openness to sexualized play, and was thus something a respectable women should avoid. The women who were the object of flirtations and harassment were ambiguously seen to carry part of the blame for *mu'aksaat*. She might be seen as a woman who invites this kind of attention, moving alone through public space and attracting the male gaze by her clothes or behavior. This partitioning of blame also resonates with views about the potential danger presented by a woman's contact with men other than her *mihrim* (husband, father, uncles, and brothers). Such contact can wreak havoc by stirring up lustful feelings in naturally weak men (Hoffman-Ladd 1987; MacLeod 1991:83–84). In the context of a lesson on the importance of the *higaab*, Amr Khaled argued that "one woman can easily entice one hundred men, but one hundred men cannot entice a single women" (cited in Bayat 2002:24).

The scene described in the *Community Times* can, however, also be read as an expression of the tensions that accompany new class configurations in Egypt's new liberal age and their manifestations in Cairo's cityscape. Women's public presence had become one of the most significant markers of the young upper-middle class culture that had developed in Cairo's new leisure spaces in the 1990s. This public presence was, however, fragile and evoked severe anxieties about the possible harm that can come to female upper-middle class bodies in the city's public spaces.

As Anna Mehta and Liz Bondi argue in their discussion of female embodiment and fear of violence in Edinburgh, "women *embody* discourse that constructs them as . . . vulnerable and physically powerless, particularly in the face of male violence, and as the object of aggressive male sexuality" (1999:77; emphasis in the original). In Cairo women, particularly young women moving on their own, were figured as objects of sexualized observation, while an ambiguous attribution of guilt for attracting such sexualized attention put them on the defensive. This type of objectification did not need a concrete agent: it was built into definitions of specific public spaces and the social identities attributed to different types of users. As I noted earlier, women literally embodied such ambivalences and the mere idea of certain social identifications—for example, being seen as disreputable—could have a physical impact. Meanwhile, daily experiences of *mu'aksaat* did continually reconfirm women's sexualized embodiment. As the earlier reference to the traumatic nature of 'a brush of hand' and my discussion of the improper gaze indicated, female upper-middle class bodies were easily injured and defiled. Looks and touches could cause injury to the female upper-middle class body, as well as a sense of defilement.

Safe Passage

The avoidance and barring of unwanted gazes and unwarranted contact featured centrally in upper-middle class strategies regarding transportation. Two common means of transport had come to symbolize the two extremes of experience in public space: the bus stood for forced proximity and possible harassment, while the car represented control, protection, and absolute freedom of movement. Everyday comments about public transport resonated with assumptions about the vulnerability and preciousness of the female upper-middle class body. A woman should not get tired, should be at ease and free of the unwanted touches of other bodies. Whereas a man might brave these nuisances, a woman should never be forced to undergo the horrors of crowdedness in an open yet closed space like the public bus, where one is condemned to the proximity of others and their unclean bodies, and worst of all, physical harassment. The cheapest 'red' public bus, charging LE0.25 (€0.05) regardless of distance traveled, had become a symbol of the 'poor Egypt' for those who took no part in it. A friend told me that her upper-middle class colleagues tended to comment on *mu'aksa* by saying, 'as if we are in a red bus.' The public bus was used as a metaphor for extreme instances of uncivilized harassment, thought to typically occur on this cheap type of transport. While buses were part of the daily routines of most Cairene men and women, most upper-middle class women told me that they had never and would never enter a public bus. The two acceptable means of public transport were the at the time new service lines of air-conditioned buses (LE2; €0.50), whose design and pricing limited physical cross-class proximity, and the subway, where two compartments are reserved for women only.

Stories of harassment in public transport abounded. Though the rumor of the taxi killer was a particularly rich one, it fit in with a larger repertoire of similar stories. I heard a number of accounts of the dangers of the mini- or microbus, which invariably featured men waiting to harass women moving on their own. These stories expressed deep seated feelings of vulnerability of young women moving on their own through Cairo's cityscape. Concerns about women's movement focused on her unscathed passage through public space. Not the presence of these women in public was seen as problematic, but rather the kind of dangers that being in public presented. Anxieties focused on the numerous dangers of harassment and defilement that were seen to accompany such being in public. These were invariably sexualized dangers that threatened a woman's sexual purity and respectability (cf. Phadke 2007:1516). Cairo was generally said to be safe, yet fears of sexual violence, especially rape, were commonplace. Whereas rape represented the ultimate desecration, even a look could harm and defile the pure, unsullied, and properly sexualized female body.

The need to take public transport or move by foot in the streets exposed upper-middle class women to infringements on their established routines and preferred lifestyles, and to the numerous sexualized dangers Cairo's cityscape was seen to harbor. Hoda commented that she had to change her way of dressing when she moved house after her marriage. Now that she took a taxi from home to the metro station located in a popular neighborhood, she had stopped wearing tight clothes and obvious makeup to avoid being too visible and thus warranting comments. "You cannot wear professional clothes, such as a skirt, unless you have a car," she said. She complained that, as a result, she was not able to present herself as a professional career woman. For many middle class women the car had become an indispensable, if for some unattainable, item. The car allowed them to dress in their preferred way and live up to their role as cosmopolitan, savvy representatives of Egypt's new generation. It also protected them from unwanted encounters. Taxis presented a favorite, but expensive option for many non-car owners.

In contrast to the stories of danger and defilement that surrounded public transport, the car thus became the symbol for and guarantor of a perfect world of professional life, self-representation, and respectable socializing. Besides physical protection, it provided a mobile framing of the self that confirmed a certain class standing, akin to the fixed spatial framing of the up-market coffee shop. As Sherif, a middle-class man in his late thirties, remarked, "A woman who takes a taxi still has a relation to the street. She will eventually return to the street and can therefore be flirted with. A woman with her own car can dress in whatever way she likes. Nobody will harass her." The public lifestyles of young upper-middle class women depended on the financial means to sit in certain places and to take certain modes of transport—in short, to move exclusively in up-market Cairo. As Armbrust notes in his discussion of moviegoing in Cairo:

> Increasingly women who spend a significant proportion of their time in public, either by choice or by necessity, wear the hijab. Women from wealthy families tend to wear the hijab less often. They are, in any case, shielded from the public view by having greater access to technology (telephones, and especially automobiles rather than public transportation), and by virtue of the more exclusive institutions they frequent. (Armbrust 1998:421)

He cites the example of an expensive upscale cinema like the Ramsis Hilton theater. "In effect," he writes, "the theater itself functions as a kind of class-*hijaab*. The Ramsis Hilton theater in particular is constructed and priced so as to exclude all but the wealthiest. At LE7.50 to LE20 the theater is too expensive for most people to attend . . . [O]ne can go to the theater by car, reach the top floor by elevator, then leave by the same route without ever being exposed to the street" (Armbrust 1998:427). The car crowned attempts to create a controlled environment. It transported women unscathed and free of unwanted interventions from one safe space to the next.

Nihal sketched her paramount image of the young upper class woman: driving a Cherokee with closed tinted windows, air-conditioning on, moving between different places dominated by her own norms of respectability and sociability. This image rings quite true. The ability of many upper-middle class women to engage in their preferred lifestyle, modes of sociability, and self-presentation depended on such class closure and control over their environment. Moving around with these female professionals, the map of Cairo seemed to shrink to include only those areas where their distinctive lifestyles were the norm: the up-market districts of Mohandisseen, Zamalek, Maadi, and Heliopolis. Safe passage between these up-market districts relied on the ring road, flyover bridges, and inner-city highway that now connect these different areas, and allow one to move from one part of up-market Cairo to the next, without having to descend into the disorder, crowdedness, and poverty that characterize Cairo's poorer spaces. For some, spaces outside of this class-specific economy became a vague and distant reality. These other spaces were marked as dirty, full of bacteria and health hazards, uncouth people, and harassment. Some of these spaces outside up-market Cairo, like the popular or informal housing sectors (*'ashwaa'iyyaat*, see Bayat and Denis 2000), were places never to be visited, unless by accident, when one gets lost and is stranded in an informal area like Dar es-Salaam, full of unknown but lurking dangers.

Gendered Fears and the Fragile Performance of Class

[The daughters of the high aristocracy] dreamt solely of a regular
sojourn abroad, lived surrounded by electronic gadgets and refused
to go out into the streets, afraid that the contact with all those poor
drifting about the sidewalks would defile them. They would only go
out by car, and then exclusively to closed establishments: restaurants,
cinemas or beaches where they could be sure they wouldn't encounter
any plebs.

They were right. Wherever they went, the atmosphere grew tense.
Their beauty was almost impermissible. Even if the girls laughed
very modestly, it looked like a provocation. When they pushed up
their hair, the gesture would become erotically charged. The pointed
breasts under their shirts inflicted more chaos than a machine gun.
Their transparent cheeks seemed made to be kissed.
Rachid Mimouni (1991:88; my translation)

This passage is taken from *Une peine à vivre*, a novel about the life of a dictator
in an unnamed country by the Algerian writer Rachid Mimouni. It describes
the lives of women in a far more privileged position than the women whose
trajectories have informed this chapter. It, however, sketches a similar ironic
situation in which elite fears and anxieties that surround less exclusive places
and their inhabitants combine with the segmented everyday realities of a
divided city. Elite norms increasingly clash with those of other city dwellers,
thereby confirming the impossibility of 'going out in the streets.' As Mimouni
writes, they were right not to leave their exclusive surroundings. Even the sim-
plest gesture could be 'misread,' creating confusion, inciting harassment and the
defilement of otherwise pure and respectable embodiments of elite femininity.

In the conspicuously cosmopolitan yet respectable spaces of the coffee
shop, female sexual respectability remained a central focus of anxieties and
contestations. This focus on female respectability rehearses the earlier centrality of women's public visibility in longstanding discursive battles over
modernity versus authenticity, colonial domination versus national liberation,
and Western secularism versus an Islamic modernity (see, e.g., Abu-Lughod
1998; Ahmed 1992; Armbrust 1999). When moving out of these safe, up-
market spaces, the focus shifted from negotiations of professional femininity
to a concern with unscathed passage through an urban space replete with sexualized pollutants and dangers.

While their class status gave them a certain leverage vis-à-vis male entitlements in the streets, most upper-middle class women I knew preferred to
resort to more reliable strategies of class closure to secure their unscathed
passage through Cairo's public spaces. Their trajectories were invariably based
on class maps. This points to a crucial contradiction at the core of their high-
mobility and rather public lifestyles: their condition of possibility was social
closure, the avoidance of any disturbance, and the ability to skirt unwanted
contacts. Only in the spaces of up-market Cairo could they be *bi-rahithum* (at
ease) and dress and socialize as they saw fit, without being annoyed or being
seen as disreputable. Other spaces held the dangers of a bad reputation that

could easily rub off on otherwise respectable upper-middle class women, and the threat of defilement posed by undeserving gazes and unwarranted touch.

The dangers that being in public represented for the upper-middle class female body were simultaneously symbolic and physical. A respectable woman was taken to have a pure, properly sexualized body. Just as upper-middle class women's reputations were easily damaged or ruined, upper-middle class bodies were easily harmed and defiled. The sense of privilege that emanated from this female presence as the manifestation of a conspicuously cosmopolitan class project was matched by a strong sense of fragility and threat. Secor argues that "Spatial stories, whether they trace tactics of anonymity or strategies of identity, should . . . be seen as political narratives operating through the streets of the city" (2004:363). The negotiations of the city discussed in this chapter evidence a form of political contestation. Upper-middle class female bodies had become a central battleground for new class configurations and contestations, literally embodying both power and fragility of Cairo's upper-middle class in Egypt's new liberal age.

As my discussion of the safe space of the coffee shop illustrated, much of these women's urban trajectories relied on class-specific 'own' spaces. In that sense they employed what according to Michel de Certeau are dominant strategies. They relied on their elite belonging and economic power to access the socially closed spaces of upscale Cairo. These spaces, in turn, depended on their presence to substantiate their upscale standing and cosmopolitan claims. These women's movement through less class-specific spaces, in contrast, comes close to de Certeau's notion of tactics that aim at creating fleeting room for maneuvering. In such encounters, the odds seemed to be against these women, despite their comfortable class positions. Starkly sexualized definitions of femininity in public, and concomitant dangers of defilement and an imputed lack of respectability mitigated against their unscathed passage through public space. Rather than fitting some of the binaries set out by de Certeau, their spatial practices thus displayed an oscillation between occupation and movement, strategies and tactics, power and powerlessness, permanence and transience (see Secor 2004 for a related critique).

These combinations of tactics and strategies have to be located in the context of Cairo's changing urban landscape in Egypt's new liberal age. Tendencies toward social closure and segregation reflect a growing reliance on 'own' spaces that provide strategic bases for the unfolding of elite strategies. Such strategies of class closure were ubiquitous in upscale Cairo. Eric Denis argues that new urban policies in Cairo are directed at the elimination of diversity, heterogeneity, and proximity (2006:67). With reference to exclusive urban developments in Sao Paulo, Teresa Caldeira argues that the tendency to spatialize social distance is connected to "the inability [of more privileged inhabitants] to impose their own code of behaviour—including rules of deference—onto the city" (2000:319). Such spatializing of social distance is an increasingly common elite strategy in Cairo. As Vincent Battesti argues, "Criticism of the public gardens is often severe among representatives of wealthier strata of society, who express regret about the 'invasion' of public spaces by the masses who 'do not know to act, who are not respectable'. . . . When the popular classes started going out, the wealthy strata of Cairo took refuge in exclusive leisure spaces and in gated communities" (2006:503). Since Cairo's upper-middle class and elite represent a minority in the cityscape that, moreover, cannot command deference in less class-specific public spaces, their privileged lifestyles and spaces are secured through closure. While new forms of segmentation and segregation are imprinted on physical and imaginary maps of the city, the desert surrounding the city becomes a new frontier where Cairo's global dreams can be realized in the most lavish manner (cf. Denis 1997, 2006; Mitchell 1999).

In many places increased crime rates form the focus of social fears that accompany growing social inequalities, and legitimize all kinds of closure in the urban landscape (see, e.g., Caldeira 2000; Low 2001). In Cairo, property crime is perceived to be relatively limited. Instead, class-based cultural differences, particularly concerning sexuality and gender, provide an important rationale for social fear and attempts to maintain or establish social distance. Assumed moral and cultural differences are the focus of anxieties and give rise to a tendency toward social avoidance and class homogeneous spaces. The privileged lifestyles of the women I have discussed are founded on exclusion. They legitimize segregation and repressive practices and policies toward less privileged Cairenes. Shilpa Phadke (2007) insightfully argues that discourses on middle class women's vulnerability and threatening lower class men contribute to the exclusion of both middle class women *and* lower class men from Mumbai's public spaces. In Cairo, arguments about gendered behavior and the need for the protection of 'classy' women similarly come to legitimize a segregated cityscape.

We can finally return to the rumor of the serial killer operating from a taxi in and around Heliopolis. This rumor can be read as a dramatized version of the ambiguity of the public presence of young female upper-middle class professionals, and I would argue, of the extent to which this presence becomes the focus of smoldering class conflicts. The taxi driver-turned-killer represents any of these women's nightmares. The taxi epitomizes a tamed meeting of privileged and unprivileged, in which a lower class man provides the logistic means for the public lifestyles of an upper-middle class female clientele. In a sadistic twist the taxi driver turns against the women he is supposed to serve, showing himself to be fatally dangerous. The taxi that was supposed to carry these women safely and unscathed through public space becomes a danger zone; the lower class man who is supposed to serve becomes a serial killer. The frightened reactions and the extensive attempts to warn female friends and acquaintances are telling. They refused to believe the public statements of the government that denied the horrid happenings, since the story of the serial killer resonated with lingering anxieties about the fragility of their negotiations of public space.

As before, class-specific, gendered practices provide a central battleground for contestations of inequality. The public presence of young, well-to-do women embodies one of the most tangible representations of changing class formations in the urban landscape. Their public visibility can come to stand in for new inequities, just as, for more privileged Cairenes, the feared reaction of men of the street serves to legitimize a further avoidance of socially open spaces as well as an increasingly exclusionary and segmented urban landscape.

Conclusion

Global Dreams and Postcolonial Predicaments

Finding Our Identity: A Search For The 'Real' Egyptian Youth

It all started with a visit to Zizo's sogo2 [sausage] place in Sayeda Zeinab [an old popular quarter close to Downtown]. [51]. . . I . . . could not help but ask myself, "Does my occasional daring meal of Zizo's sogo2 sandwiches accompanied with sugar cane juice categorize me as a 'real' representative of the Egyptian youth population?"

[I] have had the privilege to experience things only a small and insignificant percentage of Egyptian youth experience, which definitely doesn't classify me as a fair representative of the Egyptian youth, so who is? . . . Based solely on my personal speculation, the 'real' representatives of Egyptian youth are those who belong to the middle income social class, who have been educated in public schools and universities, and are exposed to the different lifestyles of both the upper income social class and the lower income social class. Those who study day and night with the aim of bettering their life, yet graduate to accept whatever form of jobs that come their way. Those who are most loyal to the country yet have completely lost faith in its development.

The country's sole chance of survival is through those who have had the privilege of leading a good life and have been given all the tools necessary to move this country forward (good education, wealth,

157

power and connections). . . . Isn't it ironic how the only social class that can ever develop this country is the only class that seems to know the least about it?!?

May El-Khishen, *Campus Magazine*, June 2004, pp. 34–36.

This essay, published in one of the numerous English-language magazines that appeared in Cairo at the start of the twenty-first century, addresses the question of belonging in a country with disjunctive fates. Against the background of a divided nation, its upper class author asks: Who are the real Egyptian youth? It is not surprising that issues of belonging and national identity come up in an increasingly segregated city marked by glaring social inequalities, where ever more rigid divisions carve up the one time iconic professional middle class. Her quest calls up many of the themes I have discussed with respect to middle class Cairo in Egypt's new liberal age.

El-Khishen's search for the real Egyptian youth brings to mind the conservative modernism of Nasserite narratives of national progress. Like these narratives, she assumes that the real representatives of Egypt are young middle class professionals, "who have been educated in public schools and universities . . . . Those who study day and night with the aim of bettering their life." Yet these exponents of the Nasserite middle class are increasingly marginalized and "graduate to accept whatever . . . job comes their way." Along the lines of the national narratives of Egypt's new liberal age, she singles out affluent Cairenes like herself as a social vanguard, Egypt's future generation. Because of their privileged backgrounds, they are the only ones who can lead the country forward, she says, but they do not seem to have either the knowledge or the commitment to take up this leading role.

El-Khishen's quest to discover representatives the real Egyptian youth takes her on a tour of Cairo's segmented landscape. While the spaces of upscale Cairo constitute the self-evident background of the lives of young affluent Cairenes like her, other places in Cairo's divided cityscape figure as icons of authenticity and almost exotic difference. Old working class areas like Sayyeda Zeinab come to harbor the authenticity of sausages and sugar cane juice—an authenticity in which even an upper class person in an adventurous mood can take part. Yet, Egypt's latest version of national modernity lies elsewhere, in the socially segregated spaces of upscale Cairo.

Reforming the Middle Class

After the 1952 Revolution, a broadened middle class was to be the carrier of the newly independent, just, and modern Egyptian nation. Cairo's budding professional middle class was the primary beneficiary of the expansion in public facilities and employment under Nasser. In the course of the 1990s, state discourses in contrast emphasized the need to catch up with global standards in light of global competition. Parallel to the revision of the national project, the Nasserite social contract between state and population has gradually been rewritten. The last decennia have witnessed the downgrading of Nasser-era public institutions, facilities, and welfare provisions, as well as the concomitant rise of a wide range of private alternatives. The public segments of the labor market and education were said to have deteriorated irrevocably. For those who can opt out of public arrangements and institutions, this 'public' has become a far-off nightmare in its incarnations of public buses, public offices, and public schools. Privatization also created new divisions within public institutions, carving out class-specific spaces that are public, yet to which access is restricted. In Cairo's public universities, the top faculties and language departments provide exclusive and privileged trajectories to graduates who have attended language schools. Government offices similarly harbor privileged islands that employ upper-middle class professionals to do the jobs that cannot be entrusted to an overstaffed and underpaid bureaucracy. Cairo's middle class has become increasingly divided between those who can afford to pay for private arrangements in all fields of life, and others who have to resort to their often rundown and dwindling public counterparts. These divisions revolve around 'local' versus cosmopolitan orientations and aptitudes.

While the public educational system, shaped by Nasser-era policies, continues to educate a relatively high percentage of the population through university, the labor market no longer awards middle class lifestyles to its graduates. The system that was once intended to produce a large urban middle class—the carrier of national dreams and aspirations—now turns out superfluous graduates who can no longer be employed in an already overflowing bureaucracy. These unemployed or underemployed graduates have instead become the targets for reform. Special programs aim to direct them away from earlier promises of a clean middle class life, and onto the insecure road of small-scale enterprise. Yet, acquired social rights and personal investments in older national narratives are not easily put aside. Many governmental statements continued to include gestures to Egypt's previous social contract, while the abrogation of established social rights was vehemently denounced and contested by erstwhile beneficiaries. Meanwhile, individual and family strategies display a subtle insistence on becoming and remaining middle class, despite exhortations to invest in other trajectories.

The explicitly localized public educational institutions and degrees of lower-middle class professionals find their counterparts in the burgeoning exclusive private institutions that provide children of more affluent families with crucial cosmopolitan capital. Those with such cosmopolitan capital and comfortable family backgrounds can aspire to jobs in up-market companies and institutions, while devalued 'local' qualifications and less privileged family backgrounds leave most middle class Cairenes to face an insecure, tight labor market that offers insecure and oftentimes unrewarding jobs. The excesses of Cairo's new liberal age are exemplified by the twin figures of the loan-defaulting business tycoon and the unemployed graduate hazarding a small business with a loan from the Social Fund for Development. The more mundane image of a lower-middle class graduate waiting on his privileged peers in an upscale coffee shop reflects everyday realities in middle class Cairo.

Such changes parallel increasingly restrictive national narratives that focus on competition in the global arena and the need to adhere to global standards and qualifications. In Egypt's new liberal age, investments were diverted to major infrastructural projects and new economy projects in attempts to capture a share of global business. The upper-middle class professionals with cosmopolitan capital who staff internationally oriented workplaces fit this national narrative and project. They are portrayed as mediators between local and global, representatives of a modern, cosmopolitan savvy Egypt that is able to face the unruly waters of the global era. Their cosmopolitan capital carries important premiums. It provides access to up-market jobs and a rapidly expanding range of upscale venues for consumption, and signals belonging in upscale Cairo. Yet, the up-market segment of the economy that employed these upper-middle class professionals has remained limited in size and was highly dependent on Egypt's fragile 'liberal' economic experiment. The crisis that has plagued the Egyptian economy since 2000 exposed its fragility. Many were afraid of getting fired, and anxiously held on to jobs they experienced as taxing, underpaid, or unrewarding. In upper-middle class circles the increasingly tight and insecure labor market and the resulting heightened competition for up-market jobs gave rise to a race for better and more exclusive qualifications.

Spatializing Reforms

Cairo, Egypt's capital and major city, the economic, political, social, and cultural hub of the country and its main node for transnational networks, has been central to the materialization of Egypt's neoliberal project. Cairo's peculiar feel, with its skyscrapers, fancy cars, and glimmer, reflects this central role. Up-market circuits of consumption and production—set apart by conspicuously cosmopolitan references and comparatively high prices—increasingly dominate more affluent areas of Cairo. They have come to constitute an upscale Cairo set amid largely neglected surroundings. This upscale Cairo is geared to and inhabited by a small section of the urban population, among others upper-middle class professionals. Conspicuously cosmopolitan lifestyles within the bounds of upper-middle class (religious) propriety have become crucial markers of privileged class membership. Within upper-middle class circles, such cosmopolitan ambitions and referencing are both normative and self-evident. Upper-middle class cosmopolitan lifestyles have, moreover, come to represent ideal lifestyles, even normative standards in commercials, music videos, and movies that portray a young, modern Egypt. This hegemony took shape in the context of Egypt's dependent integration into diverse global economic networks, importantly United States development aid and World Bank- and IMF-induced structural adjustment programs.

The upscale coffee shops that I have discussed extensively are part of upscale Cairo, yet more specifically, constitute an emergent young, upper-middle class urban presence. These social spaces, and their mixed-gender sociabilities, had an embryonic presence in upper-middle class socializing practices, in work and study spaces, as well as in imaginations of and desire for *barra*, a vaguely territorialized First World abroad. From the mid-1990s onward, they have provided upper-middle class professionals with new opportunities for socializing, finding partners, and other forms of networking and self-presentation. Coffee shops largely circumvent negative associations with the West. They heed to religious sensibilities and gendered notions of propriety, yet intimate a sense of First World inclusion. The casual mixed-gender sociabilities that characterize social life in these coffee shops are confined to such class-specific, closed, and exclusive spaces. Public leisure spaces like the upscale coffee shop express and help constitute not only a new class culture, but also new forms of social distance and segregation within the city.

A casual mixed-gender public and the presence of young, professional women are among the most important markers of Cairo's globally up-to-date exclusive modernity. While upscale spaces rely on the public presence of young upper-middle class women, the latter's public routines are fragile and depend on class-specific spaces and social avoidance and closure. They provide important rationales for the social avoidance and segregation that has become a common feature of Cairo's cityscape. Their bodies have become battlegrounds for new class configurations and contestations, illustrating both power and fragility of Cairo's upper-middle class in Egypt's new liberal age.

Cairo's public spaces have become more and more segmented as they map unto a starkly polarized income distribution. The previously outlying districts of Mohandisseen, Maadi, and Heliopolis and their desert expanses along the three main highways out of Cairo increasingly constitute *the* city for many upper-middle class Cairenes. Upscale clusters of housing complexes, malls, private schools, universities, hospitals, amusement parks, and hotels have sprung up along these three main arteries. They have contributed to a doubling of the urban surface area in the span of a few years, radically changing Cairo's lived geography and unraveling its urban fabric.

Recipe for a Divided Nation

Arjun Appadurai's essay on a world of disjunctive global flows (1990) proposed a way of understanding everyday manifestations of globalization that has become highly influential in anthropological studies. It offers ways of understanding the complex and disjunctive character of 'globalization,' and directs attention to the augmented role of imagination in a world of global flows of images and ideas. Yet, as this study has shown, such global flows have to be located in global and local histories of inequality and dominance. They feed into local social hierarchies and are taken up as forms of cultural distinction. New cosmopolitan lifestyles and matrices of belonging come into being through an intricate convergence of local distinctive class cultures and transnational economic and cultural flows. Now that Cairo has 'returned' to the global market, being connected, or conversely, being disconnected from *barra* (abroad) has again become a major denominator of difference and distinction. The social divisions of the Egyptian new liberal age gather privileged segments of Cairo's population in exclusive, conspicuously cosmopolitan spaces of work, consumption, leisure, and residence. Since these spaces are largely closed off from Cairo's other realities, they are instrumental in establishing cosmopolitan referents and standards, as well as a sense of ease and affluence as normative and self-evident features of life in upscale Cairo. In this context, hybridity and cosmopolitan savvy carry an unmistakable subtext of class-based privilege.

Eric Denis has directed attention to the parallels between Egypt's pre-Second World War liberal age and Egypt's new liberal era (1997, 2006). At the start of the twenty-first century, such comparisons seem justified. Both periods are marked by foreign dependence, conspicuously cosmopolitan lifestyles, vast social inequalities, and the disenfranchisement of the majority of the population. Elite versus popular social worlds, orientations, and lifestyles are once more increasingly figured in terms of the conspicuously cosmopolitan versus the explicitly localized. The renewed importance of cosmopolitan knowledge, skills, and tastes reproduces erstwhile lines of social stratification based on connections to the outside. Nostalgic references to pre-Nasser aristocratic times are increasingly common, and Cairo has seen the reterritorialization of an exclusive First World in upscale Cairo in the form of exclusive, conspicuously cosmopolitan, and at times, nostalgic spaces that are guarded against the city's other realities. Cairo's professional middle class had always been characterized by socioeconomic and cultural heterogeneity. However, in Egypt's new liberal age this middle class has become more and more segmented, and socioeconomic and cultural hierarchies and lines of segregation are increasingly tangible and rigid. As Anthony D. King argues, in Southern cities like Cairo "the inherently separationist structure of the colonial city and its asymmetrical power relations are being continuously reinvented, albeit in a new, internal colonialist form" (2004:142).

Upper-middle class professionals are the inhabitants of an upscale Cairo that consists of interconnected spaces that are closed off from other social worlds and lives. Such closure is, of course, mere semblance since these upscale spaces depend on the labor of working and lower-middle class Cairenes. These spaces are, however, exclusionary in the sense that they are defined and dominated by elite privileges, hierarchies, and preferences. These are spaces where, in contrast to the rest of the metropolis, privileged Cairenes are "able to impose their own code of behaviour—including rules of deference—onto the city' (Caldeira 2000:319).

Egypt's neoliberal project entails both a 'search for the global'—attempts to capture global business and reinvigorate the private sector through investments in infrastructure, showcase projects, and a range of subsidies to the private sector—*and* structural adjustment policies that aim at the downsizing of state budgets and relinquishing of the state's patronage role. These twin components of the neoliberal project can be seen as prescriptions for a divided nation. While the search for the global entails the territorialization of First World spaces in the urban landscape, structural adjustment policies seem to spell out Third World futures for the surrounding social landscape.

Feelings of exclusion from and desire for First World affluence, sophistication, and membership have long histories in postcolonial settings like Egypt. Those sections of society that have been the beneficiaries of economic restructuring, liberalization, and integration into global economic networks are able to act upon such desires. They can inhabit Cairo's territorializations of the First World, which increasingly negate previous contradictory combinations of a desire for and a felt exclusion from global dreams. The renewed popularity of the pre-Nasser Khedival period signals the abandonment of the more inclusive Nasser-era developmental project. It speaks of an increased acceptability of soaring social inequalities and the disenfranchisement of the vast majority of Egypt's population. Like those earlier times, Egypt's new liberal age awards exclusive, cosmopolitan lives to select, privileged segments of the population.

The question is what is produced around and beyond these reterritorialized First World spaces. Following Kirsten Koptiuch's assertion that a Third World is emerging in Western cities, we might say that middle class Cairo has seen materializations of a Third World (1997). It is a Third World in which social rights are rescinded and older national developmental narratives that informed middle class aspirations have been declared all but irrelevant. Redundant middle class professionals are urged to turn to informal practices and projects that were once figured as signs of tradition or lack of development, but are now promoted as paragons of capitalist savvy from below. These young professionals are therefore forced to negotiate more complex ways of being in the nation than their more privileged counterparts. They experience the abjection that James Ferguson considers central to contemporary African predicaments, "a combination of an acute awareness of a privileged 'first-class' world, together with an increasing social and economic disconnection from it. . . ." (2002:559; cf. 1999). While Cairo's exclusive First World spaces offer them merely simulacra of inclusion, many are not ready to give up on expectations of a middle class life either, and refuse to resign to the 'Third World' futures that are spelled out for them. Their contestations of neoliberal narratives and projects may give rise to other national stories yet to be dreamt.

Notes

1   According to Ragui Assaad and Malak Rouchdy, in the mid-1990s a quarter of
    the Egyptian population was poor by any standards, while another quarter was
    on the margins of poverty (1999:11). Unemployment had increased and real
    wages had decreased significantly throughout the 1980s and 1990s (see Assaad
    2002, Awad 1999).

2   In 2002 LE1,000 was worth between €200 and €250.

3   The highly segmented nature of Egyptian society and concomitant class
    differences limit the usefulness of aggregate data at the national and even local
    level. The labor force participation of women provides a good example. In 1998,
    participation of urban unmarried women with intermediate education was
    estimated at 37.3 percent, compared to 88 percent of those with a university degree
    (Assaad 2002:24). In light of these vast differences, national figures not only have
    limited explanatory value, but they can even obfuscate the existence of opposite
    trends in different segments.

    Trends in the Greater Cairo region are likely to differ significantly from other
    regions, whether rural or urban, because of the longstanding concentration of
    socioeconomic and political resources in the region. Such divergences between
    Cairo and the rest of Egypt are crucial to this study. Neoliberal policies and 'global
    city formation' have likely furthered Cairo's exceptionalism.

4   The Egyptian middle class has been taken to encompass both professionals
    and more affluent sections of the self-employed or owners of small businesses
    (see, e.g., Amin 2000:31–37; Abdel Moati 2002, Chapter Five). Following Pierre
    Bourdieu, we might define the professional middle class as consisting of those
    people who (nominally) base their middle class position on their educational,
    rather than economic, capital—such as professionals, bureaucrats, administrative
    personnel. Even though these kinds of capital are not mutually exclusive and a
    person might possess a combination of capitals, one can distinguish between
    fractions that primarily depend on one or the other form of capital for their
    reproduction (Bourdieu 1984:115). The share of professional and technical staff in

the Cairo governerate labor force (which represents only part of the Greater Cairo metropolitan area) provides an indication of the size of this urban professional middle class. In 1999 it was estimated at 31 percent, versus 19.2 percent on the national level (UNDP 2001:147).

5 Differences between the spoken, explicitly localized language, *'ammiyya*, and written, standard Arabic, *fusha*, are large in Egypt. While I grew comfortable in *'ammiyya*, my understanding of written standard Arabic has remained more limited. Ghada Tantawi helped me to review some of the Egyptian literature on the middle class.

6 In the mid-1970s consumption goods made up one-third of total imports, versus a mere 10 percent in the late 1960s (Jankowski 2000:173).

7 Alan Richards and John Waterbury (1996) suggest that labor migration did actually pick up again after the Gulf war, and that Libya has provided additional employment opportunities. However, they also argue that labor migration was not sufficient to keep pace with the growth of the Egyptian workforce (1996:385). In 2002, openings for labor migration were commonly perceived to be extremely limited. People claimed that Asians were hired for jobs that did not specifically require Arabic because they were supposedly many times 'cheaper' than Egyptians or other Arab labor migrants. Moreover, a growing number of local professionals now fill the vacancies that in earlier decades were the exclusive domain of Arab migrant workers (cf. Abdel Moati 2002:336–38).

8 See, for example, Fatma Farag, "Back to the dust," *Al-Ahram Weekly* (Issue 544, 26 July–1 August 2001).

9 See, for example, Gamal Essam El-Din, "Subsidise or Die," *Al-Ahram Weekly* (Issue 661, 23–29 October 2003) and Sherine Abdel-Razek, "Bearing the Burden," *Al-Ahram Weekly* (Issue 686, 15–21 April 2004).

10 Richard H. Adams Jr. suggests that this is the case (2000:267–68). UNDP reports similarly indicate risen levels of social inequality. Whereas the Gini coefficient for Cairo in 1995 was 33.7, in 2000 it had risen to 39, the highest in the country (UNDP 2001:158; UNDP 1999:160). According to 'human development indexes' (a combination of indexes for health, education, and income), Greater Cairo had three out of five highest and three out of five lowest scoring areas in the country (UNDP 2003:44).

Actual social inequality might be considerably higher than the quoted statistics indicate. Egyptian income distribution statistics are rather unreliable, as Bartsch has noted. He found that half of the country's consumer expenditure was missing from the statistics on which these income distribution figures are based. Most of the missing expenditure is likely to belong to a small section of affluent households (discussed in Mitchell 2002:286–87).

11 The same imagery featured on the website of the Future Generation Foundation. The Foundation optimistically echoed IMF policies that suggest that eventually, greater integration into the global market will bring improved life standards for everyone. According to its mission statement, the foundation's aim was to "contribute to Egypt's economic growth and global competitiveness efforts" by "helping in upgrading local corporate culture." These upgraded human resources "will translate into greater fiscal well-being for the nation at large, a leading role

in the regional economy, and a strong position on the global market" (http://www.fgf-egypt.com/english/foundation/fgf14.asp [accessed July 2003]).

12 As Lila Abu-Lughod notes, "while the everyday forms of piety that are so much a part of life in Egypt are occasionally reflected in the popular serials—older characters or simple peasants are sometimes shown praying or using religious phrases—the new forms of piety are never portrayed. One never sees the young in the cities asserting an Islamic identity. . ." (1993:399). The *higaab* is the most common sign of such Islamic identities. While, in the early years of the twenty-first century there was a growing offer of religious programming (Quran recitations, religious sermons and programs, and religious television serials), religious programs were clearly set apart from other types of programming (ibid., cf. Abu-Lughod 1995). The result was a portrayal of modern Egyptian everyday life as largely secular and often relatively affluent, in which only older and more 'traditional' people engage in religious practices.

13 This is a probably unwitting reworking of the official name, *Jiil al-Mustaqbal*, the Future Generation.

14 Such a wholesale reinvention of present, future, and past is certainly not unique to Egypt. Emanuela Guano discerns a similar invention of such an industrial past—a move she terms "historical cannibalism"—in the development of a gentrified 'First World' waterfront in Buenos Aires (2002:189).

15 While upper-middle class cosmopolitan lifestyles had come to represent common advertising ideals, television commercials also portrayed and spoke to less affluent consumers. This diversity mirrors the diverse languages of advertising that Rajagopal (2001, see also Rajagopal 1999) discerns in India's television landscape. Different viewers are educated differently into national consumer citizenship. An Ariel commercial, for example, employed the tested formula of door-to-door visits in popular areas, where faithful female consumers were rewarded with a locally sensible gift, in this case golden coins. Egyptian state television also featured many humorous commercials that played on well-known television epitomes of *sha'bi* characters. The characters, themes, and phrases of these commercials were readily taken up in everyday humor.

16 Cf. Bayat and Denis 2000, which includes maps of Cairo that detail the distribution of educational attainment in Cairo.

17 Besides these exclusive compounds, there were also new housing projects in the desert that catered to less affluent Cairenes. Some privately built gated communities catered to middle to upper-middle class Cairenes with a higher building density and a large share of high-rise apartment buildings, rather than villas (Kuppinger 2004). Public housing projects offered affordable housing to lower-middle to middle class Cairenes.

From the mid-1970s onward, the government has tried to divert Cairo's population growth to new cities in the desert around Cairo (Stewart 1999:140). While the relatively nearby Sixth of October City has been successful, more outlying cities have not attracted the predicted numbers of inhabitants. These cities suffered from lack of facilities and their distance from Cairo and the lack of good transportation made them unattractive for people whose work and social lives remained located in the city. The latest public addition to Cairo is New Cairo, located at the outskirts of Nasser City. Some of New Cairo's spaciously laid-out apartment blocks offer affordable housing to (lower) middle class Cairenes (cf. De Koning 2001).

18 These central terms in Egyptian social life are discussed elaborately by, among others, Armbrust (1996:26–27), Singerman (1997:11–14), Ghannam 2002.

19 A law stipulating this employment guarantee for university graduates was promulgated in 1961; a second law in 1964 extended this right to holders of degrees from higher institutes and secondary technical education. This right has been effectively abrogated through a gradual increase in the waiting period for a guaranteed job, from ten months in 1982 to five or six years in 1987 and thirteen years in 1995 (Tourné 2003:22ff.).

20 According to official figures, which tend to overstate actual school attendance, overall enrollment in basic and secondary education was 42 percent in 1960 (women only: 32.1 percent); by 2000/2001 it had risen to 86 percent (women only: 83 percent) (UNDP 2003:125). The enrollment in higher education (universities and higher institutes) went up from 6.9 percent of those between 17 and 22 in 1970 to 20.2 percent in 1996 (Galal 2002:2).

21 Sixty-six percent of the private schools were located in Greater Cairo (taken here to be Cairo governorate and urban Giza) versus merely 28.5 percent of the public schools (calculated from unpublished ministry of education statistics).

22 Until the mid 1990s Egypt had only one private university, the American University in Cairo (AUC). Despite debates about allowing private universities to operate in Egypt beginning as early as the late 1970s, the establishment of private universities long remained a touchy political issue (Waterbury 1983:241). However, this 'affront' to Nasserite educational and developmental philosophy was ratified in the mid-1990s. In 1996 four new private universities were authorized. In 2003 a French and a German university opened their doors. These private universities are all located on the outskirts of Cairo.

23 The choice to move from private intermediate to public high school was motivated by the belief that private 'Arabic' secondary schools are actually worse than governmental ones. The former were seen as catering to those pupils who did not score well in the preparatory school exams and were therefore not eligible for a place in a governmental high school.

24 In 1997, fifty-eight foreign tourists and four Egyptian policemen were killed in an Islamist attack at a pharaonic site in Luxor.

25 Professionals who had been educated in French or German commonly used the same mix of Arabic and English, except when all persons present had followed similar educational trajectories. In these settings they could indulge in the French-Arabic or German-Arabic pidgins of their school days.

26 A number of upper-middle class professionals used 'A- and B-classes' to talk about class in Egypt. These terms derive from marketing terminology. Maureen O'Daugherty similarly notes that middle class Brazilians use these terms to talk about class (2002:97). The use of such terms indicates familiarity with marketing discourses and the growing importance of these discourses to imaginations of society. Income differences and the related ability to consume were clearly seen as distinguishing characteristics within Cairo's upper-middle class. Those who used the terminology seemed to employ 'A-class' primarily for those who could

engage in lavish cosmopolitan consumption, for example, frequent travel abroad. It is striking that only A- and B-classes were ever mentioned. As both these consumption segments fall within the upper-middle class/elite, it seems that anyone below this income threshold was simply irrelevant to such discussions of Egypt's new generation or Cairo's new urban landscape.

27 While distribution was initially restricted to Cairo, since 2003 the magazine has also been distributed in a small number of locations in Alexandria.

28 Whereas unemployment was nearly nonexistent among those who could at most read and write, it was extremely high among those with an intermediate degree, and remained considerable among men and women with a higher education. The available statistics show an increase in the numbers of highly educated, unemployed men between twenty-two and thirty-five from 10 percent in 1988 to 16 percent in 1998. Among their female counterparts there was an increase from 18 percent to 26 percent (Amer 2002:232). Overall unemployment was predominantly concentrated in the younger generations, among new entrants into the labor market (Assaad 2002:34). Ragui Assaad, however, argues that unlike other regions, Greater Cairo has actually experienced falling unemployment ratios (2002:26). He does not specify how this decline is distributed with respect to educational status. Though such a divergent trend in metropolitan Cairo would be important with respect to the present study, a lack of further data makes it difficult to draw any conclusions. These figures cover the years before the economic slowdown that set in after 2000. During the years in which this study was conducted, the situation is likely to have worsened considerably.

29 Since it is nearly impossible to delineate this up-market sector, it is difficult to indicate its size. The number of employees in foreign enterprises hardly captures the size of this up-market segment. Despite a significant growth in the number of people employed in foreign enterprises, their total was estimated at a mere 0.15 percent of the total number of employed persons nationwide (from 0 in 1976 to 10,000 in 1986 and 23,000 in 1996) (UNDP 2001:97). The percentage of students in private secondary general education provides an indication of the share of the upper-middle class in Cairo's professional middle class. In Greater Cairo, 20 percent of the students in secondary general education attended private schools in 1999/2000, versus 8.5 percent nationwide (calculated from statistics of the ministry of education). These numbers would indicate that the relative share of the upper-middle class lies between 15 and 20 percent of Cairo's professional middle class, and around 5 to 7 percent of all Cairenes. These estimates concur with Timothy Mitchell's estimate that only 5 percent of Egypt's population could afford to engage in the consumption of upscale goods and services (2002:286–87).

30 In 2002, LE1,000 was equivalent to €250, devaluating to €200 toward the end of the year. Average per capita income was estimated at some LE560 per month (calculated from http://devdata.worldbank.org).

31 See, for example, *Al-Ahram Weekly*'s report on the 2004 conference of the NDP, the ruling party. It discusses Gamal Mubarak's dominance in the NDP, his increased influence on policy directions, and his outspoken preference for economic liberalization and further integration into the global market (http://weekly.ahram.org.eg/2004/709/fr1.htm) (accessed December 14, 2008).

32 http://www.fgf-egypt.com/english/foundation/fgf14.asp (accessed July 2003).

33 Cf. Abdel Malek in *Al-Ahram Weekly* (Issue 611, 7–13 November 2002) for similar doubts about the efficacy of the Fund.

34 *Law faatak il-miirii, itmarragh fi turaabu.*

35 Fatma Farag, 'Back to the dust,' *Al-Ahram Weekly* (Issue 544, 26 July–1 August 2001). Whereas 'dust' obviously refers to the saying, it also evokes some widely shared associations with government employment: dusty offices overstaffed with listless employees. Since government employment is so widely associated with bad pay, severely overstaffed offices and stagnant careers, an ironic reading would suggest that all these job seekers fight for is dust.

36 Despite the de facto abolishment of employment guarantees and stated intentions to curb or even downsize the bureaucracy, the number of civil servants has continued to grow steadily. Ragui Assaad argues that this growth is mainly due to the greater persistence of older, mostly female civil servants in government employment. This greater persistence is not sufficiently compensated by a lower rate of hiring (2002:45).

37 *Hubb fi hadabit al-haram* ('Love at the Pyramids Plateau,' 1984) is based on a short story by Naguib Mahfouz that was published in 1979. The film addresses the problems of Ali, a university graduate who works in the government bureaucracy. He comes from an educated family and his neighbors respectfully address his father with *effendi*, the now somewhat archaic title for the educated. He falls in love with a new colleague of his, but they cannot get married because of his dire financial situation. The film tells the story of their struggle to remain true to their mutual love, despite adverse circumstances.

38 In 2002 the Egyptian parliament accepted a new labor law that grants employers in the private sector more extensive rights to fire employees. While this 'liberal' labor legislation abrogated many of the legal protections of the older Nasser-era law, the freedom of independent collective organization, strikes, or bargaining remains severely curtailed (Fergany 1998).

39 Cf. Armbrust (1996:225 n.6). I also noted a related expression that equates being a foreigner/Westerner with a higher level of expertise. *Il-agnabi bita'na* literally means 'our (Western) foreigner,' but is used in the sense of 'our own expert.'

40 Eileen Moyer's work on street workers in Dar es Salaam, for example, shows that while large parts of the educated middle class experience declining living standards and the children of state employees have a hard time reproducing their parents' middle class living standard, Tanzania's 'liberal era' has brought new chances in the urban informal sector for rural-to-urban migrants, who were previously banned from the city (Moyer 2003, see, e.g., also Zhang 2002 and Anagnost 2004, who discuss the differential impact of China's late socialist phase). While this might be an obvious point, the social locatedness of such stories of enfranchisement and disenfranchisement is, for example, lacking in Achille Mbembe and Janet Roitman's otherwise insightful discussion (1995) of the 'crisis of the subject' in the wake of the collapse of the Cameroonian state, which implicitly tells a clearly middle class story.

41 Colonial and imperial histories provide important inspiration for affluent lifestyles in postcolonial and postimperial settings. These 'colonial' styles

constitute one of the distinctive, privileged styles of First World spaces across the world. They rehearse specific local colonial and postcolonial trajectories, as, for example, Anthony D. King argues with respect to Indian compounds whose names refer to Oxford or Cambridge (2004:133).

42　While *higaab* is used to refer to 'the veil' in a general sense, it also denotes a more specific form of the veil, the headscarf, as distinct from other forms of covering: the *khimaar*, the veil covering the upper part of the body, and the *niqaab*, the full body cover with face veil. The headscarf, often worn with tight yet covering clothes in matching colors, was the most common form of dress among upper-middle class *muhaggabaat*. Some *muhaggabaat* would opt for a style one could call 'Islamic chic,' consisting of flowing, smartly cut robes with a matching scarf.

43　Restaurants that cater to the same young affluent public, like TGI Friday's and Chili's, are, in contrast, franchises of North American chains.

44　Mona Abaza notes that *bii'a* has eclipsed *baladi* as a derogatory term. In contrast to my argument, she states that the term is used to designate the bad taste of the lower classes (2001:120, n. 13).

45　Mona Abaza comments on a similar deployment of such purified popular traditions in Cairo's shopping malls (2001b:111). This 'traditional Egyptian' style had become increasingly common in less exclusive establishments, particularly during Ramadan. The more widespread adoption of this style has resulted in a mixing of actually existing local practices with their orientalistic renditions, which has diminished some of its more flagrant orientalistic portent.

46　For a detailed discussion of the story see *Al-Ahram Weekly*, 28 February–6 March 2002, (http://weekly.ahram.org.eg/2002/577/eg9.htm#3, accessed December 14, 2008). A short notice in the 14–20 March 2002 issue announces the arrest of the culprit who allegedly sent the e-mails.

47　While people's reports on veiling are part of contentious and highly politicized analyses of the development of religiosity in society, they generally noted a recent increase of *muhaggabaat* in the upper-middle class. Changes in a number of upper-middle class companies confirmed such an increase. Whereas *muhaggabaat* used to present a rare sight in most up-market companies and institutions, significant numbers of their female employees began wearing the veil from the late 1990s onward.

48　Maroush was a crossover between a *'ahwa baladi* and a coffee shop. It was located on the sidewalk of a busy square in Mohandisseen. Maroush presented an exception to the general rule that coffee shops with an upper-middle class public are closed off from views from the street. It, however, did attract a middle to upper-middle class public that would equally frequent coffee shops.

49　See Wilson for a critique of the universalistic assumptions regarding the male gaze (2001:83).

50　Streets in elite areas like Zamalek and Maadi differ significantly from streets in popular areas, as do shopping streets from big thoroughfares and more residential streets. Despite such significant differences, a dominant male presence and women's liminality as marginalized passersby are shared features of Cairo's street life. Streets moreover share a certain indeterminacy with respect to class. Some popular areas constitute marked exceptions to these gendered definitions of the street, while women peddlers who occupy sidewalks in central streets defy notions of women's liminality.

51 In *Campus Magazine*, Arabic words are transcribed according to an informal transcription system that many Cairenes use in their English language e-mail communications. The *'ain* (ع) is represented by a 3, the *hah* (ح) by a 7, and the *qaf* (ق) and *hamza* by a 2. *Suguq* thus becomes sogo2 and, e.g., *higaab* is written as 7igab.

Bibliography

Abaza, Mona

    2001   "Shopping Malls, Consumer Culture and the Reshaping of Public Space in Egypt," *Theory, Culture & Society* 18(5):97–122.

    2006   *The Changing Consumer Cultures in Modern Egypt: Cairo's Urban Reshaping.* Cairo: The American University in Cairo Press.

Abdel-Fadil, Mahmoud

    1980   *The Political Economy of Nasserism: A Study in Employment and Income Distribution Policies in Urban Egypt, 1952–72.* Cambridge: Cambridge University Press.

Abdel Moati, Abdel Basset

    2002   *It-tabaqaat il-igtimaa'iyya wa mustaqbil Masr* [Social Classes and Egypt's Future]. Egypt 2020 Library. Cairo: Dar al-Merit.

Abdelrahman, Maha M.

    2004   *Civil Society Exposed: The Politics of NGOs in Egypt.* Cairo: The American University in Cairo Press.

    2005   "Consumerism, Islam and Fashion in Egypt Today." Paper presented at the conference "Muslim Fashions–Fashionable Muslims," Amsterdam, 15–16 April 2005.

    2007   "NGOs and the Dynamics of the Egyptian Labour Market," *Development in Practice* 17(1):78–84.

Abécassis, Frédéric et al.

    1997   "Histoires de Familles: Processus d'Appropriation des Langues Étrangères en Égypte, au XXe Siècle," *Égypte/Monde Arabe* 29(1):83–99.

Abu-Lughod, Janet L.

    1971   *1001 Years of the City Victorious*. Princeton: Princeton University Press.

Abu-Lughod, Lila

    1993   "Finding a Place for Islam: Egyptian Television Serials and the National Interest," *Public Culture* 5:493–513.

           "Movie Stars and Islamic Moralism in Egypt," *Social Text* 42:55–67.

    2005   *Dramas of Nationhood: The Politics of Television in Egypt*. Chicago: Chicago University Press.

Abu-Lughod, Lila, ed.

    1998   *Remaking Women: Feminism and Modernity in the Middle East*. Cairo: The American University in Cairo Press.

Adams, Richard H. Jr.

    2000   "Evaluating the Process of Development in Egypt, 1980–97," *International Journal of Middle East Studies* 32:255–75.

Ahmed, Leila

    1992   *Women and Gender in Islam*. New Haven: Yale University Press.

Amer, Mona

    2002   "Youth Labor Market Trajectories: A Comparison of the 1980s and 1990s." In *The Egyptian Labor Market in an Era of Reform*. Ragui Assaad, ed., 233–57. Cairo: The American University in Cairo Press.

Amin, Galal

    1999   "Globalization, Consumption Patterns and Human Development in Egypt." ERF Working Paper 9929. Electronic Document. http://www.erf.org.eg/uploadpath/pdf/9929.pdf (accessed March 10, 2004).

    2000   *Whatever Happened to the Egyptians: Changes in Egyptian Society from 1950 to the Present*. Cairo: The American University in Cairo Press.

Anagnost, Ann

    2004   "The Corporeal Politics of Quality *(Suzhi)*," *Public Culture* 16(2):189–208.

Anderson, Benedict

    1991   *Imagined Communities: Reflections on the Origin and Spread of Nationalism*. Revised ed. [1983]. London: Verso.

Appadurai, Arjun

    1990   "Disjuncture and Difference in the Global Cultural Economy," *Public Culture* 2(2):244–55.

Armbrust, Walter

    1996   *Mass Culture and Modernism in Egypt*. Cambridge: Cambridge University Press.

1998   "When the Lights Go Down in Cairo: Cinema as Secular Ritual," *Visual Anthropology* 10(2–4):413–42.

1999   "Bourgeois Leisure and Egyptian Media Fantasies." In *New Media in the Muslim World: The Emerging Public Sphere*. Dale F. Eickelman and Jon W. Anderson, eds., 106–32. Bloomington: Indiana University Press.

Assaad, Ragui

1997   "The Effects of Public Sector Hiring and Compensation Policies on the Egyptian Labor Market," *The World Bank Economic Review* 11(1):85–118.

2002   "The Transformation of the Egyptian Labor Market: 1988–98." In *The Egyptian Labor Market in an Era of Reform*. Ragui Assaad, ed., 3–64. Cairo: The American University in Cairo Press.

Assaad, Ragui and Malak Rouchdy

1999   "Poverty and Poverty Alleviation Strategies in Egypt," *Cairo Papers in Social Science* 22(1).

Awad, Ibrahim

1999   "Employment Policy under Economic Reform," *Cairo Papers in Social Science* 21(3):50–72.

Ayubi, Nazih N.M.

1982   "Implementation Capability and Political Feasibility of the Open Door Policy in Egypt." In *Rich and Poor States in the Middle East: Egypt and the New Arab Order*. Malcolm Kerr and El-Sayyed Yassin, eds., 349–413. *Cairo:* The American University in Cairo Press.

Baraka, Magda

1998   *The Egyptian Upper Class between Revolutions*. Reading, NY: Ithaca Press.

Barsoum, Ghada Fakhry

1999   "Jobs for *"Wilad al-nas"*: The Jobs Dilemma of Female Graduates in Egypt." MA thesis, American University in Cairo.

Battesti Vincent

2006   "The Giza Zoo: Reappropriating Public Spaces, Reimaging Urban Beauty." In *Cairo Cosmopolitan: Politics, Culture, and Space in the New Middle East*. Diane Singerman and Paul Amar, eds., 489–512. Cairo: The American University in Cairo Press.

Bayat, Asef

2002   "Piety, Privilege and Egyptian Youth," *ISIM Newsletter* 10(02):24.

Bayat, Asef and Eric Denis

    2000   "Who is Afraid of *Ashwaiyyat*," *Environment & Urbanization* 12(2):185–99.

Beal, E. Anne

    2000   "Real Jordanians Don't Decorate Like That! The Politics of Taste among Amman's Elites," *City & Society* 12(2):65–94.

Bondi, Liz and Mona Domosh

    1998   "On the Contours of Public Space: A Tale of Three Women," *Antipode* 30(3):270–89.

Bourdieu, Pierre

    1984   *Distinction: A Social Critique of the Judgment of Taste.* Translated by Richard Nice. London: Routledge.

    1986   "The Forms of Capital." In *Handbook of Theory and Research for the Sociology of Education.* J.G. Richardson, ed., 241–58. New York: Greenwood Press.

Buck-Morss, Susan

    1995   "The City as Dreamworld and Catastrophe," *October* 73:3–26.

Caldeira, Teresa P.R.

    2000   *City of Walls: Crime, Segregation, and Citizenship in Sao Paulo.* Berkeley and Los Angeles: University of California Press.

Calhoun, Craig

    2003   "'Belonging' in the Cosmopolitan Imaginary," *Ethnicities* 3(4):531–68.

de Certeau, Michel

    1984   *The Practice of Everyday Life.* Berkeley: University of California Press.

Cheah, P.

    1998   "Introduction Part II: The Cosmopolitical—Today." In *Cosmopolitics: Thinking and Feeling beyond the Nation.* P. Cheah and B. Robbins, eds., 20–41. Minneapolis: University of Minnesota Press.

Clammer, John

    2003   "Globalisation, Class, Consumption and Civil Society in Southeast Asian Cities," *Urban Studies* 40(2):403–19.

Cochran, Judith

    1986   *Education in Egypt.* London: Croom Helm.

Cole, Donald P. and Soraya Altorki

    1998   *Bedouin, Settlers and Holiday Makers: Egypt's Changing Northwest Coast.* Cairo: The American University in Cairo Press.

Dawson, Ashley and Brent Hayes Edwards

    2004   "Introduction: Global Cities of the South," *Social Text* 22(4):1–7.

Denis, Eric
    1997   "Urban Planning and Growth in Cairo," *Middle East Report*, Winter 1997:7–12.
    2006   "Cairo as Neo-liberal Capital? From Walled City to Gated Communities." In *Cairo Cosmopolitan: Politics, Culture, and Space in the New Middle East.* Diane Singerman and Paul Amar, eds., 47–72. Cairo: The American University in Cairo Press.

Elsheshtawy, Yasser
    2006   "From Dubai to Cairo: Competing Global Cities, Models and Shifting Centers of Influence?" In *Cairo Cosmopolitan: Politics, Culture, and Space in the New Middle East.* Diane Singerman and Paul Amar, eds., 235–50. Cairo: The American University in Cairo Press.

Elyachar, Julia
    2002   "Empowerment Money: The World Bank, Non-Governmental Organizations, and the Value of Culture in Egypt," *Public Culture* 14(3):493–513.
    2003   "Mappings of Power: The State, NGOs, and International Organizations in the Informal Economy of Cairo," *CSSH* 45(3):571–605.
    2005   *Markets of Dispossession: NGOs, Economic Development and the State in Cairo.* Durham and London: Duke University Press.

El-Khishin, Khaled
    2003   "Bidding for 'Global City' Status: A Prescription for Sustaining Cairo's Financial Health," *Cities* 20(2):129–34.

Fergany, Nader
    1998   "Impact of the Proposed Labour Law on Labour Market Flexibility and Social Conditions in Egypt: A Preliminary Assessment." Electronic document. http://www.almishkat.org/engdoc98/labour_law/labour_law.htm#3 (accessed February 27, 2005).

Ferguson, James
    1999   *Expectations of Modernity: Myths and Meanings of Urban Life on the Zambian Copperbelt.* Berkeley: University of California Press.
    2002   "Of Mimicry and Membership: Africans and the 'New World Society,'" *Cultural Anthropology* 17(4):551–69.

Ferguson, James and Akhil Gupta
    2002   "Spatializing States: Toward an Ethnography of Neoliberal Governmentality," *American Ethnologist* 29(4):981–1002.

Fernandes, Leela

2000a "Nationalizing 'the Global': Media Images, Cultural Politics and the Middle Class in India," *Media, Culture & Society* 22:611–28.

2000b "Restructuring the New Middle Class in Liberalizing India," *Comparative Studies of South Asia, Africa and the Middle East* 20:88–104.

2004 "The Politics of Forgetting: Class Politics, State Power and the Restructuring of Urban Space in India," *Urban Studies* 41(12):2415–2430.

Fine, Ben

2000 "The Developmental State is Dead—Long Live Social Capital?" *Development and Change* 30:1–19.

Friedman, Jonathan

2003 "Globalizing Languages: Ideologies and Realities of the Contemporary Global System," *American Anthropologist* 105(4):744–52.

Galal, Ahmed

2002 "The Paradox of Education and Employment in Egypt." Electronic document. http://www.worldbank.org/wbi/mdf/mdf4/papers/galal.pdf (accessed March 10, 2004).

Ghannam, Farha

2002 *Remaking the Modern in a Global Cairo: Space, Relocation, and the Politics of Identity.* Berkeley: University of California Press.

Gordon, Joel

2000 "Nasser 56/Cairo 96." In *Mass Mediations: New Approaches to Popular Culture in the Middle East and Beyond*, Walter Armbrust, ed., 161–81. Berkeley: University of California Press.

2002 *Revolutionary Melodrama: Popular Film and Civic Identity in Nasser's Egypt.* Chicago: University of Chicago Press.

Guano, Emanuela

2002 "Spectacles of Modernity: Transnational Imagination and Local Hegemonies in Neoliberal Buenos Aires," *Cultural Anthropology* 17(2):181–209.

Gupta, Akhil

1992 "The Song of the Nonaligned World: Transnational Identities and the Reinscription of Space in Late Capitalism," *Cultural Anthropology* 7(1):63–79.

Haeri, Niloofar

 1997 "The Reproduction of Symbolic Capital: Language, State and Class in Egypt," *Current Anthropology* 38(5):795–816.

Hamel, Rainer E.

 1998 "On Language, State, and Class in Egypt," *Current Anthropology* 39(3):354–55.

Hammam, Hussam and Patrick Haenni

 2003 "Chat Shows, Nashid Groups and Lite Preaching: Egypt's Air-conditioned Islam," *La Monde Diplomatique*. Electronic document. http://mondediplo.com/2003/09/03egyptislam (accessed October 5, 2003).

Hirschkind, Charles

 2006 *The Ethical Soundscape: Cassette Sermons and Islamic Counterpublics.* New York: Columbia University Press.

Hoffman-Ladd, Valerie J.

 1987 "Polemics on the Modesty and Segregation of Women in Contemporary Egypt," *International Journal of Middle East Studies* 19:23–50.

Ibrahim, Saad Eddin

 1982 "Oil, Migration and the New Arab Social Order." In *Rich and Poor States in the Middle East: Egypt and the New Arab Order*, Malcolm Kerr and El-Sayyed Yassin, eds., 17–70. Cairo: The American University in Cairo Press.

 1987 "A Sociological Profile." In *The Middle East City: Ancient Traditions Confront a Modern World*. Abdulaziz Y. Saqqaf, ed., 209–26. New York: Paragon House Publishers.

Jankowski, James

 2000 *Egypt: A Short History*. Oxford: Oneworld.

Kaviraj, Sudipta

 1997 "Filth and the Public Sphere: Concepts and Practices about Space in Calcutta," *Public Culture* 10(1):83–113.

Kienle, Eberhard

 2001 *A Grand Delusion: Democracy and Economic Reform in Egypt*. London: I.B. Taurus.

King, Anthony D.

 1990 *Global Cities: Post-Imperialism and the Internationalization of London*. London: Routledge.

 2004 *Spaces of Global Cultures: Architecture, Urbanism, Identity*. London: Routledge.

Koptiuch, Kirsten

    1997   "Third-Worlding at Home." In *Culture, Power and Place: Explorations in Critical Anthropology*. Akhil Gupta and James Fergusson, eds., 234–48. Durham: Duke University Press.

Koning, Anouk de

    2001   "Dreams of Leaving: Suburbia in Cairo," *Etnofoor* 14(1):103–106.

Kuppinger, Petra

    2004   "Exclusive Greenery: New Gated Communities in Cairo," *City & Society* 16(2):35–61.

Kusno, Abidin

    2004   "Whither Nationalist Urbanism? Public Life in Governer Sutiyoso's Jakarta," *Urban Studies* 41(12):2377–94.

Low, Setha M.

    2001   "The Edge and the Center: Gated Communities and the Discourse of Urban Fear," *American Anthropologist* 103(1):45–58.

MacLeod, Arlene Elowe

    1991   *Accommodating Protest: Working Women, the New Veiling, and Change in Cairo*. New York: Columbia University Press.

Mahmood, Saba

    2001   "Theory, Embodiment, and the Docile Agent: Some Reflections on the Egyptian Islamic Revival," *Cultural Anthropology* 26(2): 202–36.

    2003   "Individual, Family, Community and State-Ethical Formation and Politics of Individual Autonomy in Contemporary Egypt," *Social Research* 70(3):837–68.

    2005   *Politics of Piety. The Islamic Renewal and the Feminist Subject*. Princeton: Princeton University Press.

Massey, Doreen

    1994   *Space, Place and Gender.* Cambridge: Polity Press.

Mazarella, William

    2003   "'Very Bombay': Contending with the Global in an Indian Advertising Agency," *Cultural Anthropology* 18(1):33–71.

Mbembe, Achille and Janet Roitman

    1995   "Figures of the Subject in Times of Crisis," *Public Culture* 7(2): 323–52.

McMichael, Philip

    1998   "Development and Structural Adjustment." In *Virtualism: A New Political Economy*. James G. Carrier and Daniel Miller, eds., 95–116. Oxford: Berg.

Mehta, Anna and Liz Bondi

1999   "Embodied Discourse: On Gender and Fear of Violence," *Gender, Place and Culture* 6(1):67–84.

Mimouni, Rachid

1992   *Straf voor het leven*. Translation of *Une peine à vivre* [1991]. Amsterdam: Maarten Muntinga.

Mina, Fayiz Murad

2001   *It-ta'lim fi Masr: il-waaqa' wa il-mustaqbil hita 'aam 2020*. [Education in Egypt: The present and the future until the year 2020]. Egypt 2020 Library. Cairo: al-Anglo al-Misriyya.

Mitchell, Timothy

1999   "Dreamland: The Neoliberalism of Your Desires," *Middle East Report* Spring 1999:28–33.

2002   *Rule of Experts: Egypt, Techno-Politics, Modernity*. Berkeley: University of California Press.

Moore, Clement Henry

1994   *Images of Development: Egyptian Engineers in Search of Industry*. 2nd revised ed. [1980]. Cairo: The American University in Cairo Press

Morley, David

2001   "Belongings: Place, Space and Identity in a Mediated World," *European Journal of Cultural Studies* 4(4):425–88.

Moyer, Eileen

2003   "In the Shadow of the Sheraton: Imagining Localities in Global Spaces among Dar es Salaam Street Youth." PhD dissertation, University of Amsterdam.

Navaro-Yashin, Yael

2002   *Faces of the State: Secularism and Public Life in Turkey*. Princeton: Princeton University Press.

Nederveen Pieterse, Jan

2000   "Globalization North and South: Representations of Uneven Development and the Interaction of Modernities," *Theory, Culture & Society* 17(1):129–37.

Newcomb, Rachel

2006   "Gendering the City, Gendering the Nation: Contesting Urban Space in Fes, Morocco," *City and Society* 18(2):288–311.

Nuwayr, 'Abd al-Salaam

2000   "Al-Ta'lim wa al-hiraak al-ijtimaa'i fi Misr" [Education and social mobility in Egypt], *Ahwal misriyya* 9:37–57.

2002 *Consumption Intensified: The Politics of Middle Class Daily Life in Brazil.* Durham: Duke University Press.

Öncü, Ayse

1997 "The Myth of the 'Ideal Home' Travels across Cultural Borders to Istanbul." In *Space, Culture and Power: New Identities in Globalizing Cities.* Ayse Öncü and Petra Weyland, eds., 56–72. London: Zed Books.

Öncü, Ayse and Petra Weyland, eds.

1997 *Space, Culture and Power: New Identities in Globalizing Cities.* London: Zed Books.

Osman, Magued I. and Laila S. Shahd

2003 "Age-Discrepant Marriages in Egypt," *Cairo Papers in Social Science* 24(1/2):51–61.

Ossman, Susan

1994 *Picturing Casablanca: Portraits of Power in a Modern City.* Berkeley: University of California Press.

Pain, Rachel H.

1997 "Social Geographies of Women's Fear of Crime," *Transactions of the Institute of British Geographers* 22:231–44.

Peck, Jamie and Adam Tickell

2002 "Neoliberalizing Space," *Antipode* 34(3):380–404.

Phadke, Shilpa

2007 "Dangerous Liaisons: Women and Men: Risk and Reputation in Mumbai," *Economic and Political Weekly* April 28:1510–1518.

Rajagopal, Arvind

1999 "Brand Logics and the Cultural Forms of Political Society in India," *Social Text* 60, 17(3):131–49.

2001 "The Gift, the Commodity and the Televisual Imagination: Advertising and Technologies of Perception in South Asia." Paper presented at the ASSR, University of Amsterdam, 20 March.

Rashad, Hoda and Magued Osman

2003 "Nuptiality in Arab Countries: Changes and Implications." *Cairo Papers in Social Science* 24(1/2):20–50.

Reid, Donald Malcolm

1991 *Cairo University and the Making of Modern Egypt.* Cairo: The American University in Cairo Press.

Richards, Alan and John Waterbury

1996 *A Political Economy of the Middle East.* 2nd ed. Boulder: Westview Press.

Robbins, R.

    1998   "Introduction Part I: Actually Existing Cosmopolitanism."
Cosmopolitics: Thinking and Feeling beyond the Nation. P. Cheah and
B. Robbins, eds., 1–19. Minneapolis: University of Minnesota
Press.

Robinson, Jennifer

    2002   "Global and World Cities: A View from off the Map," *International
Journal of Urban and Regional Research* 26(3):531–54.

Rodenbeck, Max

    1999   *Cairo: The City Victorious*. Cairo: The American University in Cairo
Press.

Rose, Gillian

    1993   *Feminism and Geography: The Limits of Geographical Knowledge*.
Cambridge: Polity Press.

Sassen, Saskia

    1998   *Globalization and Its Discontents: Essays on the New Mobility of People
and Money*. New York: New Press.

    2000   "Spatialities and Temporalities of the Global: Elements for a
Theorization," *Public Culture* 12(1):215–32.

    2001   *Global City: New York, London, Tokyo*. 2nd revised ed. Princeton:
Princeton University Press.

Secor, Anne J.

    2002   "The Veil and Urban Space in Istanbul: Women's Dress, Mobility
and Islamic Knowledge," *Gender, Place and Culture* 9(1):5–22.

    2004   "'There is an Istanbul that Belongs to Me': Citizenship, Space
and Identity in the City," *Annals of the Association of American
Geographers* 94(2):352–68.

Singerman, Diane

    1997   *Avenues of Participation: Family, Politics, and Networks in Urban
Quarters of Cairo*. Cairo: The American University in Cairo Press.

Singerman, Diane and Paul Amar, eds.

    2006   *Cairo Cosmopolitan: Politics, Culture, and Space in the New Middle
East*. Cairo: The American University in Cairo Press.

Singerman, Diane and Barbara Ibrahim

    2003   "The Cost of Marriage in Egypt: A Hidden Variable in the New
Arab Demography," *Cairo Papers in Social Science* 24(1/2):80–116.

Smart, Alan and Josephine Smart

    2003   "Urbanization and the Global Perspective," *Annual Review of
Anthropology* 32:263–85.

Smith, Michael D.

    1996   "The Empire Filters Back: Consumption, Production and the Politics of Starbucks Coffee," *Urban Geography* 17(6):502–25.

Smith, Michael Peter

    2001   *Transnational Urbanism: Locating Globalization.* Malden: Blackwell.

Smith, Neil

    2002   "New Globalism, New Urbanism: Gentrification as Global Urban Strategy," *Antipode* 34(3):427–50.

Starrett, Gregory

    1998   *Putting Islam to Work: Education, Politics, and Religious Transformation in Egypt.* Berkeley: University of California Press.

Stewart, Donna J.

    1999   "Changing Cairo: The Political Economy of Urban Form," *International Journal of Urban and Regional Research* 23(1):128–46.

Tourné, Karine

    2003   "Figures of Youth in Egypt: The Young Graduates Between Visibility and Illegitimacy." Paper presented at the Fourth Mediterranean Social and Political Research Meeting, Florence, 19–23 March.

UNDP (http://hdr.undp.org/)

    1998   *Human Development Report 1997/98: Public Spending.*

    1999   *Human Development Report 1998/99: Education.*

    2001   *Egypt Human Development Report 2000/2001: Globalization.*

    2003   *Egypt Human Development Report 2003: Local Participatory Development.*

Veltmeyer, Henry, James Petras, and Steve Vieux

    1997   *Neoliberalism and Class Conflict in Latin America: A Comparative Perspective on the Political Economy of Structural Adjustment.* Basingstoke: Macmillan.

Vignal, Leïla and Eric Denis

    2006   "Cairo as Regional/Global Economic Capital?" In *Cairo Cosmopolitan: Politics, Culture, and Space in the New Middle East.* Diane Singerman and Paul Amar, eds., 99–152. Cairo: The American University in Cairo Press.

Waterbury, John

    1983   *The Egypt of Nasser and Sadat: The Political Economy of Two Regimes.* Princeton: Princeton University Press.

Werner, Karin

1997 *Between Westernization and the Veil: Contemporary Lifestyles of Women in Cairo.* Bielefeld: transcript.

White, Louise

2000 *Speaking with Vampires: Rumor and History in Colonial Africa.* Berkeley: University of California Press.

Wikan, Unni

1980 *Life among the Poor in Cairo.* Ann Henning (translation). London: Tavistock.

1996 *Tomorrow, God Willing: Self-made Destinies in Cairo.* Chicago: The University of Chicago Press.

Wilson, Elizabeth

2001 *The Contradictions of Culture: Cities: Culture: Women.* London: Sage.

Winegar, Jessica

2006 "Cultural Sovereignty in a Global Art Economy: Egyptian Cultural Policy and the New Western Interest in Art from the Middle East," *Cultural Anthropology* 21(2):173–204.

Yousry, Mahmoud, Tarek Abu-Zekry, and Ahmed M. Yousry

1998 "Cairo as a World City: The Impact of Cairo's Orientation towards Globalization." In *Globalization and the World of Large Cities.* Lo Fu-Chen, ed., 270–313. Tokyo: UNUP.

Zhang, Li

2002 "Spatiality and Urban Citizenship in Late Socialist China," *Public Culture* 14(2):311–34.

Index

infrastructure, 29–30; map of, xiv; up-market, 17–19, 30–31, 43, 127, 130, 151–52, 161

Caldeira, Teresa, 42, 155

Campus Magazine, 65, 101, 158. *See also* English-language magazines

capital: different forms of, 54–56, 66, 88–90; cosmopolitan, 6–9, 45, 55, 61, 63, 128, 160; cultural, 9, 54–55, 56, 62, 68, 71, 107, 136; economic, 54, 55–56, 57, 119; social, 13, 54, 67, 87–88

Carrefour, 17–19

Catholic education, 50, 55, 115

de Certeau, Michel, 133, 154

charity, 123

Cilantro, 104–107, 121–22

class, 10–11, 45. *See also* elites; lower class; middle class; social level; upper-middle class; upper class; closure, 152–154. *See also* social closure; coffee shops, 111, 115, 121–22, 130; membership, 67–70

closure, social, 119–20, 129–30, 139, 153–55. *See also* segregation

clothing: upper-middle class styles, 134, 140; in public spaces, 147, 151

clubs, social and sporting, 103–104, 128

Coffee Roastery, 102–104

coffee shops, 2, 7, 14–15, 86, 97–130, 138–44, 160; class and, 111, 115, 121–22, 130; configurations of closeness and distance, 124–29; contested modernities of leisure, 111–19; cosmopolitan belonging, 107–108, 127–30; exclusivity and closure, 119–21; geographies of belonging, 121–24; global flows and, 106–109; history of, 102–103; mixed-gender

leisure culture in, 110, 112–18, 138–39; as public spaces, 110, 111, 119, 130, 132, 146; and religious sensibilities, 99, 109, 113; social life, 98–100, 108–11; women and, 98, 116–18, 138–44

commercials, 31–37, 42, 167n15

compounds, 41–43. *See also* gated communities

configurations of closeness and distance, 121–29

consumption, 7, 8, 18–19, 33, 36, 38–39, 67–68, 107, 109, 128; goods, 8, 21, 37, 109, 166n6, 169n26

contested modernities of leisure, 111–19

corruption, 76, 80

cosmopolitanism, 12, 38, 46–47, 64, 112–13; 'cosmopolitan', 8–9; cosmopolitan belonging, 108, 127–28, 130; cosmopolitan Cairo, 18–19, 29–30, 34, 37, 39, 126, 160; cosmopolitan capital, 6–9, 45, 55, 61, 63, 128, 160; cosmopolitan lifestyles, 6, 8–9, 113, 128, 161–62; cosmopolitan styles and practices, 7–8, 37, 102, 106–107, 110, 113, 126, 128, 137–38

courses, English and computer, 76–78. *See also* remedial courses

craftsmen, 83–84

defilement, sense of, 141, 146–47, 150–54

degrees, 45, 52, 56, 86, 88, 92; American and British, 51, 52, 54; value of, 84. *See also* education

Denis, Eric, 4, 5, 19, 40, 42, 96, 123, 128, 154, 162

Downtown Cairo, 14, 27–28, 34–36, 42, 121

dreams, 1, 4, 16, 31, 37, 41, 43, 96, 155, 159, 163

Dubai, 18, 128. *See also* Gulf states

economy: Egyptian, 3–4, 20–25, 160; liberalization, 21–23, 51; state involvement in, 19–25; urban, 5–6; up-market segment of the urban, 6, 74, 78, 91, 160, 169n29. *See also* labor market

education, 4, 12, 45, 47–59, 70–71; being middle class, 12, 46–47; dual nature of the educational system, 51, 87; Catholic, 50, 55, 115; college-age population, 48; democratization, 47, 49; history of, 49–51; investments, 50, 55, 70; language schools, 49–56, 60, 71, 91; languages, 59–66; lines of relative nobility, 54, 70; national system, 49–51; private, 49–57, 70; privatization, 51–53; public, 51–52, 57, 159; statistics, 12, 21, 48, 168nn20, 21, 169n29; strategies, 55–59; upper-middle class contestations, 66–70. *See also* degrees; universities

Egyptian Arabic, 13, 68. *See also* 'ammiyya

Elyachar, Julia, 10, 79

elites, 21, 67–68, 154–55. *See also* upper class; areas, 41–42; culture, 7–9, 61, 64, 153; leisure, 112, 136; membership, 9, 46, 55; orientations, 61, 108

employment, 24, 169n28; government, 4, 20, 24, 81–82, 92–93, 170n36;

guaranteed government, 47, 168n19; insecure, 81, 86, 91, 95, 160; private sector, 75, 78, 82, 86–87; up-market, 75, 78, 88, 92; women, 13

English, 6, 9, 54–55, 58–65, 76–77, 106–108

English-language magazines: 62, 65–66, 71, 101

Enigma, 101, 117

entrepreneur as role model, 78–80

exams, 49, 51–53, 58

exclusivity of spaces, 31, 37, 43, 106–107, 119–20, 129

family backgrounds, 15, 55–56, 67–70, 78, 88

Ferguson, James, 8, 164

Fernandes, Leela, 4, 36–37, 39, 64, 91

fieldwork in middle class, 13–15

films, 9, 113, 170n37

First World, 6, 18, 64, 164. *See also* globalization; belonging, 108, 126. *See also* global belonging; desire for, 8–9, 19, 38, 126–27; lifestyles, 8, 19, 43, 127–28; reterritorializations of, 19, 102, 127, 163–64

flirts: in coffee shops, 108, 116, 120; in public spaces, 111, 138, 143, 145–46, 148, 151

food: in coffee shops, 101, 105–107, 121; subsidies, 22, 24

foreign appearances, 89

France, 8, 61, 107

French language, 49–50, 58, 61–62, 108

fusha, 63

future generation, 31–32, 65–66, 71, 158

Future Generation Foundation, 31–32, 36, 77, 166n11

Mubarak, Gamal, 31, 77

muhaggabaat (veiled women), 32, 89, 103, 171nn42, 47. *See also higaab*; veil

multilinguism, 63–64

multinational companies, 2, 26, 63, 74, 91, 92

Mumbai (Bombay), 33, 39, 135, 140, 155

mustawa. See social level

Nasser era, 4, 19–20, 48, 95; education, 47, 49–50; institutions, 24, 159; modernism, 47, 113, 158; nostalgia for, 95–96, 163; professional middle class, 6, 9, 36, 47, 95, 158; state-led development, 4, 19–20, 78

Nasserite social contract, 21, 23, 25, 43, 159

national development, 4, 23, 43

national project, 19, 26, 32, 159

national narratives, 4, 6, 9, 31, 42, 45, 71, 158–60, 164

neoliberalism, 23, 26, 38. *See also* new liberal era; neoliberal landscape, 38, 126; neoliberal policies, 23–25, 43, 95; neoliberal precepts, 4, 23, 79, 95; neoliberal project, 26, 31, 38–39, 78, 160, 163; neoliberal reforms, 24, 26, 29, 42–43

new generation, 31–32, 65–66, 71, 158

new liberal era, 2, 4, 10, 42, 45, 95, 123, 154, 160–62; narratives of, 6, 31, 36, 63, 70, 158

Nile City Towers, 26–27

Nineteen Fifty-Two (1952) Revolution, 4, 19

nobility, lines of relative, 54–55, 70, 78

non-governmental organizations (NGOs), 5, 25, 79; as employers, 75, 78, 87, 91

nouveaux riches (new rich), 21, 56, 67–68

nostalgia, 95–96, 163

Ossman, Susan, 143

outside *(barra)*, 7, 38, 65, 109, 127, 162

The Paper, 65–66, 101

Phadke, Shilpa, 135, 140, 155

pollution. *See* defilement

popular classes *(ish-sha'b)*, 7, 46, 103. *See also* classes

popular areas, 29, 171n50. *See also 'ashwaa'iyyaat*

postcolonial predicaments, 11, 36, 127, 163

poverty, 6, 12, 24, 123

prerevolutionary Egypt, 96, 163–64

private schools, 49–51, 52, 54–55, 70, 168n21

private sector, 6, 19, 21, 23, 24, 50, 80, 84, 87, 95, 163; employment 75, 78, 82, 86–87

privatization, 22–24, 159; of education, 51, 70; of public assets, 23

professionals. *See also* middle class, upper-middle class; definition of professional middle class, 12, 164n4; definition of professional upper-middle class, 6, 74; upper-middle class, 2, 6, 13, 37–38, 42, 62, 68, 74, 95, 104–105, 110, 160–61; young, 1–3, 12–13

prostitutes, 140–43, 147

public education, 51–52, 57, 159. *See also* education

public spaces, 14, 110–11, 129, 133; coffee shops as, 110, 111, 119, 130, 132, 146; gardens, 41, 103, 155;

standards, 6; global, 23, 33, 36–37, 159; of living, 47–49, 59, 90, 170n40; Third World, 95
Starbucks, 108
status: elite, 112, 135; global city, 3, 28, 43; social, 49, 61, 67, 84, 86, 110, 146, 153; up-market, 101, 123
strategies: of class closure, 153, 154; education, 57, 67; employment, 85; reconversion, 55–56, spatial, 133–34, 157, 150, 154
subsidies, food, 22, 24; private sector, 23, 24, 27, 163
Suez Canal, 21, 22, 36

tabaqa (class), 46. *See also* classes
taxis, 131–32, 150, 155–56
trajectories: educational, 50, 51, 57; upper-middle class, 64, 87, 94; women's urban, 134, 138, 147, 153–54
Telecom Egypt, 32–36
television, 9, 32, 109, 167n12; commercials, 31–37, 42, 167n15; serials, 67, 80
Third World standards, 95
tourism, 5, 22, 29, 168n24
transportation, public, 30, 150–51
tuition fees, 49, 52, 53, 56. *See also* education

'udit il-khawaaga, 89
unemployed university graduates, 73–74, 77, 80, 85, 159
unemployment, 24, 77, 110, 169n28. *See also* employment
United States of America, 38; American cultural influences, 102–103, 106, 107–108, 122

American University in Cairo (AUC), 52, 121
universities, 52, 86; AUC, 52, 121; private 51, 52, 160n22; public, 52–53, 158. *See also* education
university graduates, unemployed, 73–74, 77, 80, 85, 159
up-market Cairo, 17–19, 30–31, 43, 127, 130, 151–52, 161
up-market coffee shops. *See* coffee shops
up-market segment of the urban economy, 6, 74, 78, 91, 160, 169n29
up-market workspaces, 89, 108, 110, 160
upper class, 8, 21, 41, 118. *See also* elites; areas, xiv, 39
upper-middle class. *See also* class, elites, up-market Cairo; definition of professional upper-middle class, 6, 74; lifestyles, 6, 37, 55, 68, 71, 111, 130, 135–36, 161, 170n41; professionals, 2, 6, 13, 37–38, 42, 62, 68, 74, 95, 104–105, 110, 160–61; as new/future generation, 31–32, 65–66, 71, 158
urban economy, 5–6
urbanism, national, 11, 27

veil *(higaab)*, 20, 89, 99–100, 103–104, 136–47, 147, 171nn42, 47. *See also muhaggabaat*; in media representations, 32, 167n12
visibility, women's public, 137, 143–44, 153, 156

wages, 6, 74–75, 81, 82, 91, 93; decline of real, 5, 22, 24
wasta (connections), 76, 88, 94–95

women: and coffee shops, 98, 116–18, 138–44; negotiations of public space, 132, 137, 139, 143, 145–50, 153–54; public lifestyles, 118, 136, 138–39, 143, 144, 151–53, 155–56; public visibility, 137, 143–44, 153, 156; reputation of, 83, 113–14, 115, 137, 138, 146, 154; urban trajectories, 134, 138, 147, 153–54

World Bank, 23, 29, 79, 94

young professionals, 1–3, 12–13

Zamalek, 18, 39, 41, 121